PALESTINE ON THE AIR

A supplement to
JOURNAL OF CIVIL AND HUMAN RIGHTS

by Karma R. Chávez

COMMON THREADS
An anthology from the
University of Illinois Press

Library of Congress Control Number: 2019948995

ISBN 978-0-252-08485-0 (paperback)

Journal of Civil and Human Rights ISSN 2378-4253 (online)

CONTENTS

PREFACE

Michael Ezra

Thank you for taking the time to examine *Palestine on the Air*, which marks the first venture by the *Journal of Civil and Human Rights* into the Common Threads series by the University of Illinois Press.

It is my pleasure to help bring to you this important new volume about the Palestinian freedom struggle. As editor of the *Journal of Civil and Human Rights*, I feel a sense of pride and accomplishment from my small role in helping this work get published. I would also like to offer sincere thanks to *JCHR* editorial board member Karma Chávez for giving our journal the opportunity to sponsor this work.

Palestine on the Air takes the form of ten interviews that Professor Chávez conducted between 2013 and 2016 for her show *A Public Affair* on the community FM radio station WORT while she was teaching in Madison at the University of Wisconsin. Professor Chávez's interviews bring you first-hand, extended testimony from Palestinian people, something that most U.S. media consumers will never experience.

Some of the Palestinian people you will meet in the pages of *Palestine on the Air* include

- Johayna Saifi, director of the nonprofit organization Hirakuna, who talks about what life is like for Palestinians who live in Israel and her efforts to organize them;
- Haitham Salawdeh, an activist with the U.S. Palestinian Community Network, who travels back-and-forth between Milwaukee, Wisconsin, and Duma, Palestine, where he was born and raised; and
- Ghadir Shafie, the codirector of Aswat, who helps Palestinian LBTQI women living in Israel.

As you read *Palestine on the Air*, you will notice a central theme emerges that makes clear just how deeply the United States is implicated in the ongoing occupation and apartheid conditions in the West Bank and the subjugation of Palestinian authority and self-determination. One of the reasons Professor Chávez and I are excited about the publication of this book is because we believe it is crucial that a U.S. audience become more involved in this conversation.

Israel is the U.S. government's second-highest aid recipient. A disproportionate percentage of settlers illegally living in the occupied West Bank are U.S. American citizens. U.S. law enforcement depends upon Israeli military and security technology. The U.S. Senate introduced a bill known as the Combatting BDS Act. Academics and state employees who publicly embrace a pro-Palestinian perspective have been censured or fired. Even the Birmingham Civil Rights Institute took issue with one of the city's greatest freedom fighters, Angela Davis, primarily because of her solidarity with Palestine and support of the Israel boycott. *Palestine on the Air* makes plain the U.S. government's antagonistic role in the Israel/Palestine conflict and how American citizens have followed that lead.

But *Palestine on the Air* also details how individual Americans have found ways to organize in support of the Palestinian freedom struggle. It is in this latter spirit that we bring to you this work. Therefore, in *Palestine on the Air*, you will meet American allies such as

- Charlotte Silver, a journalist with the website *Electronic Intifada*, which brings pro-Palestinian coverage to a worldwide audience;
- Jeff Halper, the anthropologist who cofounded the Israeli Committee Against House Demolitions, and
- Sarah Schulman, the esteemed writer and historian who explains how Israel "pinkwashes" its occupation of the West Bank by using Gay Pride as a public relations mechanism.

The reason we are publishing *Palestine on the Air* is to give people a meaningful, accessible, and brief study of important issues related to the Palestinian people over the last twenty years. Readers without much knowledge of Israel/Palestine will find the text to be plentiful but digestible. Those with a deep understanding of the subject will still discover an assortment of new perspectives and first-hand testimony not found anywhere else.

Karma Chávez says that she would never have felt bold enough to publish on Palestine if it had not been for her trip there in 2015. While most of us reading this book will likely never make that journey, we hope *Palestine on the Air* will nonetheless bring you one step closer to understanding what is actually going on in that part of the world. I hope you find this book to be as meaningful as I do.

Rohnert Park, CA
August 2019

ACKNOWLEDGMENTS

Karma R. Chávez

This book would not be possible without the generous support and encouragement of several people and entities. Thank you to Penelope Mitchell and the Palestinian American Research Center (PARC) for sponsoring my 2015 trip to Palestine, without which I would have never felt bold enough to publish on Palestine. PARC afforded me the opportunity to meet the Palestinians who inspired me to put together this collection. Thank you to J. Kēhaulani Kauanui for the idea of publishing my radio interviews. I had very kind hosts during my visit to the West Bank and Israel, including Ayelet Ben-Yishai, Ofer Schorr, Ghadir Shafie, and many folks who came out for my talk at Isha L'Isha: The Haifa Feminist Center. I want to thank my friend Ahmad Yacoub, a Palestinian poet who publishes beautiful poems in Spanish. We met in a café in Ramallah one afternoon in 2015 and spent the day conversing in Spanish about politics and life over coffee, beers, and cigarettes.

I am immensely appreciative of staff and volunteers at WORT-FM in Madison, Wisconsin, particularly Molly Stentz, Susan Sheldon, Amanda Zhang, Cynthia Lin, various phone answerers, and engineers for support when I hosted for the station; and the Board of Directors for granting permission to publish these interviews. Barbara Olson of the Madison-Rafah Sister City Project helped connect me with radio guests and kept me informed on Palestine issues more broadly when I was in Madison. The Institute for Middle East Understanding introduced me to Alex Kane, who expertly fact checked this entire volume. I am very grateful for his labor. Hana Masri deserves a special shout out: not only did she transcribe all of these interviews as an hourly worker for me across several summers, but she also filled in all of the citations in proper style after Alex's fact checks and gave feedback on the introduction. The book would not be done without Hana's excitement for it and for justice in Palestine. Thank you to my best friends, Leah Mirakhor, for offering her insights on the introduction, and Kimberlee Pérez, for always being there. Thanks to Ira Dworkin for helping me articulate a key contribution of the book.

Dawn Durante of the University of Illinois Press initially took this idea and put it into motion, and for that I will always be grateful. I have since had the pleasure of working with both Alexa Colella and Mike Ezra on thinking through many logistics of what this experimental volume will look like, and working around the inevitable obstacles that emerge when publishing about Palestine. I am grateful for their excitement about this volume and their creativity in ensuring it would be published.

My partner, Annie Hill, has been an incredible interlocutor as I thought through aspects of this project, and she has offered very helpful editing as well. As in all things, I am thankful for Annie. Finally, thank you to every person who let me interview them to talk about these crucial issues. I have learned (and continue to learn) so much from each of you.

INTRODUCTION
From the Mexico-U.S. Borderlands to Palestine

Karma R. Chávez

I first learned something of substance about the Palestinian struggle in 2006 when I volunteered with Coalición de Derechos Humanos, which is an anti-border-militarization and immigrant-justice organization in Arizona. Derechos Humanos often brings delegations of would-be allies and interested groups to the Mexico-U.S. border to facilitate understanding of the borderlands migrant death crisis; destruction of communities and environment due to border walls and militarized zones; and human rights violations enacted by U.S. economic and immigration policies in the late twentieth and early twenty-first centuries. In 2006, Derechos Humanos hosted a Palestinian delegation. This specific delegation endeavored to connect the plights of occupied Palestinians with North American indigenous communities whose lands cross the United States and Mexico as well as with migrants and other peoples of color in Arizona and Sonora who are impacted by U.S. *and* Israeli militarization policies, practices, and technologies.[1] During the delegation, Derechos Humanos cofounder Isabel Garcia and a member of the Palestinian group collectively proclaimed, "Your struggle is our struggle, your wall is our wall."

Although this coalitional claim between two constituencies does not capture the complexity of what Palestinians in the occupied territories share with North American indigenous peoples and migrants in the Mexico-U.S. borderlands, it does convey the need to create conceptual and activist connections against state violence across the globe. State violence includes border walls and surveilled crossing points, blurred lines of responsibility between law enforcement and military forces, and policy that relegates and designates indigenous people and ethnic minorities for lethal state interventions (e.g., settler and Israeli military violence against Palestinians in the West Bank or the "deterrence through death" polices of U.S. Immigration and Customs

Enforcement that drive migrants into the most dangerous parts of the Arizona desert). The coalitional claim also helps to underscore the violence of building infrastructure that separates indigenous peoples from one another on their own lands. Participating in the delegation pushed me toward developing a transnational analysis of state violence in order to better fight it, but the issue of Palestine did not become central for me for another few years.

Context for this Collection

The American Studies Association (ASA) asked its membership to vote on supporting the academic boycott of Israel in 2013 (an issue Professor David Lloyd discusses in his interview). To cast an informed vote, I wanted to learn more about the political, historical, and social context of the Israeli state. In 2005, members within Palestinian civil society called for a Boycott, Divestment, and Sanctions (BDS) global movement against the Israeli state until it complied with international law and principles of human rights.[2] The members of civil society who joined together to make this call included associations, unions, political parties, and others representing Palestinian refugees around the world, Palestinian citizens of Israel, and Palestinians living under occupation in Gaza and the West Bank. They made this call due to Israel's ongoing violations of international law, the hundreds of United Nations (UN) resolutions that have condemned Israel, and because no actions thus far have ensured that Israel complies with international law, respects human rights, or ends the occupation and oppression of Palestinians. Like the South African call for BDS to end apartheid, the Palestinian call asks people across the globe to boycott Israeli goods and institutions, divest from companies with ties to the Israeli army, and demand government sanctions against Israel until it fulfills the following:

1. Ending its occupation and colonization of all Arab lands and dismantling the Wall
2. Recognizing the fundamental rights of the Arab-Palestinian citizens of Israel to full equality
3. Respecting, protecting, and promoting the rights of Palestinian refugees to return to their homes and properties as stipulated in UN resolution 194[3]

For several years, ASA leadership built support for an affirmative vote by hosting delegations to Palestine and educating its membership, but I was a relatively new member with this academic association and the proposed boycott was my first encounter with this issue institutionally. I not only began to learn about Palestinian struggles under occupation, but I also witnessed the vitriol directed at pro-Palestinian efforts by Zionists who wanted to preserve Israel as an ethno-religious state with the right to settle historic Palestinian lands—everything between the Jordan River and the Mediterranean Sea—and persist in treating Palestinian citizens of Israel (roughly 20 percent of its current population) as second-class citizens (a topic Ghadir Shafie and Johayna Saifi discuss in their interviews).[4]

During that time, I hosted a live, hour-long weekly public affairs radio program for Madison, Wisconsin's, community radio station, WORT-FM. I began using that platform as a way to host in-depth conversations with people who knew about the politics of Palestine/Israel and could speak to a wide audience. From 2013–2016, I conducted eleven radio interviews on issues related to Palestinian life and resistance, Israeli state and settler violence, Israel's practice of pinkwashing—using its gay rights record as an alibi for its record of human rights abuses—as well as BDS and other forms of solidarity activism in the United States (see Nora Barrows-Friedman and Sarah Schulman's interviews for more on these last points). Most interviews were sought in response to specific events, including the release of important books on the subject, the ASA vote, the firing of Professor Steven Salaita, and the 2014 attack on Gaza and its aftermath (see Charlotte Silver's interview), among other topical issues. Beyond being responsive to the events of the day, some interviews emerged after I traveled to the West Bank in 2015 as part of a trip for U.S. academics to meet with Palestinian academics.

This two-week trip was life-changing for me. Our group toured Palestinian universities and met with academics in our fields of study while we learned about the horrific conditions of teaching and researching under occupation. We met with cultural producers, activists, people in charge of cultural and historic preservation efforts, and ordinary Palestinians. We saw firsthand the realities of living under a constant Israeli military presence, the persistent threat of settler violence, and the lack of mobility and land rights, among many other hardships. When I returned to the United States, I hosted shows with people I met or learned about while in Palestine, and whose viewpoints offered insight and information about the everyday experience of apartheid conditions. When I left Madison in 2016, I also left my radio show. As I searched for a way to preserve the public service of that show, I recalled a conversation with a friend and colleague from the West Bank trip, Kēhaulani Kauanui, about transcribing radio interviews to reach a wider audience. That conversation inspired this collection of Palestine-related interviews, which contribute to conceptual and activist connections against state violence and, akin to the original live radio interviews, to inform a lay audience in the United States.

A U.S. audience remains important in conversations about Palestine, not just so that people will make conceptual connections like "their walls are our walls," although such basic links are valuable. Instead, a U.S. audience is important because the United States is so deeply implicated in the ongoing occupation and apartheid conditions of Palestine/Israel. The U.S. government planned $3.1 billion in foreign aid to Israel in fiscal year 2017,[5] making Israel the second-highest aid recipient.[6] In 2016, President Barack Obama increased the amount of U.S. aid to Israel, signing a $38 billion aid deal, giving Israel roughly $3.8 billion per year in military aid for ten years.[7] Furthermore, between 9 and 15 percent of settlers illegally living in the occupied West Bank are U.S. American citizens, numbers significantly higher than other Jewish immigrants to Israel who mostly settle within Israel's 1948 boundaries.[8] Thus the political and material conditions that enable occupation and Israel's standing in the world can be traced, concretely, to U.S. support.

The United States has also grown dependent on Israel in matters of security, and that contributes to U.S. backing of Israeli policies and practices against Palestinians and in occupied Palestinian land. As Jeff Halper elaborates in the interview based on his book *War Against the People*, and as has become especially stark during President Donald Trump's administration, Israel's policing, security, and military strategies and technologies are the gold standard for modern states the world round.[9] For example, given Israel's woeful human rights record, human rights groups have drawn attention to U.S. law enforcement entities from cities including Baltimore; Washington, DC; Houston; Miami; Los Angeles; and New York City receiving training in Israel from its military, police, and security forces.[10] Such exchange programs are regular and often privately funded by organizations like the Anti-Defamation League.[11] These ties further bind the United States to Israel, as U.S. law enforcement becomes dependent on Israel's cutting-edge technology and methods. Reliance on and replication of Israeli policing, security, and military strategies and technologies are further evidenced in Trump's references to the success of Israel's wall (although it is often unclear which barrier he means since Israel has several) as a model for his dream wall on the Mexico-U.S. border.[12] Moreover, in late 2018, Trump ordered U.S. military troops to the border because of the supposed crisis of Central American migrant caravans arriving there.[13] He also told troops to regard rock throwing as gunfire.[14] These displays of force at the border bear a strong resemblance to conduct by the Israeli Defense Forces at borders and checkpoints.[15] Even some critics of Trump's wall still turn to Israel's methods of border fortification, especially its smart fencing along the borders with Egypt and Lebanon, as inspiration for the United States.[16] Israeli company Magal Security Systems, which built the wall along Gaza, has been vying to build Trump's Mexico-U.S. border wall.[17] Thus, the United States and Israel, from government entities to private enterprise, have manufactured a symbiotic relationship around police, security, and military in which there is little regard for the people who suffer from Israeli state violence.

This collection adds valuable perspectives to the extant body of scholarly work that offers in-depth considerations on the Palestinian struggle for self-determination.[18] It also makes an innovative methodological contribution. As a scholar trained in rhetoric who conducts archival research, I am interested in how archives can intervene in and disrupt political temporality and distortions. Archives, particularly resistant archives, afford us the opportunity to make past events endure in alternative forms and contest entrenched narratives, often through ongoing research and publication. In one sense, this book serves as an archive of significant events that had tremendous impacts on people's lives. It also archives the live radio interviews I conducted, giving them new life as texts for a wider audience. Furthermore, as a scholar and interviewer, at times I responded to what I understood to be a political exigence, and, at other times, I created an exigence for certain voices to receive airtime on issues that I, and the communities I am accountable to, deemed important. In both instances, the interviews on the Palestinian struggle for justice, land, and self-determination, when aired live and now as published in this collection, intervene in the world of public and political argument. In each interview, I was more than a witness or facilitator; I relied on my skills as a rhetoric scholar who understands discursive framing and claims-making and who holds an informed viewpoint on the issues discussed. I conducted interviews as rhetorical interventions and generous acts of public scholarship to augment perspectives for an audience willing to hear about the Palestinian struggle and learn more about its complexity.

Rhetoric scholars should not only analyze what others have said and written. We can and must use our methodological training to produce incisive texts of our own outside of conventional scholarly publications. We have an active role in amplifying voices and airing different points of view. Beyond the methodological contribution of this text, my intervention also enacts a political commitment. The interviews in *Palestine on the Air* are vital and timely due to the U.S. mainstream media's one-sided presentation of Palestine/Israel, tacit and active support for Israel and its policies, and routine silence on Israeli violence, occupation, and settlement.[19] Diverse viewpoints should be heard because U.S. mainstream media often rely on pro-Zionist perspectives to frame Palestine/Israel,[20] which limits and distorts the information available to the average person in the United States. This book resists such distortions and creates a dialogic archive. *Palestine on the Air* presents a series of interviews and an accessible entry point for readers who care about issues of occupation and colonialism and want to know more about Palestine and struggles for Palestinian liberation.

What's Happened since the Interviews Aired

Since I completed my last interview in 2016, significant events related to the politics of Palestine, Israel, and the United States have transpired that highlight many of the themes in this collection of interviews. The themes include Israeli state and settler violence against Palestinian civilians leading to maiming and death, unwavering U.S. support for Israel's policies and actions, and the U.S. state and public targeting of intellectuals and activists for speaking out against the state of Israel. Detailing all that has happened in the past several years would be impossible, but a few instances are worth noting to provide an update and contemporary contextualization for reading these interviews.

I began writing this introduction just days after May 15, 2018, the 70th anniversary of the Nakba—the Arabic word for catastrophe that honors the mass expulsion of Palestinians from their historic lands,[21] and President Trump's relocation of the U.S. Embassy from Tel Aviv to Jerusalem on May 14, 2018, the anniversary of Israel's declaration of independence. Although perhaps obvious to some readers, it is necessary to explain briefly why Trump's decision remains so controversial. By moving the U.S. Embassy, the United States essentially acknowledges Jerusalem as the capital of Israel, despite an international consensus otherwise. The international community refuses to accept Jerusalem as Israel's capital for many reasons, but mainly because the original partition plan in 1947 divided the city between Israel and Jordan. Even after the 1967 war when Israel took control of the entirety of Jerusalem, the original boundary puts East Jerusalem within Palestinian territory in the West Bank, and many who want a two-state solution hope it will be the capital of a future Palestinian state.[22] Trump's decision, in light of the immense power of the United States in bolstering Israel's actions and influence in global politics, essentially kills that possibility and Palestinians' broader struggle for land and self determination in their historic lands.

The relocation of the U.S. Embassy represents only one recent event. Each year on March 30, Palestinians commemorate Land Day to honor those who lost their lives on that day in 1976 while resisting Israeli aggression and confiscation of lands.[23] March 30, 2018, sparked a new campaign dubbed "The Great March of Return," as Palestinians living in the blockaded Gaza Strip began protesting at the border fence with Israel. The vast majority of Gazans are refugees, and most were displaced during the 1948 creation of Israel. They protest for their right of return to their historic homes and against the eleven-year-old Israeli siege that continually restricts their air, land, and sea movement and access.[24] The Israeli siege restricts not only Gazans ability to travel but also their access to the sea to fish and to outside goods and raw materials. Although Israel has blocked Gazan movement in various ways since the early 1990s, the formal blockade began in 2007 after Hamas, which Israel and the United States regard as a terrorist organization, won in Gaza's legislative elections.[25] Since then, Israel has launched attacks on Gaza twice, both in 2008–2009 (Operation Cast Lead) and in 2014 (Operation Protective Edge). Operation Cast Lead is largely regarded as an offensive attack by Israel, resulting in the deaths of roughly 1,400 Palestinians and the injuring of over 5,300.[26] Three Israeli civilians and ten Israeli soldiers were killed, including four in "friendly fire." The catalyst to Operation Protective Edge is widely disputed, but it resulted in more than 2,100 Palestinian deaths and 11,000 injuries.[27] Sixty-six Israel soldiers and six Israeli civilians were killed. In both instances, Gazans' homes, schools, hospitals, and civilian infrastructure were destroyed, and the blockade has restricted the import of materials to rebuild.[28] My description of these events in no way encompasses all of the suffering in the Gaza Strip, often described as an "open-air prison,"[29] or the reasons Israel has offered for its actions, but it helps to contextualize how Gazans are forced to live.

At the time of this writing in January 2019, Gazan protestors continue The Great March of Return every Friday by agitating at the Israeli security fence. Their protracted struggle to return to their lands is framed by the U.S. Embassy move and the increasingly, but everlasting cozy relationship between the United States and Israel. Since the beginning of The Great March of Return protests, more than 250 Palestinians have been killed by Israeli military forces and more than 23,000 have been injured.[30] The United Nations Office for the Coordination of Humanitarian Affairs reports one

Israeli casualty and three injuries related to these protests between their start and the end of 2018.[31] Gazans' resolve in the face of so much continued devastation speaks to the need for more understanding of the Palestinian struggle in order for these conditions to change.

The intensity of protests in Gaza, the violence of Israeli occupation forces, the chummy relationship between President Trump and Israeli Prime Minister Benjamin Netanyahu, and the growing BDS movement have led more people to speak out in public forums for Palestinian self determination and, as a result, for more people to be targeted and punished in the United States. Since 2014, twenty-seven states have enacted anti-BDS laws, and several others are considering them.[32] The first bill proposed in the U.S. Senate in 2019 was a previously introduced bill known as the Combatting BDS Act, this time called the Strengthening America's Security in the Middle East Act.[33] Among other provisions, it sought to protect local and state governments that refuse to work with companies that boycott Israel. It narrowly failed the 60-vote threshold to move forward without the risk of filibuster, with a 56–44 vote.[34] Senate Republicans, seeking out divisions among Democrats, reintroduced the bill in late January, and it is set for another full Senate vote.[35]

Nevertheless, state laws are already having a chilling effect. For instance, due to a similar Texas law, a contracted, elementary school speech pathologist, Bahia Amawi, was told she could no longer work at the school because she refused to sign an oath indicating that she "does not" and "will not" boycott Israel.[36] The law used to take away Amawi's job emerged in response to academic organizations' boycott resolutions, including the ASA's historic vote to endorse the academic and cultural boycott of Israel in 2013. Amawi is legally fighting her case, but it remains unclear what the outcome will be. Additionally, the major news network CNN fired professor and media commentator Marc Lamont Hill after he spoke to the UN in late November 2018 in favor of Palestinian equal rights and a free Palestine.[37] Efforts to threaten his position as a tenured professor at Temple University mounted but did not result in his firing.[38] Still, activists and commentators drew important parallels between Hill and Steven Salaita, interviewed in this volume, who the University of Illinois at Urbana-Champaign fired because of his tweets criticizing Israel during the 2014 bombardment of Gaza (see also the interview with Sarah T. Roberts and Katherine Franke).[39] On the heels of Hill's CNN dismissal, Black radical internationalist activist and retired professor Angela Y. Davis learned that the Birmingham Civil Rights Institute (BCRI) would no longer award her the Fred Shuttleworth Human Rights Award after some members of the local Jewish community objected. The BCRI's Board explained that parts of her record did not meet the criteria for receiving the award, and as came out later, this claim was directly connected to Davis's positions in solidarity with Palestine and in support of a boycott of Israel.[40] The BCRI eventually reversed its decision and honored Davis. Certainly, losing an award pales in comparison to losing a job, having one's home demolished, or suffering the murder of one's family (as discussed by Haitham Salawdeh in his interview), but that a globally known and renowned civil and human rights activist would be treated like this on the basis of her positions on Palestine/Israel indicates the fervor that this issue has reached in U.S. public discourse. That the BCRI did, in the end, honor Davis's lifetime of human rights work also speaks to the power of the Palestine solidarity movement.

Overview of the Volume

Given the complex historical and contemporary context, my hope is this collection of interviews reaches readers who do not have time to consume the many brilliant books on the history of Israel's state formation or the conditions of occupation, or who do not know where to turn for diligent and digestible media reporting. This collection can serve as a resource for teachers and community organizers looking for accessible texts on Palestine from informed writers, activists, and academics. Although some people featured are noted experts and activists, such as Steven Salaita, Sarah Schulman, and Jeff Halper, others may be less known in the West, such as Johayna Saifi, Haitham Saladweh, and Ghadir Shafie. The people presented in this book often work and think across the intersections of the United States and Palestine/Israel.

I begin the collection with three Palestinians, Haitham Salawdeh, Ghadir Shafie, and Johayna Saifi, who introduce readers to life under occupation in the West Bank and in close proximity to Israeli settlers or to life as a Palestinian citizen of Israel. I then turn to journalist Charlotte Silver, who reported on the situation in Gaza one year after Operation Protective Edge. From there, I turn attention to the Palestine solidarity movement in the United States, beginning with David Lloyd of the ASA and the U.S. Campaign for the Academic and Cultural Boycott of Israel, who discusses the ASA's decision to support the academic boycott. The next two interviews address Steven Salaita's firing, from the viewpoints of Katherine Franke and Sarah T. Roberts, who each helped to lead the campaign in support of Salaita, followed by an interview with Salaita after the publication of his book *Uncivil Rites*. Building on the theme of U.S. solidarity, Nora Barrows-Friedman discusses her book, *In Our Power*, which details the social movement on college campuses in support of Palestine. Sarah Schulman's interview is next, as she discusses her book *Israel/Palestine and the Queer International*, which reflects on her own journey toward Palestine solidarity as a U.S. Jew and a queer woman in the United States. I conclude the volume with Jeff Halper's interview, where he assists readers in understanding the answer to the question: how does Israel get away with it? These interviews, given in real time and without the benefit of on-hand sources and fact checkers have now been supplemented with endnotes supplied by regional expert and freelance journalist Alex Kane. I gave interviewees the opportunity to look at Kane's suggestions and offer their own take if they wanted (only Salawdeh offered a post-script to his interview). My graduate research assistant Hana Masri offered additional sources in these notes in order to provide readers with further resources should they want them.

The interviews were conducted between 2013 and 2016 because that is when I hosted my show. But this time period was also significant for many reasons, as I hope will be transparent in reading the interviews. This time period included the publication of several important books, key votes on BDS resolutions by academic and religious organizations, Operation Protective Edge, and more. Other than cleaning up vocal ticks (e.g., "um," "you know," "sort of," etc.), I've left the interviews in their original form, which includes my original introduction for my guests, moments when calls dropped, questions from callers who listened to the live show, and the ways that people speak that don't always translate into grammatically correct writing. Additionally, because my scripts for the shows were created for live radio and aired sporadically over several years, sometimes the introductions to the interviews are repetitive. Rather than correcting this, I left the content as it was and hope that readers will skip over what they may have already read in another interview. The whole process of publishing this collection was an experiment of sorts, and I felt the most important thing was to keep the interviews in their original form to reflect their character and content as interviewees and I jointly created them.

Talking about Palestine/Israel is a complicated and fraught project where facts are disputed, emotions run high, and every statement is political. I have attempted to be fair and accurate in the way I have presented and sourced this volume, and in how I conducted the original interviews. The voices in this volume, including my own, speak in solidarity with the many Palestinian movements against apartheid and for self determination.

NOTES

1. "U.S.-Israel Strategic Cooperation: Homeland Security Collaboration," *Jewish Virtual Library*, June 2017, https://www.jewishvirtuallibrary.org/u-s-israel-homeland-security-collaboration; Todd Miller and Gabriel M. Schivone, "Gaza in Arizona: How Israeli High-Tech Firms Will Up-Armor the U.S.-Mexico Border," *Mother Jones*, January 26, 2015, https://www.motherjones.com/politics/2015/01/us-mexico-border-gaza-israeli-tech-wall/; Jimmy Johnson, "A Palestine-Mexico Border," *NACLA*, June 29, 2012, https://nacla.org/blog/2012/6/29/palestine-mexico-border.

2. "Palestinian Civil Society Call for BDS," BDS Movement, July 9, 2005, https://www.bdsmovement.net/call.

3. "Palestinian Civil Society Call for BDS." UN Resolution 194, adopted by the United Nations General Assembly in 1948, resolves that "refugees wishing to return to their homes and live at peace with their neighbours should be permitted to do so at the earliest practicable date, and that compensation should be paid for the property of those choosing not to return and for loss of or damage to property which, under principles of international law or equity, should be made good by the Governments or authorities responsible" ("Resolution 194," United Nations Relief and Works Agency for Palestine Refugees in the Near East, accessed May 16, 2019, https://www.unrwa.org/content/resolution-194). "The wall," in point one, refers to the separation wall that Israel continues to erect between Israel's 1948 boundaries and the occupied West Bank. When completed, the wall will likely be between 420 and 440 miles long, more than twice the length of the border. The excess length is because the wall twists well into the West Bank to encompass Israeli settlements. It also surrounds East Jerusalem ("Israel and International Law: The West Bank Wall," Institute for Middle East Understanding, April 1, 2015, https://imeu.org/article/israels-west-bank-wall).

4. "Discrimination against Palestinian Citizens of Israel," Institute for Middle East Understanding, September 28, 2011, https://imeu.org/article/discrimination-against-palestinian-citizens-of-israel; Yousef Munayyer, "Not All Israeli Citizens are Equal," Opinion, *New York Times*, May 23, 2012, https://www.nytimes.com/2012/05/24/opinion/not-all-israeli-citizens-are-equal.html; Ben White, "Explained: Palestinian Citizens of Israel," *Middle East Monitor*, December 28, 2016, https://www.middleeastmonitor.com/20161228-explained-palestinian-citizens-of-israel/.

5. "Israel Foreign Assistance," accessed June 27, 2018, https://www.foreignassistance.gov/explore/country/Israel.

6. Ann M. Simmons, "U.S. Foreign Aid: A Waste of Money or a Boost of World Stability? Here are the Facts," *Los Angeles Times*, May 10, 2017, http://www.latimes.com/world/la-fg-global-aid-true-false-20170501-htmlstory.html.

7. Peter Baker and Julie Hirschfeld Davis, "U.S. Finalizes Deal to Give Israel $38 Billion in Military Aid," *New York Times*, September 13, 2016, https://www.nytimes.com/2016/09/14/world/middleeast/israel-benjamin-netanyahu-military-aid.html.

8. This first article claims 9 percent of new West Bank settlers are U.S. citizens. The second claims that 15 percent of current West Bank settlers are U.S. citizens. Judy Maltz, "Americans Disproportionately Leading the Charge in Settling the West Bank," *Haaretz*, June 23, 2017, https://www.haaretz.com/israel-news/.premium.MAGAZINE-americans-disproportionately-leading-charge-in-settling-west-bank-1.5486975; JTA, "15% of Settlers are American, New Research Claims," *Times of Israel*, August 28, 2015, https://www.timesofisrael.com/15-of-west-bank-settlers-are-americans-new-research-finds/.

9. Jeff Halper, *War against the People: Israel, Palestinians, and Global Pacification* (London: Pluto Press, 2015).

10. Edith Garwood, "With Whom are Many U.S. Police Departments Training? With a Chronic Human Rights Violator—Israel," *Human Rights Now Blog*, Amnesty International, August 25, 2016, https://blog.amnestyusa.org/middle-east/with-whom-are-many-u-s-police-departments-training-with-a-chronic-human-rights-violator-israel/; Alice Speri, "Israel Security Forces are Training American Cops Despite History of Rights Abuses," *Intercept*, September 15, 2017, https://theintercept.com/2017/09/15/police-israel-cops-training-adl-human-rights-abuses-dc-washington/; See also the database: https://palestineishere.org/places/police/.

11. Henry Schwan, "New England ADL Sends Wayland Police Chief to Israel for Specialized Training, *Metrowest Daily News*, December 1, 2018, https://www.metrowestdailynews.com/news/20181201/new-england-adl-sends-wayland-police-chief-to-israel-for-specialized-training; Spencer Ho, "Israel Trains U.S. Law Enforcement in Counter-Terrorism," *Times of Israel*, October 8, 2013, https://www.timesofisrael.com/israel-trains-us-law-enforcement-in-counter-terrorism/.

12. Isabel Kershner, "Trump Cites Israel's 'Wall' as Model: The Analogy is Iffy," *New York Times*, January 27, 2017, https://www.nytimes.com/2017/01/27/world/middleeast/trump-mexico-wall-israel-west-bank.html.

13. David Jackson, Susan Page, and John Fritze, "Exclusive: President Trump Vows to Send as Many Troops to the Border 'as Necessary' to Stop Caravan," *USA Today*, October 22, 2018, https://www.usatoday.com/story/news/politics/2018/10/22/trump-halt-migrant-caravan-many-troops-necessary/1731717002/.

14. Courtney Weaver and Katrina Manson, "Trump Suggests U.S. Troops Should Fire on Rock-Throwing Migrants," *Financial Times*, November 1, 2018, https://www.ft.com/content/12ed8f9e-de27-11e8-9f04-38d397e6661c.

15. "Palestinian Who Threw Rock at Israeli Soldier Shot Dead in West Bank," *i24 News*, June 6, 2018, https://www.i24news.tv/en/news/israel/176497-180606-palestinian-killed-by-israeli-fire-in-flashpoint-west-bank-village; Yuval Shany, "Is Israel Justified in Shooting Protestors on Gaza Border?," Opinion, *Forward*, April 7, 2018, https://forward.com/opinion/398307/is-israel-justified-in-shooting-protestors-on-gaza-border/.

16. Bret Stephens, "What Real Border Security Looks Like," Opinion, *New York Times*, January 10, 2019, https://www.nytimes.com/2019/01/10/opinion/border-wall-israel-lebanon-egypt.html.

17. Chloe Farand, "The Israeli Company that Built a Wall Along Gaza's Border Wants to Build Donald Trump's Wall on the Mexican Border," *Independent*, February 6, 2017, https://www.independent.co.uk/news/world/americas/israeli-company-magal-security-gaza-build-wall-donald-trump-us-mexico-border-a7564271.html; Jonathan Ferziger, "Israeli Company that Fenced in Gaza Angles to Help Build Trump's Mexico Wall," *Bloomberg*, January 29, 2017, https://www.bloomberg.com/news/articles/2017-01-29/israel-s-magal-pushes-for-mexico-wall-deal-as-trump-buoys-shares.

18. The following short list includes important books detailing Israel's security regime and the relationships between Israel and the West, particularly the United States: Halper, *War against the People*; John J. Mearsheimer and Stephen M. Walt, *The Israel Lobby and U.S. Foreign Policy* (New York: Farrar, Straus and Giroux, 2008); Ilan Pappé, *The Idea of Israel: A History of Power and Knowledge* (New York: Verso, 2014); Pappé, *The Bureaucracy of Evil: The History of the Israeli Occupation* (Oxford: Oneworld, 2012); Pappé, *The Israel-Palestine Question* (London: Routledge, 2006); Nadera Shalhoub-Kevorkian, *Security Theology, Surveillance and the Politics of Fear* (Cambridge: Cambridge University Press, 2015); Timothy P. Weber, *On the Road to Armageddon: How Evangelicals Became Israel's Best Friend* (Grand Rapids, MI: Baker Academic, 2005); Ben White, *Cracks in the Wall: Beyond Apartheid in Palestine/Israel* (London: Pluto Press, 2018).

19. The problem of the U.S. media's preference for Israel over Palestine has been well documented, most famously by Edward W. Said in *Covering Islam: How the Media and the Experts Determine How We See the Rest of the World* (New York: Routledge and Keagan Paul, 1981); Said, *The Question of Palestine* (New York: Routledge and Keagan Paul, 1980). See also: Seth Ackerman, "Al-Aqsa Intifada and the U.S. Media," *Journal of Palestine Studies* 30, no. 2 (2001): 61–74; Marda Dunsky, "Missing: The Bias Implicit in the Absent," *Arab Studies Quarterly* 23, no. 3 (2001): 1–29; Marda Dunksy, *Pens and Swords: How the American Mainstream Media Report the Israeli-Palestinian Conflict* (New York: Columbia University Press, 2008); Robert Fisk, "Fear and Learning in America," *Independent*, April 17, 2002, https://www.independent.co.uk/voices/commentators/fisk/robert-fisk-fear-and-learning-in-america-9210590.html; D.D. Guttenplan, "Parallax and Palestine," *Nation*, February 21, 2002, https://www.thenation.com/article/parallax-and-palestine/; Luke Peterson, *Palestine-Israel in the Print News Media: Contending Discourses* (London: Routledge, 2015); Susan Dente Ross, "Unequal Combatants on an Uneven Media Battlefield: Palestine and Israel," in *Images that Injure: Pictorial Stereotypes in the Media*, 2nd ed., ed. Paul Martin Lester and Susan Dente Ross (Westport, CT: Praeger, 2003), 57–64; Barbie Zelizer, "How Bias Shapes the News: Challenging the *New York Times*' Status as a Newspaper of Record on the Middle East," *Journalism: Theory, Practice, and Criticism* 3, no. 3 (2002): 283–307.

20. This bias is evident through reporting that 1) includes few, if any ordinary Palestinian voices (but many images of Palestinian protestors and mourners). The Palestinian voices included are often leaders quoted making comments that incite Western fears (e.g., Daniel Estrin and Abu Bakr Bashir, "Hamas Leader Implies 'Hundreds of Thousands' of Palestinians may Breach Israel Border," *NPR's All Things Considered*, May 10, 2018, https://www.npr.org/sections/parallels/2018/05/10/610062464/hamas-leader-implies-hundreds-of-thousands-of-palestinians-may-breach-israel-bor); 2) relies on notably pro-Israel and Zionist U.S. Americans to offer their assessments of the situations in news reporting with no comparable Palestinian point of view (e.g., Ari Shapiro, "Former U.S. Ambassador to Israel Weighs in on Embassy Move to Jerusalem," *NPR's All Things Considered*, May 14, 2018, https://www.npr.org/2018/05/14/611097661/former-u-s-ambassador-to-israel-weighs-in-on-embassy-move-to-jerusalem); 3) gives opinion and editorial space to those who rely on old tropes of Palestinians as the extremists and Israelis as rational actors with no comparable alternative viewpoints featured (e.g., David Brooks, "The Gaza Violence: How Extremism Corrupts," Opinion, *New York Times*, May 17, 2018, https://www.nytimes.com/2018/05/17/opinion/gaza-israel-palestinian-extremism.html).

21. "Quick Facts: The Palestinian Nakba," Institute for Middle East Understanding, May 13, 2015, https://imeu.org/article/quick-facts-the-palestinian-nakba.

22. Oren Liebermann, "Why Moving the U.S. Embassy to Jerusalem Is So Controversial," *CNN*, December 6, 2017, https://www.cnn.com/2017/01/24/middleeast/donald-trump-us-embassy-israel-explainer/index.html; Ian Black, "Why Would Moving the U.S. Embassy to Jerusalem Be So Contentious," *Guardian*, December 5, 2017, https://www.theguardian.com/us-news/2017/dec/05/jerusalem-embassy-move-can-the-saudis-stay-trumps-hand.

23. Nasim, Ahmed, "Palestine Land Day Remembered," *Middle East Monitor*, March 30, 2018, https://www.middleeastmonitor.com/20180330-palestine-land-day-remembered/.

24. Rebecca Stead, "What Everyone Should Know about Israel's Siege of the Gaza Strip," *Middle East Monitor*, August 10, 2018, https://www.middleeastmonitor.com/20180810-what-everyone-should-know-about-israels-siege-of-the-gaza-strip/.

25. "Big Hamas Win in Gaza's Election," *BBC News*, January 28, 2005, http://news.bbc.co.uk/2/hi/middle_east/4214375.stm; Scott Wilson, "Hamas Sweeps Palestinian Elections, Complicating

Peace Efforts in the Mideast," *Washington Post*, January 27, 2006, http://www.washingtonpost.com/wp-dyn/content/article/2006/01/26/AR2006012600372.html.

26. "Operation Cast Lead," Institute for Middle East Understanding, January 4, 2012, https://imeu.org/article/operation-cast-lead; "Eight Years After the 2008–2009 (Cast Lead) Hostilities in Gaza: Lack of Accountability Persists," *Monthly Humanitarian Bulletin*, United Nations Office for the Coordination of Humanitarian Affairs, February 2017, https://www.ochaopt.org/content/eight-years-after-2008-2009-cast-lead-hostilities-gaza-lack-accountability-persists.

27. "The 2014 Israeli Attack on Gaza ('Operation Protective Edge') One Year Later," Institute for Middle East Understanding, July 8, 2015, https://imeu.org/article/2014-israeli-attack-on-gaza-one-year-later; "Gaza Crisis: Toll of Operations in Gaza," *BBC News*, September 1, 2014, https://www.bbc.com/news/world-middle-east-28439404.

28. "Aid Groups Appeal for End to Gaza Blockade," *YNetNews*, August 26, 2015, https://www.ynetnews.com/articles/0,7340,L-4694757,00.html; Sam Masters, "Gaza, a Year on from Operation Protective Edge: A Growing Population and a Compromised and Depleted Aquifer Leaves Water in Scarce Supply for Palestinians," *Independent*, July 7, 2015, https://www.independent.co.uk/news/world/middle-east/gaza-a-year-on-from-operation-protective-edge-a-growing-population-and-a-compromised-and-depleted-10373143.html.

29. Noam Chomsky, "Noam Chomsky on Gaza, the World's Largest Open-Air Prison," *In These Times*, November 7, 2012, http://inthesetimes.com/article/14148/gaza_the_worlds_largest_open_air_prison; Alistair Dawber, "Tales from Gaza: What is Life Really Like in 'the World's Largest Outdoor Prison'?" *Independent*, April 13, 2013, https://www.independent.co.uk/news/world/middle-east/tales-from-gaza-what-is-life-really-like-in-the-worlds-largest-outdoor-prison-8567611.html.

30. "Israel Killed 253 Palestinians during Great March of Return," *Middle East Monitor*, December 27, 2018, https://www.middleeastmonitor.com/20181227-israel-killed-253-palestinians-during-great-march-of-return/.

31. "Humanitarian Snapshot: Casualties in the Context of Demonstrations and Hostilities in Gaza, 30 March–31 December 2018," United Nations Office for the Coordination of Humanitarian Affairs—Occupied Palestinian Territory, January 21, 2019, https://www.ochaopt.org/content/humanitarian-snapshot-casualties-context-demonstrations-and-hostilities-gaza-30-march-31-0.

32. "Anti-Boycott Legislation around the Country," Palestine Legal, April 10, 2019, https://palestinelegal.org/righttoboycott.

33. Ryan Grim, "U.S. Senate's First Bill, in the Midst of the Shutdown, Is a Bipartisan Defense of the Israeli Government from Boycotts," *Intercept*, January 5, 2019, https://theintercept.com/2019/01/05/u-s-senates-first-bill-in-midst-of-shutdown-is-a-bipartisan-defense-of-the-israeli-government-from-boycotts/.

34. "S.1: Strengthening America's Security in the Middle East Act of 2019," *Govtrack*, January 11, 2019, https://www.govtrack.us/congress/bills/116/s1/summary.

35. Catie Edmondson, "Senate Advances Pro-Israel Bill as GOP Searches for Democratic Divisions," *New York Times*, January 28, 2019, https://www.nytimes.com/2019/01/28/us/politics/senate-israel-boycott-democrats.html?module=inline.

36. Glenn Greenwald, "A Texas Elementary School Speech Pathologist Refused to Sign a Pro-Israel Oath, Now Mandatory in Many States—so She Lost Her Job," *Intercept*, December 17, 2018, https://theintercept.com/2018/12/17/israel-texas-anti-bds-law/.

37. Benjamin Fearnow, "Why did CNN Fire Marc Lamont? Pro-Palestine Comments at UN, Seen as Anti-Israel, Lead to Network Cutting Ties," *Newsweek*, November 29, 2018, https://www.newsweek.com/marc-lamont-hill-cnn-fired-palestine-hamas-boycott-israel-united-nations-anti-1237748.

38. Craig R. McCoy, "UN Speech by Temple Prof Draws Fire from University's Board Chair," *Inquirer*, November 30, 2018, http://www.philly.com/philly/news/breaking/marc-lamont-hill-temple-israel-anti-semitic-20181130.html.

39. Dima Khalidi, "Marc Lamont Hill Is Not Alone," *Jacobin Magazine*, December 13, 2018, https://www.jacobinmag.com/2018/12/marc-lamont-hill-palestine-censorship-israel.

40. Sherry Wheeler Stewart, "Civil Rights Award Rescinded from Angela Davis after Jewish Community Objections," *NPR*, January 8, 2019, https://www.npr.org/2019/01/08/683250815/civil-rights-award-rescinded-from-angela-davis-after-jewish-community-objections.

HAITHAM SALAWDEH

"Settler Violence in Duma Village, West Bank," September 9, 2015

https://www.wortfm.org/palestinian-activist-haitham-salawdeh/

KARMA CHÁVEZ: At the end of July, an eighteen-month-old Palestinian boy was burned to death after Israeli settlers set fire to his family house in Duma village, south of Nablus city, in the occupied West Bank of Palestine. While I did not visit Duma village, I was in Nablus during my visit at the start of the summer. The parents of Ali Dawabsheh and his four-year-old brother were also injured in the attack. His father, thirty-two-year-old Saad Dawabsheh succumbed to his injuries eight days after the attack. And just this week, Ali's mother, twenty-seven-year-old Riham Dawabsheh passed away this week in an Israeli hospital, leaving four-year-old Ahmad as the only survivor in the attack.[1] The attack is attributed to Israeli extremists living on settlements in the West Bank that international law deems illegal. The word "revenge" in Hebrew and a star of David were spray painted on the burned home.[2]

This tragic incident is unfortunately not isolated despite the international attention it received. The United Nations reports that prior to this incident and since the start of 2015, there were 120 documented attacks by Israeli settlers against Palestinians in the West Bank.[3] In both 2013 and 2014, the Palestinian government logged more than 1,000 settler acts of violence and property destruction.[4] The Israeli human rights organization Yesh Din also reports that 92.6 percent of complaints that Palestinians file with Israeli police go without charges.[5]

The Israeli government strongly condemned this act of racist terrorism when it happened. The Israeli army's Lieutenant Colonel Peter Lerner said in a statement: "This attack against civilians is nothing short of a barbaric act of terrorism. A comprehensive investigation is under way in order to find the terrorists and bring them to justice."[6] Prime Minister Benjamin Netanyahu also used the word "terrorism" and condemned extremism.[7] Unfortunately, forty days and three deaths later, the publication *Mondoweiss* reports that Israel has not charged anyone with the murders.[8]

Today, we have a special show. Our guest, Haitham Salawdeh, was born and raised in Duma, Palestine, where the atrocity took place. He is a neighbor and relative of the victims. Haitham left Duma to pursue his university studies in Germany and later the United States. He lives in Milwaukee and has been in Wisconsin since 1992, but he visits his family regularly and arrived in Duma just days after the fire-bombing took place. He will thus provide us with a close and personal depiction of the situation in the West Bank, this atrocity, and what people in the U.S. are doing in response.

In addition to his personal connection to this atrocity, Haitham is an activist with the USPCN (U.S. Palestinian Community Network). USPCN is a network of community organizations and activists chartered to organize the U.S. Palestinian community and educate the public on Palestinian issues.

Haitham Salawdeh, welcome to *A Public Affair*.

KC: First of all, I just would like to say that I'm very, very sorry for your losses. I know, another one this week. How are you doing?

HAITHAM SALAWDEH: I'm doing—I'm doing okay because I get to be busy and I get to not see the family day in and day out. I get to not see the father of Saad who is in his late seventies, on kidney dialysis, and has diabetes and struggling to really just stay on his feet. And so, when you are away from the situation, you are going to be much less in distress as the family back home. And sometimes that can affect you negatively because you get to forget during the day, but you're always so reminded by the messages I get day to day from how the family's doing and how everybody is handling it in Duma. Duma is a very small, very tightly knit community, I mean, these are people that have been living together for hundreds of years. There are two families in Duma, the Dawabsheh and the Salawdeh and there is no way that you cannot make a connection between these two families through anything—just, the proximity, the local proximity has generated one big—really one big family and what affects one affects the other, basically, so . . .

KC: And so how—about how many people live in the village?

HS: Duma, today, has about two thousand people or around two thousand people. You have to remember that a lot of the people—when you count them, a lot of them are also in exile. Basically, either, like me, who cannot go back or others in exile; they are on the outside and they're working because there are not many opportunities, and hopefully we can get to talk about that, too, in the show. There are not many opportunities given and afforded to these people in Duma. So, you have a demographic that has a lot of children, you have a demographic that has a lot of elderly people. And the in-betweeners, you know, the young and especially the men leave the village and they go to the Gulf states and other areas to work. And when I say two thousand, it is actually a village, like many other Palestinian villages, mainly of children, women, and elderly people. When I was there in August and people were trying to talk about ways to defend the village—and of course, they have no weapons, so when you say "defend" you mean holding a stick and trying to basically be an alarm system for the village. You have a lot of teenagers basically coming and volunteering to do that task because that's all you've got in a village like Duma.

KC: Well I know this summer when I visited Nablus there is a lot of industry in terms of the big soap industry there seemed to be—candy making industry, shoemakers. We saw a very vibrant industry there. Do those translate into the village at all or not?

HS: Not directly. The soap industry and all these industries that have been in Nablus for many years actually, and yes, you're right they do provide work. You have to remember that the eighty thousand population of Nablus needs work as well. And so, the unemployment is staggering; unless you go out to work for the settlements or Israel, there is not much to do. You have the government that provides work. Riham, the woman who died over the weekend, the mother, was a teacher, and so a lot of the Palestinian population, if they are not working for a teaching position or a doctor or something like that, your only choice is the Palestinian security forces or probably the settlements. But there isn't really a lot of opportunity in the village or around the village. Nablus work is very difficult, and it's kind of hard to get somebody from Duma to go work in the factories there.

KC: And so, just to—I'm just wanting to paint a little bit of a picture of this place. I grew up in a town of about two thousand people, also very kind of close knit, probably in a different way, but this is probably very familiar to a lot of rural Wisconsinites who grew up in a similar place that didn't have a lot of economic opportunities. The small families—so the Dawabsheh family is one of the two major families, you said there in the town but the tiny family here that was in this home, Ali, Riham, and Saad as well as Ahmed, did you know them well? Will you tell us a little bit about them?

HS: So, I left Duma in 1984 and by then—Saad's brother was the only son of Abu Nasr at that time and Saad was, I don't remember if he was—if his mom was pregnant with him or not born yet, I think, even. So, when I left, Duma wasn't in my mind in terms of—I know the old generation, I know some of the younger generation but not all of them. I am very good friends with his brother Nasser because at my time I was able to see him. But I'm very familiar with the family as a whole. We are very related through marriage and other ways. I know that Riham, like I said, is a teacher in

Qusra, the village next door. And they've been married for just five or six years. When I went back usually I would see Abu Nasr, who is the father of Saad, the grandfather. But I have to say, I haven't had the opportunity or the privilege to meet Saad and his family, it's just—when I go home what you usually see (and my family will tell you, and my wife will tell you—who is American, by the way, and not used to the reception that happens) you usually come in the house when you arrive and you just have people after people walking in and walking out for a week. You don't even know who's coming and who's going, and the door is open and so on. And so, I have known the people before or when I was living there, it's very hard for me to keep track [*laughing*] of the new gen—of the newcomers to the village, so to speak.

KC: Sure. Now, you arrived in Duma just after this atrocity, will you describe what people were experiencing and what they were talking about in those days just after this tragic incident?

HS: Certainly, I mean, from the minute I arrived to the minute I left, I have to say that—and they want to relay this message, because I think that's the most important message of all—the most affected in this atrocity, in addition to the immediate family and the families in general, are the children. I have to say that every—almost every child under five and certainly the children who are not living in the heart of the village, who are on the outskirts of the village—and maybe to paint the picture, when you talked about Wisconsin villages, you are absolutely right, I mean, it is very similar, the relationships are very similar. The only difference is that Palestinian villages are very separated from their farmland. So, people live in the village proper and then the farmland is on the outskirts. Which means that you live like door to door. People are kind of close and next to each other more so than in Wisconsin where there is distance and people can afford to live on their farm and their farm is huge, between one farm and another farm you have to take a car sometimes. In Duma this is not the case, everybody just kind of lives close to each other, except there are houses that happen to be on the outskirts. And the impact on the children in these houses is really huge. I mean, they are not sleeping well. The general psychological effect on children that we see with trauma happens here, where bedwetting is a common occurrence. Refusing to sleep in the house, one of my cousins' daughters insists they go to their grandparents' house and they leave their house. The feeling of unsafety is unparalleled.

I have been in Duma before, and I have seen Palestinians go through many—many—problems, but this one is unique for the village. Because the village has never really experienced anything like this. Nablus used to be the problem spot, and so when we go to Palestine, usually if there is any sort of problem we would go to Duma because, you know, nothing happens in Duma. And when this happens in a place where nothing happens, every feeling of safety falls off because there is nothing you can do about it, first of all. And you talked about the fact that forty days later nothing had happened; these people are still at large. And I want to remind your listeners of the fact that if a Palestinian child were to throw a stone at a military jeep, the whole village will be summoned, and everybody will be questioned, his house will be probably demolished, and the child will probably go to jail. We just saw that two weeks ago when a soldier was trying to arrest a Palestinian boy, and if it weren't for the courageous act of the women around who actually yanked him from the soldier, that child would be in jail right now.[9] So any small act of a Palestinian against the occupation will be met with an iron fist. And, at the same time, people who saw the end of the killings of Saad and his family gave directions as to where these settlers ran, and we know the direction they went to, and the Israeli ministry could have at least questioned someone, they could have done something like that. But of course, they are not doing anything. The Palestinian villagers in general, and in Duma in particular, they have no guns, they have no way of defending themselves, which means they are very at the mercy of kind of shouting if they see something and hoping that Palestinian Authority or somebody will come and intervene. But fear is, I would say, bigger than anger, which is kind of unusual, right? In a situation like this where four people died, you would think that it would be a huge amount of anger—and there is, but fear is the prominent factor here, I think.

KC: Wow. It's really—I mean, it's very terrifying, Haitham, to hear that fear has trumped anger in this situation and hearing there's no recourse, really, to protect oneself. I read an article from *Al Jazeera* about a week ago that talked about these sort of informal patrols of young men, teenagers, I think you alluded to this earlier in the interview, university students who are essentially a kind of neighborhood watch—a weaponless neighborhood watch to keep an eye on the village. Do you know some of the young men who are participating in this effort?

HS: Yeah, I was there when this effort was being put together, and I know some of these young men who are trying to patrol the streets and watch out. I can tell you that, while that effort is appreciated, people are afraid for the men more than anything else. Because, again, when you are running with a stick there's really not much you can do against a well-armed—the

Jewish-only settlements around us, they have fences and they have electronic monitoring equipment, and then they have soldiers manning the entrances and so on; they can feel safe. In Duma, that's kind of open bordered and there is—there are no walls, and people don't want to have walls, and there are no fences, and there's no electronic equipment to monitor movements. But the whole—which, by the way, two weeks ago there was another attack on another house in Duma, close to the first house. And the house did get burned, but people were able to get out early, and people are more alert now, and the whole village came to their aid, and luckily nobody was hurt but property, which is replaceable right?

So, the main thing is that the children and the people were out and are safe. But you can see there are too many entry points for somebody to be able to man and look at. So, yeah of course, I don't want to tell them that their efforts are very ineffective, but you want to encourage that kind of being vigilant and looking around. But, honestly, this is at a scale where young people on their own cannot really manage. You need protection, you need government protection. And at least you need some kind of weaponry that can make them defend themselves because a guy with a stick when you're faced with five settlers with guns, he might not even have the opportunity to alert the village. Duma being in what's described by Oslo as Zone C, Duma is really under Israeli commission. And people tend to forget the fact that in the equation of occupier and occupied, the occupier is always responsible for anything that happens to the occupied. And it's no different than the POW—the prisoner of war and the jail. You know, the jail is responsible for the well-being of the prisoner of war, and in this equation, Israel is the number one responsible for what happens. And the occupied's job is really just to resist the occupation. Really, that's their main job the same way it's the main job of a POW to escape prison. And so, we try to protect ourselves, but Israel has to basically get their guards back, and it is basically their responsibility to manage the settlers. And these are men and women that are mostly rich white folks from New York and Brooklyn who come to Palestine thinking that they want to be closer to God and the best way they can get closer to God is by turning our people in. You know, they are insane, and they need to be managed by the government that supports them in the first place. It's not our job.

KC: Yeah, no, absolutely. And I think this is maybe what a lot of people don't understand. You mentioned Area C as the region which, in the Oslo Accords, Duma is under. And so, just briefly—correct me if I'm wrong—Area C, that means it's both under Israeli civilian and security control.

HS: Yes, yeah.

KC: And that actually represents—I think people don't necessarily realize, they think the West Bank is Palestinian territory, but about 75 percent of the West Bank is under both Israeli civilian and security control, including your village, is that correct?

HS: You're right, and that's totally correct. I mean, other than the major cities, really, the Palestinian Authority has very little to do—in Duma and any other village next to Duma—outside of Nablus, they have absolutely no control, civilian or otherwise. There are Area Bs that are kind of closer to Nablus proper, you know Area A, Ramallah proper. But villages like Duma, and so on, they are all under Israeli occupation, and they control the entrances and the lives of people and everything else.

KC: And so, it's for this reason why—it's not—villagers can't appeal to the Palestinian Authority, you actually have to appeal to Israel for some sort of justice here, that's the only authority.

HS: Yes, that's true. And when you—the person you're appealing to is both the judge and the jury, and the executioner and the imprisoner, it's really, at the end of the day, they play the same role because we talk about settlers, but we have to remember these settlers did not come from Mars. These settlers were brought there by government sponsorship, Israel sponsors—directly or through government sponsored organizations that do the same thing. We should not forget a few years ago[10] when Bibi Netanyahu went to France and asked the Jews to come back to Palestine.[11] The whole collecting of people to bring back is a big effort, and they are willing to take anyone and everyone. And when it comes to the West Bank and that area, in hope of grabbing as much land as possible to change the demographics of the area, I don't think that questions are asked. Anyone who is willing to come will be given tax advantages and tax privileges, will be protected by the military, and they can come and live and farm and so on. And that's government sponsored. The military paves the way for these people to come in. The settlements are—most of them are created based on a very old Turkish law where if land is standing unused for x number of years, the state has a right to take it. And Israel and the military perfect the idea of putting legal veneers around their action. And so, what they will do, many times, they will come and declare a specific piece of land—they will declare it a closed military area, so you cannot come into it,[12] and if you do, you will be shot.[13] So for a couple of years nobody comes into the land. And then three years later, that area is then considered to be unused; because they will kill you, nobody's using it.[14] So they will turn it into a state land,[15] and then that goes into the Jewish fund for people to use.[16] And that's where the settlements are built, always. So, you have a state-sponsored—settlers coming into our midst and it's kind of hard for the state, who brought them in the first place, to put a stop to them.

KC: Well, and I think what you described there is something maybe a lot of people don't understand. I know I didn't understand this until I actually visited the region, which is the way that the building of settlements gets facilitated by—not a lot of people are in, and then because people aren't in because they would be shot or—or detained, now the land is unusable, and so it can be settled by someone else as dictated by the Israeli government. How many settlements are near Duma and how far are they?

HS: So, there are a few outposts, there are like two or three outposts just two kilometers from Duma. There are big settlements that are about five—there are three big settlements that are about five to seven kilometers, four or five miles from Duma. And then, from the Jordan Valley side, of course, it's all settlements. And Duma sits on the hill—on the hills on top of the Jordan Valley. And so, below us, you just see settlements. Ma'ale Efraim and other kinds of settlements and outposts. There is a lot. When I left Palestine, there were about eighty thousand settlers in the West Bank and Gaza. Now you're talking about half a million settlers.

KC: And the concept of the outpost—can you explain what an outpost is in relation to a settlement?

HS: So, these outposts are basically a group of people who come and declare land theirs, themselves, structures and Palestinian lands that even the Israeli government itself, it's like—the veneer of legality needs to be maintained somehow and they would say, "These are illegal, these have not gone through the regular confiscation kind of model." And so, these are usually more aggressive people, they are more ideological, if you like. And so, they come, they build almost always temporary structures, and they take over a piece of land.

Given the fact that they all have guns, that sets the whole notion of the—that possession is 99 percent of ownership. And so, they kind of on their own, take over the land that—and sometimes would—many times, actually, would burn trees down, would intimidate people from even going onto the roads that are close to them. So, enforcing this whole thing. On the top of Duma there used to be an outpost, about in 2006–2008, where the Jewish-only road that goes up—which is the only road that Duma could take, so it's not like we had a lot of choice but to take that road—a guy was with his family of twenty, I think, or so was manning that road and would be shooting at people and basically terrorizing, if you want, in the area. And they are usually outlawed and considered illegal even by Israel itself.

KC: Just to kind of clarify what you just said there: so, on a road—on the road—because, of course, in the West Bank there are two road systems, there's a set of road systems for Israeli settlers and then there's a set of roads for Palestinians. So, on the road that Palestinians—the only road that you could take out of the village there was a settler who was at an outpost who was shooting people for using the road?

HS: Yup. And it—to some extent it was by him, it was not just force but intimidation tactics. And maybe that brings me back to experiences that further—because sometimes occupation—the Palestinian occupation is quite a bit different. The consequences of occupation and overall oppression that's happening to Palestinians is not new news. It's something Americans saw in this country. The difference was the requirement of the system. You know, so in America the old system needed Black slaves, so they uprooted the Blacks from *their* country and brought them to America. In Palestine it's slightly different, where the system is really invested in the resources but not the people. Every effort is being made to slowly, slowly drain the land from its people, either by stealing their resources away or making threats to them, or fear. In every single way, if you—and I don't know how much you've seen from how people kind of move in Palestine when you were in Palestine, but if you noticed, every single thing that happens in Palestine is meant to really make your life hard and horrible and make it easier for you to make the decision to move on your own. So, although differences in systems existed where, like I said, Israel is invested in empty land, America was invested in the Blacks. Yet the results kind of are the same. You did have an apartheid system here, you had, you know, Black-only schools, Black-only neighborhoods, Black-only this, Black-only that. And you do the same in Palestine. The Jewish-only cities—I mean you couldn't even—like, I couldn't even live there if my life depended on it, right? So, the situations existed—the lynching and burning of people happened—in two places. While it's really interesting to see that oppression had maybe different requirements, but the tools are the same. And one of the tools is intimidation; intimidation was happening here in America to many people of color, and it's happening in Palestine the same way. It's—the tactics are the same, and the impacts on the people are the same.

KC: I want to go back a little bit to put this night—again, July 31—in the context of what you've been describing. And, from what you've described—this question may be irrelevant, but I want to know what people are saying, which is—what exactly happened, what is the motivation as people understand it? Because it's not an isolated, random act, because these things happen, although it's new, you said to Duma. But do we have a sense of—like is there a story in the village about who did this and why specifically they targeted this house? . . . Oh, are we there? Do we have you still Haitham? Oh, I think we lost you. To get Haitham back on the air here, Mike will give him a call . . . I think we got Haitham back on the air here, sorry we lost you for a second!

HS: Yeah, sorry, I think it must be a conspiracy [*laughing*]. But if it's possible for you to repeat your questions, I think the last thing I heard was you talking about the night of the 31st.

KC: Sure, yeah, what I was going to ask—and in part asking a question about motive, based on the context you've just provided for us, it seems a little bit irrelevant, but I'm wondering, maybe, how the villagers are talking about how they understand the motivation of what happened, if there is a specific reason why *this* house or *this* family—specific family—was targeted, was there an interaction earlier? What are people saying about how they're making sense of what happened, or is it just this is what happens when you have settlers so close in proximity to villagers?

HS: This is a great question because had this happened, maybe five years ago, I think that question would be much more relevant. But you have to remember that this is not the first time. Mohammed Abu Khdeir, the Palestinian American[17] who was beaten and burned to death[18] just a year ago[19] by settlers[20] is still in the memory of many Palestinians. Abu Khdeir was given gasoline, and his mouth was filled with gasoline and was set aflame[21] and was captured, captured on camera.[22] And people—people tend to remember these things. It's not difficult—it's difficult to forget a heinous act like that. And so, the Duma villagers don't see themselves as being singled out as much as being part of a systematic effort to terrorize and scare Palestinians to leave, at large. This is really the main point. And for the last years, if you go back and look, I mean, mosques have been burned, churches have been burned. There isn't a month that went by for a while that there wasn't a burning happening. One that happens more frequently are trees being burned, knowing that Palestinians in the area—if you saw, that's their livelihood, olive trees and fig trees and so on. And when you burn somebody's livelihood, basically, you might as well have killed them. You are uprooting them from that area, removing any connection from them. These things happen and happen a lot. Now, that house happens to be not totally in the outskirts of Duma but kind of remote, and that's what people think is happening. It is kind of a less central home, and so people with homes that are kind of farther from the village center are being extra cautious and are being scared, to tell you the truth.

KC: And so, it's actually the sort of encroaching that—you become more vulnerable—or potentially more vulnerable on the outskirts as the settlements move closer.

HS: Absolutely. The joke was let's do like the penguins do, can we move the houses around, you keep rotating them. But of course, we can't do that. But that's really—kids and adults would feel safe. I think that the biggest, really—and I said it at the beginning—the thing that's really shocked me the most is how little kids that usually you wouldn't expect to vocalize their feelings that much, I mean usually kids are not as vocal about it, they internalize it, and they grow up with it, and they become screwed up. But I've seen so many kids that are vocalizing their fear. It's unusual, to say the least.

KC: Some people are talking about this as what's known as the quote/unquote "price tag" movement, which essentially is this kind of loose movement of settlers who specifically attack Palestinians but also Israeli Defense Forces property, and it's a retaliatory price to be paid, right, for when the Israeli Defense Forces actually try to push back settlements.[23] Is this kind of discourse of the "price tag" movement something that's discussed in Duma at all?

HS: I don't think that's really there. You have to think about somebody who is in Duma—and Duma's very sheltered. They don't really care about the geopolitical impact of what happens. They actually don't know much about the settlers either. They only see the word "revenge," and they only see the David star. And it's kind of hard for a Palestinian who has gone through this to get them to start to rationalize and analyze and see the state—other organizations that are in one way or another state sponsored. But it's really—I think people know somewhat justly that it's settlers, some settler movements. The details of that, I don't think that it's very clear to Palestinians. Because remember there has been no investigation, so everything is speculation at this point. It's like—like I said, if a Palestinian kid were to throw a rock at a military jeep, you would see the village being summoned, collected. And when something like this happens, the army doesn't move, nobody moves. In fact, the only movement the army made is in Duma and around Duma to stop the villagers from throwing stones and fulfilling their anger. So as far as the village is concerned, to be honest with you, I think they believe the army is as much responsible as anyone else. We don't make a distinction, I don't think.

KC: Mhm. We have just about ten minutes left in the show, and I wanted to turn attention a little bit at least to efforts to respond—not just, you have these young men who are patrolling, if nothing else, to maybe psychologically make themselves feel safer and empowered. But you—at the very start you were talking about the—the worst impact of this is on the children. Are there resources—psychological resources or therapy kinds of resources or what's available for people to deal with this trauma in the village of Duma?

HS: Duma has absolutely no psychological facilities. We barely have clinics or anything like that. Anything that happens has to be delivered to Nablus. This is a poor community. And poverty comes with big price tags. Some of it is the fact that these children, while they need proper health, will never be able to get the proper health they need. The schools lack school counselors. In fact, the school was the place where the family has been kind of receiving—people are coming to give their sympathies from all over the world, I have to say. So, the school girls are going to go back to school this September and they are going to be reminded of that atrocity by two things: One, the house that sits right next door, it's about two houses from the girls' elementary school. And then the other thing is by the flags and everything else, the remnants of the place that people used to live, to meet and greet people coming to the family outside of the village. Kids are going to be reminded of this for a long time. And there is really no way of combating—of combating that damage that already has happened or is happening day in and day out.

And if I might digress, I think as somebody who grew up in that village, I have to tell you, when I was growing up as a kid, I was afraid of things that are so irrational. I just remember hearing about things like typhoons in India and things like that and not being able to sleep because, what happens if a typhoon would come to my village? You have—you've seen it, you know it's a desert, there's no danger of any water let alone a typhoon. And yet I was afraid of it. And I look at these children and I see a danger that's *not* unrealistic. It's very real, and it's very realistic, and they know it. And their family knows it, their parents know it. It is really, really difficult to handle and manage and combat. And I don't really know, without the professional help—and many, many professionals need to be involved—I don't know that the village alone will be able to come to terms with it.

KC: You mentioned at the school, where there was sort of a memorial being created, that there's been—from around the world people have sent their regards. Has there been any international effort to provide this sort of service to the village?

HS: Not that I'm aware of. No one has ever really indicated, mentioned, offered, or thought of doing that. I think the atrocities that Palestinian children go through, and Gaza is an example, wars and wars and there's just—the need is so much. There is absolutely no effort being made to make these Palestinian children whole psychologically.

KC: And you—I wanted to give you a chance, we just have about three or four minutes left here, but I wanted to give you a chance to talk a bit about the U.S. Palestinian Community Network and any efforts that you're coordinating or other organizations you work with are coordinating here in the U.S. to support the village or to support the family in Palestine.

HS: I think so far Duma as a village has gotten more help from our brothers and sisters in Israel proper in '48, the Palestinians who have a little bit more freedom to move than us. I don't think that there are efforts that are directly to benefit the village Duma, per se, that we are doing here other than your usual shows like this, trying to educate people about what happened. But I think that we cannot take it—take the Palestinian issue and piecemeal it, Gaza is one, Duma is another, Nablus is another—the issue is really the same across, and any work that is being done to educate on Palestine and to try to make people aware of what's happening, any work is good and will benefit everybody. Referring our legislative bodies to hold these people responsible to see to the fire. You know, Palestinian children are like other children, too. And you cannot be talking about human rights and children's rights and not including us. And so, all the work we have been doing in terms of education and outreach, that is catching all of these areas and not just for Duma but for the rest of Palestine.

KC: And just really quick, if someone—one of the ways to get people connected to issues is to tell them personal stories, and if someone has been very compelled by your story and the story of your village today and they wanted to do something specifically in response to this, is there a place that you would direct them? Should they get in touch with the U.S. Palestinian Community Network, or is there another organization you would recommend them contacting?

HS: Absolutely, I think there's a great organization in Madison, the Madison-Rafah Sister City Project that they can reach out to. In Milwaukee they can reach out to me, to my organization USPCN at uspcn.org. And, you know, there's a lot of—as a connection of networks and individuals, we will be able to put these people in touch with whoever they would like, what kind of topics they want to take a look at from right of return to refugee issues to education and other issues, we would be able to help facilitate that connection. Also, people who need speakers or are looking for education events, we'll be able to help with that as well.

KC: Great. Well, we're going to have to leave it there, but Haitham I just really want to thank you for sharing your story and for being with us today.

HS: Thank you, thank you so much for having me.

KC: For sure. Again, our guest today, Haitham Salawdeh, who is a Palestinian and an activist located in Milwaukee but who is originally from the Duma village, which was the site of a firebombing by Israeli settlers in late July. A family of three—a family of four, three of which were killed, the last one so far has died this week and we hope the four-year-old Ahmed will make it. Again, his organization is the U.S. Palestinian Community Network at uspcn.org if you're interested in learning more. He also mentioned the Rafah Sister City Project here in Madison, which you can google and check out online as well.

Postscript from Salawdeh, April 2018

HS: Since the incident, my village has seen other attacks as well.[24] One of the attacks was against the home of a witness to the burning of the family.[25] The village has been very vigilant, and as a result no injuries happened. People's response to these attacks has been instantaneous, and fires are put out, and people are rescued. The sole survivor of the attack is going to school now and lives with his uncle. He lives with many medical problems and still requires a lot of medical attention. He is seen as a symbol of hope and testament to Palestinian resilience.

NOTES

1. Siobhan Fenton, "Mother of Palestinian Toddler Burned to Death in West Bank Arson Attack Dies from Injuries," *Independent*, September 7, 2015, https://www.independent.co.uk/news/world/middle-east/mother-of-palestinian-toddler-burned-to-death-in-west-bank-arson-attack-dies-from-injuries-10489232.html.

2. Associated Press, "Israel Indicts Jewish Extremists for Arson Attack that Killed Palestinian Family," *Guardian*, January 3, 2016, https://www.theguardian.com/world/2016/jan/03/israel-indicts-jewish-extremists-for-arson-attack-that-killed-palestinian-family.

3. The United Nations Office for the Coordination of Humanitarian Affairs reported 127 Israeli settler attacks "on Palestinians and their property across the West Bank, including Jerusalem," from January 1, 2015 to August. "Suspected Settler Violence Claims the Lives of a Palestinian Father and Son," *Monthly Humanitarian Bulletin*, United Nations Office for the Coordination of Humanitarian Affairs, August 28, 2015, https://www.ochaopt.org/content/suspected-settler-violence-claims-lives-palestinian-father-and-son#_ednref3.

4. The numbers are actually lower according to the Women's Center for Legal Aid and Counseling (WCLAC), with 400 acts of settler violence in 2013, and 331 in 2014. WCLAC, "Israeli Settler Violence in the West Bank and East Jerusalem," Report prepared for the UN Special Rapporteur on Violence against Women and the UN Special Rapporteur on the situation of human rights in the Palestinian Territories Occupied since 1967, September 2, 2015, http://www.wclac.org/english/userfiles/SETTLER%20VIOLENCE%20-%20SEP%202015.pdf.

5. Yesh Din, "Prosecution of Israeli Civilians Suspected of Harming Palestinians in the West Bank," data sheet, May 2015, http://files.yesh-din.org/userfiles/Prosecution%20of%20Israeli%20Civilians%20Suspected%20of%20Harming%20Palestinians%20in%20the%20West%20Bank_May%202015.pdf.

6. "Palestinian Baby Burned to Death in Settler Attack," *Al Jazeera*, July 31, 2015, https://www.aljazeera.com/news/2015/07/palestinian-baby-burned-death-extremist-attack-150731035331224.html.

7. In a call to Palestinian president Mahmud Abbas, Netanyahu said, "We must fight terrorism together, regardless of which side it comes from." "Palestinians Bury Baby Killed in West Bank Arson Attack," *Al Jazeera*, July 31, 2015, https://www.aljazeera.com/news/2015/07/palestinians-bury-baby-killed-west-bank-arson-attack-150731130550655.html.

8. Allison Deger, "Palestinians in Duma are Angry that No One Has Been Charged for Murders, After 38 Days," *Mondoweiss*, September 7, 2015, http://mondoweiss.net/2015/09/palestinians-charged-murders/. In early 2016, Israel charged two teenagers in connection with the arson attacks. Allison Deger, "Israel Charges Two Jewish Extremist Youths in Duma Killings," *Mondoweiss*, January 3, 2016, http://mondoweiss.net/2016/01/extremist-charged-killings/. As of June 2018, the two men are on trial. Yotam Berger, "Right-Wing Extremists Protest West Bank Arson Murder Trial: 'Your Grandson's on the Grill,'" *Haaretz*, June 20, 2018, https://www.haaretz.com/israel-news/.premium-right-wing-extremists-protest-west-bank-arson-murder-trial-1.6196907.

9. Technically, this occurred about twelve days before the interview. See: TOI Staff, "Palestinian Women, Kids Attack IDF Soldier Trying to Arrest Boy," *Times of Israel*, August 29, 2015, https://www.timesofisrael.com/palestinian-women-kids-attack-idf-soldier-trying-to-arrest-boy/.

10. Netanyahu did this in February 2015. See Peter Beaumont, "Leaders Reject Netanyahu Calls for Jewish Mass Migration to Israel," *Guardian*, February 16, 2015, https://www.theguardian.com/world/2015/feb/16/leaders-criticise-netanyahu-calls-jewish-mass-migration-israel.

11. Netanyahu was calling for them to come to Israel, which Salawdeh refers to here as historic Palestine. As Salawdeh explained in response to fact checking, Netanyahu "knows that many of the people he calls upon to come and live in Israel will come to live in the settlements. These settlements are not in Israel, but in places still considered Palestine." See Beaumont, "Leaders Reject Netanyahu."

12. Amos Harel, "How Israel Keeps Palestinians off a Third of All West Bank Land," *Haaretz*, September 25, 2015, https://www.haaretz.com/.premium-how-israel-keeps-palestinians-off-a-third-of-west-bank-land-1.5402260.

13. Suzanne Goldberg, "Israelis to Set Up Buffer Zone in West Bank," *Guardian*, September 6, 2001, https://www.theguardian.com/world/2001/sep/07/Israel; "Squeeze them Out," *Economist*, May 4, 2013, https://www.economist.com/middle-east-and-africa/2013/05/04/squeeze-them-out.

14. Fact checking did not produce any current source confirming this specific process. Salawdeh points to an older source, Ian Lustick's book *Arabs in the Jewish State*. Lustick writes: "Still another technique employed quite often to expropriate Arab land involves the use of Article 125 of the Emergency Regulations. . . . Typically the process works this way: An area encompassing Arab-owner agricultural lands is declared a 'closed area.' The owners of the lands are then denied permission by the security authorities to enter the area for any purpose whatsoever, including cultivation. After three years pass, the Ministry of Agriculture issues certificates which classify the lands as uncultivated. . . . The lands are then expropriated and become part of the general land reserve for Jewish settlement. Permission to enter the 'closed area' is granted to Jewish farmers; alternatively, the classification of the area to 'closed' is lifted altogether." Ian Lustick, *Arabs in the Jewish State: Israel's Control of a National Minority* (Austin: University of Texas Press, 1980), 177–78.

15. It is unclear if this is the process for all closed military zones, but it does happen. See Noga Kadman, B'Tselem, *Acting the Landlord: Israel's Policy in Area C: The West Bank*, June 2013, https://www.btselem.org/download/201306_area_c_report_eng.pdf.

16. "Jewish fund" is not entirely accurate here. However, the Israeli army has historically redistributed land in this way either to the Israeli state or to the World Zionist Organization. See "Squeeze Them Out."

17. Mohammed Abu Khdeir is not a U.S. American citizen. Salawdeh misspoke here: Mohammed's cousin Tariq Abu Khdeir, a Palestinian American who visited Jerusalem and was beaten by Israeli police after Mohammed's death, was also on the news during July 2014. Salawdeh confused the two. See Ryan Grim, "Tariq Abu Khdeir Was Beaten by Israeli Police," *Huffington Post*, July 7, 2014, https://www.huffingtonpost.com/2014/07/07/tariq-abu-khdeir-beaten_n_5565266.html.

18. Jason Hanna and Amir Tal, "Israeli Teens Sentenced for Palestinian Boy's Burning Death," *CNN*, February 4, 2016, https://www.cnn.com/2016/02/04/middleeast/israeli-teens-sentenced-palestinian-death/index.html.

19. It was July 2014, so technically a year and two months ago at the time of this interview. See Hanna and Tal, "Israeli Teens Sentenced."

20. The ringleader of the crime is a settler, as in, he lives in a West Bank settlement. One of the others lives in Beit Shemesh, which is not a West Bank settlement. The other one convicted for the crime is said to be from Jerusalem—though press reports do not indicate whether it is a Jerusalem settlement or West Jerusalem, which is not a settlement. See Itamar Sharon, "Abu Khdeir Murder Suspect Gives Chilling Account of Killing," *Times of Israel*, August 12, 2014, https://www.timesofisrael.com/we-said-they-took-three-of-ours-lets-take-one-of-theirs/.

21. Lizzie Dearden, "Mohammed Abu Khdeir Murder: Israeli Man Convicted of Burning Palestinian Teenager to Death in Revenge Killing," *Independent*, April 19, 2016, https://www.independent.co.uk/news/world/middle-east/mohammed-abu-khdeir-murder-israeli-man-convicted-of-burning-palestinian-teenager-to-death-in-revenge-a6991251.html.

22. The way Salawdeh says this indicates that the killing itself was caught on camera. It was not, though there is security footage of the kidnappers leading up to the killing. See Robert Tait, "Revealed: CCTV Shows Moment Palestinian Boy is Kidnapped Before Being Killed," *Telegraph*, July 3, 2014, https://www.telegraph.co.uk/news/worldnews/middleeast/palestinianauthority/10943882/Revealed-CCTV-shows-moment-Palestinian-boy-is-kidnapped-before-being-killed.html. Salawdeh notes that he misspoke here, but that "the point still stands. The horrible acts against Palestinians have not been secret and the facts are not in dispute. It is the moral implications of these acts that seem to not take hold in the western world. Israel defends itself and as such these acts are forgotten here but not in the rest of the world and definitely not in Palestine. We cannot forget."

23. Allison Deger, "Palestinian Toddler Killed in Settler Price-Tag Attack," *Mondoweiss*, July 31, 2015, https://mondoweiss.net/2015/07/palestinian-toddler-settler/; Uri Friedman, "The 'Price Tag' Menace: Vigilante Israeli Settler Attacks Spread," *Atlantic*, October 3, 2011, https://www.theatlantic.com/international/archive/2011/10/price-tag-menace-vigilante-israeli-settler-attacks-spread/337218/.

24. MEE Staff, "Dawabsheh Family 'Miraculously' Survives Second Arson Attack," *Middle East Eye*, May 18, 2018, http://www.middleeasteye.net/news/Palestine-dawabsha-family-illegal-settlements-arson-attack-duma-West-Bank-Israel.

25. Allison Deger, "Arsonists Attack House of Witness in Duma Arson Attack (Updated)," *Mondoweiss*, March 21, 2016, http://mondoweiss.net/2016/03/arsonist-set-ablaze-house-of-witness-in-duma-arson-attack/.

GHADIR SHAFIE

"Pinkwashing and the Boycott, Divestment, and Sanctions Campaign," May 25, 2016

https://www.wortfm.org/ghadir-shafie-and-the-bds-movement-in-palestine/

KARMA CHÁVEZ: In 2005, Palestinian civil society issued a call for a campaign of boycotts, divestment, and sanctions (BDS) against Israel, similar to that against South Africa during its apartheid era, until it complies with international law and Palestinian rights. Palestinians appealed to people around the globe to pressure their respective states to impose embargoes and sanctions against Israel. They also invited conscientious Israelis to support this call, for the sake of justice and genuine peace.

> "These non-violent punitive measures should be maintained until Israel meets its obligation to recognize the Palestinian people's inalienable right to self-determination and fully complies with the precepts of international law by:
>
> 1. Ending its occupation and colonization of all Arab lands and dismantling the Wall
> 2. Recognizing the fundamental rights of the Arab-Palestinian citizens of Israel to full equality; and
> 3. Respecting, protecting and promoting the rights of Palestinian refugees to return to their homes and properties as stipulated in UN resolution 194."[1]

In the ten-plus years since this original call, the BDS movement has gained significant traction around the world, including most recently locally the UW-Madison Teaching Assistants Association voted overwhelmingly (81 percent of voting members) in favor of adopting a resolution to divest from Israeli state institutions and international corporations complicit in the Israeli occupation of Palestine and the ongoing violations of Palestinians' human rights.[2]

Despite its spread, the mainstream on the right and the left is adamantly opposed to the BDS movement in the United States. During a speech to the American Israeli Public Affairs Committee (AIPAC) in March, Democratic presidential hopeful Hillary Clinton called the Israel boycott movement "alarming" and characterized BDS activists as anti-Semitic, accusing them of "bullying" Jewish students on college campuses.[3] Meanwhile, Republican presumptive nominee Donald Trump, while not weighing in on BDS, said to AIPAC that he is "a lifelong supporter and true friend of Israel."[4] For his part, Bernie Sanders has added BDS backer Cornell West to the Democratic National Committee's policy platform committee, along with pro-Palestinian activist James Zogby, president of the Arab American Institute.[5] What does all this mean for the future of BDS in an election year in the U.S.?

To talk through such questions, I've invited my friend Ghadir Shafie, a Palestinian activist and citizen of the state of Israel. Ghadir is codirector of Aswat—Palestinian Gay Women. Aswat is a group of lesbian, bisexual, transgender, intersex, questioning, and queer Palestinian women that came together in 2002 and established a home for Palestinian LBTQI women to allow safe, supportive, and empowering spaces to express and address their personal, social, and political struggles as a national indigenous minority living inside Israel; as women in a patriarchal society; and as LBTQI women in a wider heteronormative culture. Ghadir Shafie is an internationally known activist and speaker who talks on BDS, LGBTQ, and feminist rights, as well as the Israeli strategy known as pinkwashing around the world. She joins us by phone from Akka in the north of Israel/Palestine.

Ghadir Shafie, welcome to *A Public Affair*.

GHADIR SHAFIE: Hi Karma, thank you so much for this introduction. It's always a pleasure to talk to you and your listeners.

KC: Well thank you so much for being here, and I was thinking about how just a year ago I was there with you in Israel-Palestine and really getting my eyes opened to all of these issues, front and center, and so it's nice a year later to be able to have the opportunity to have this conversation with you.

GS: Thank you.

KC: Ghadir Shafie, I'd like to just get a chance to know you a little bit better, for listeners to know about you and ask how you got involved in the Palestinian struggle for rights and self-determination. Is this something all Palestinians living in Israel do?

GS: Well, basically, it was extremely important for all Palestinians to get involved in the BDS—boycott, divestment, and sanctions known as BDS, because first, the Palestinian boycott, divestment, and sanctions is the first and only effort that addresses and unites the rights of all Palestinians in calling for Israel to meet its obligations under international law, like you referred in the introduction. Second, and in fact, BDS is a rights-based movement, it is democratic and inclusive, it is endorsed and led by the largest coalition of Palestinian civil society, representing Palestinians in '67, '48, and in exile. And more specifically, as a Palestinian living inside Israel for many years, we've always been called many names—we've been called Arab-Israelis, Palestinians of '48, Palestinians living inside Israel, and we were ignored in all peace treaties, accords, and negotiations. And BDS is the only effort that acknowledges and emphasizes the need to recognize our rights as Palestinians.

And certainly, one of the most important successes of BDS is bringing human rights and the discourse of human rights back to the agenda after they had been omitted entirely from the Oslo peace process and from many accords. And by focusing on rights rather than political solutions, BDS has unified Palestinians everywhere despite political and geographic division that exists today. So, yes, why BDS? Why not? BDS is not just about boycotting; it is first and foremost about self-determination for the Palestinian people in accordance with international law and the universal principles of human rights. BDS is primarily about freedom, justice, and equality. And, just to be more particular, why BDS should work for us: according to the latest statistics, there are approximately twelve [million] Palestinians in the world today.[6] Fifty percent, amounting to approximately six million Palestinians, are living outside historic Palestine, mainly refugees ethnically cleansed during the Palestinian Nakba in 1948 and ever since. So 50 percent of Palestinians live outside of Palestine and Israel,[7] 38 percent amounting to almost four million Palestinians live in the West Bank, besieged Gaza, and East Jerusalem.[8] And 12 percent, about two million, live inside Israel and are defined as citizens of the state of Israel.[9] And for many years the conversation about Palestine was confined to ending occupation, meaning addressing most of the rights of a mere 38 percent of the people in Palestine, meaning those who live in the occupied Palestinian territories, the West Bank, and Gaza Strip. I say "occupation"—or the "end of occupation" addresses the rights of most Palestinians because even among the residents of Gaza Strip and the West Bank, almost half of them are refugees. So aside from ending occupation, their most important right is the right to return to their homes of origin from which they were systematically expelled.

So BDS, again, is the only call that actually unites all our demands despite the constant attempts to divide my people. And I think, finally, and one of the most significant successes of the BDS discourse is that BDS is not just morally consistent and compelling, it actually works. It is powerful; it's efficient. I think we have to give credit to Mr. Benjamin Netanyahu who gives a great deal of credit to BDS.[10] BDS is inspired by global solidarity in the '70s and

'90s with the antiapartheid movement in South Africa. The Palestinian-led BDS movement is universal, and it's appealing to international civil society, and this is basically, I think, why many people consider it a threat.

You referred to the presidential candidates and more specifically to Hillary Clinton and her speech addressing AIPAC earlier this March. And I think Hillary, I think more than other candidates, placed special attention and emphasis on BDS during her speech, again, pledging she will do everything in her power to limit the rise of BDS and how she wants to protect all the Jewish students at universities from the anti-Semitic Palestinian BDS activists. Basically saying, you know, human rights defenders have become the greatest threat to America. This is ridiculous, and I think that people are more aware of the threat of trying to criminalize BDS for the sake of the security issue. We see this trend happening in many other parts of the world, not just in Israel or the U.S. And I think that—I think that it's our right and duty as activists, or human rights defenders, to be more concerned with this trend to criminalize human rights defenders and movements that are actually calling for justice, freedom, and equality.

KC: Mhm. Now, there's a lot in there that I want to pick up on in what you've said. And I guess the place I'll begin, just to kind of make sure everyone's on the same page here, is one of the things you mentioned is that one of the big differences between the BDS and other efforts at what we might call peace in that part of the world is that BDS centers human rights and not political process. Will you expand upon what you mean by that?

GS: Well in all attempts—peace treaties, peace accords—people were trying to focus on the solution. "How do we solve the problem for Israelis and Palestinians?" They turned us into a Swiss cheese state, they enforced more blocks, they made it impossible for us to exist in this reality. And I think looking for solutions will actually let Israel continuously negotiate in saying that "We have turned every stone, there is no Palestinian partner." And constantly pointing fingers at the Palestinian freedom fighters, and painting them as criminal terrorists only buys Israel time and gives them more time to build more settlements, kill and exile more Palestinians, and regulate more laws to act against us and criminalize our—even our most peaceful efforts together, acts of solidarity from international allies and partners because here we feel completely helpless. We are not decision makers, we don't have the power to change policies from within, we don't have the power to end occupation, we don't have the power to stop building of settlements, confiscation of lands, targeting every aspect of our life. So, I think the main point here is to try and bring it back to the human rights. Just like all the attempts that they're doing today with BDS, trying to criminalize it, so that we talk about our right to BDS as a rights-based movement, and that is something that every government can criminalize.

KC: Mhm. Ghadir Shafie, what do you say to someone who hears that and then poses back to you the question, "Well, what about Israeli human rights?"

GS: Well, obviously, Israeli human rights defenders—we all have heard about what happened to organizations like Breaking the Silence[11] and many others—are also being targeted by the government, they're being outcasted, they're being criminalized, and a lot of attempts to try and control their resources and outlaw them. I think—I think that in the beginning of the 2000s, a lot of Israeli human rights defenders just joined the public scene that built some kind of a consensus around the Palestinians and the Palestinian conflict, and we've seen it among the Israeli left, I think there is no one left from the Israeli left today. We don't see it in the Israeli Parliament, who issued more than fifty laws against Palestinians.[12] We don't see it in the work of organizations that are constantly widening the gaps between our struggle and their struggle. And let's look at the LGBT organizations. I think in the past decade or so they have become more right-wing, we've seen the rise of homonationalism,[13] we're seeing more and more LGBT organizations being explicitly complicit in pinkwashing and being completely complicit with the state of Israel along with its agencies, with the Ministry of Education, the Ministry of Foreign Affairs, and other institutions who are being complicit in advocating the pinkwashing agenda, both internationally and internally.

So, there's a consensus around the Palestinians, and this is one of the greatest challenges. We've seen it during the aggression—the latest brutal aggression on Gaza in 2014, when I personally felt that humanity has left this country, where years of trying to be involved in all kinds of processes to bring both sides closer were shattered. And we—I personally, and I think every Palestinian—saw the true face of Israel and the consensus around the issues where a mere expression of sympathy with victims and men, women, and children being slaughtered was considered a threat to the state of Israel, to the existence of the state of Israel, and to the security of the state of Israel. And I think—and I think if Israel continues to go in that direction, then it will be more difficult to impose—or to try and make Israel to be more—to comply with international law and human rights.

KC: I wanted to follow up on some of the stuff you're talking about, too, related to the 12 percent of Palestinians, the two million people who are citizens of Israel. So, a few weeks ago, I had Jeff Halper on here, and he's the cofounder of the Israeli Committee Against House Demolitions, and he was talking about the differences between how Jewish and Palestinian citizens of Israel are treated legally. And of course, a caller called to dispute him, and I suspect some might call us today. But, as yourself a Palestinian who's a citizen of Israel, you experience those differences firsthand, and I think over here, we hear about the 2014 aggression, but we don't really hear about the everyday differences about what it means to be a Jewish citizen and what it means to be a Palestinian citizen of Israel. Will you talk about some of those differences?

GS: Absolutely. I think a lot of people when they talk about land confiscation, home demolition, you know, the building of settlements—these are very political, these are very intense issues that people don't really think about logically, they don't make sense when they think about them, they just take sides. And, you know, taking sides is very, very easy in this conflict. You're either a Zionist or a human rights defender. But I think I would like to talk about education. And if you talk about education, I think most people would agree that education should be accessible, free, and equal for all.

But in the case of Israel, the Ministry of Education operates two systems. All schools in Israel operate under the Ministry of Education,[14] and the Ministry of Education operates two segregated systems, two separated sets of rules, procedures, and resources to Palestinian schools and Israeli schools.[15] And in creating these two different realities, obviously—and this is an admission of the success of the Israeli government over the past six decades or so, that the government of Israel has invested in previous years one third of its budget on Palestinian students when compared to Israeli students,[16] and today, according to the latest studies and research by the OECD (Organization for Economic Cooperation and Development), they say that Israel is investing one ninth in Palestinian students when compared to Israeli students.[17] And you can see that if Israel is investing in Palestinian students, in Palestinian education, training for teachers in the facility, in programs, in extracurricular activities, it means that it is actually aiming at a policy and a practice to create huge socioeconomic gaps and sometimes even two legal systems, two systems of resources in education. So, if education, or discrimination in education, is extremely visible, so you can imagine the allocation in resources in other fields being very much affected by the politics of the government of Israel, especially the latest government.

So, you can see the Israeli Parliament has more than fifty laws discriminating between Israelis and Palestinians in all—in anything you can think of, in job opportunities, education opportunities. We get less from the government from the first grade, and then both Israelis and Palestinians are supposed to comply to the same standards when they have to seek higher education. Of course, in terms of rights of Palestinian students—again, for security issues, they don't serve in the army,[18] and then they get—so everything is conditioned with army service, whether you want to buy a house,[19] get a job,[20] even get married,[21] they interfere. I'm not free to choose who to fall in love with and who to marry, I can only marry people who live inside the state of Israel. I can't fall in love with a Palestinian who lives in Gaza Strip or the West Bank because the citizenship law actually prevents me from bringing my spouse to live in my own city or prevents me from going and living there. So there all kinds of laws and regulations that organizations like Adalah, the human rights association, and many others work against inside the state of Israel.

And also, if we look at government policies in terms of the pinkwashing policies, pinkwashing has long been promoted as an international agenda in order to divert international attention from the gross violation of human rights, occupation, criminalization, and apartheid. But in fact, through the experience of Aswat, now we know that pinkwashing is an internal agenda which is deliberately implemented by the Ministry of Education to keep us constantly at a disadvantage when it comes to issues related to sexuality, sexual orientation, and gender identity.[22] Where programs are operated in Israeli schools monitoring—training for teachers is offered and is totally blocked in Palestinian schools. So perhaps we can elaborate on that much later. So, you can see it in all aspects of life. And I think one of the most—one of the greatest threats to our personal security today as women or as citizens, Palestinians living inside Israel, is that after the aggression on Gaza, it became extremely dangerous to be a Palestinian in Israel. We have witnessed a lot of targeted assassinations of innocent people, bystanders, university students, mothers, going home and, simply because they were wearing hijab or because they looked Arab or Palestinian, they were targeted either by the mob or security forces. It has become extremely dangerous to speak Arabic in public spaces. I feel threatened every time I speak Arabic on a public—on a train or in the public sphere. Because any expression of anything different than the right-wing Israeli settler is becoming a threat to Israel security. So, the feeling of safety and security in your own home is, I think—and in my opinion the worst feeling that we can endure as Palestinians.

And of course, there are constant escalations, and there's targeting and the incitement from everyone. You know, government officials compete to crack harder on Palestinians and label us as terrorists. People from academia call for assassination of Palestinian mothers so they won't have more Palestinian children[23] who will become terrorists. The Minister of Justice is constantly[24] calling on the murder of Palestinian children and Palestinian mothers, referring to us as snakes,[25] which has a very Satanic Biblical interpretation in the Bible. Obviously, the media is being extremely complicit, whether local or international media, especially in the U.S. If you watch CNN and Fox News, you can see that there's no ounce of justice in their reporting, and complicity. It's not just Israeli institutions, the embassies—just to give you an example, the U.S. embassy in Tel Aviv, every year around Pride, they issue—they invite for a reception in honor of LGBTs in Israel, and this year they're honoring a reception in honor of the Jewish Federation of North America LGBT Mission for Israel, which is a very—which is probably one of the most racist anti-Palestinian defenders of Israel's violation of human rights and international law. So, you can see that a lot of agencies are complicit with policies of pinkwashing and policies of trying to shrink the spaces for Palestinian human rights defenders, and, you know, shrink the resources for Palestinian human rights defenders, whether in Israel or elsewhere.

KC: And we do have a caller who has some feelings he'd like to share, so, Ed, welcome to *A Public Affair*.

ED: Howdy and thank you.

KC: Thank you.

ED: Yes, I've been following this problem with Israel's abuse of Palestinians for some time, and I've heard several lectures by an Anna Baltzer, who is a Jewish person who talks in favor of helping Palestinians against the Israeli aggression. But this seems like such a severe problem, it's not publicized at all, you don't hear much about how bad it is. But one thing that I noted is that we look at the United States—the United States has veto power in the United Nations. And the majority of all the vetoes the United States did of actions in the United Nations involve vetoing action against Israelis' international crimes against the Palestinians. That's the largest source of the vetoes by the United States in the United Nations. This seems to be a real problem, and I appreciate you having this broadcast on the radio about it.

KC: Yeah, thanks a lot for that, Ed. You bring up a really great point. Ghadir, I'd like for you to respond to this question of the U.S.'s veto power in the UN, which is part of what has allowed the human rights violations of Israel to continue. What do we make of that and maybe how the BDS intends to address that?

GS: Yeah, absolutely, I think the UN is starting to play some kind of role in the Israeli-Palestinian conflict. And most recently by issuing a statement calling for Israel to stop its targeting of human rights defenders and more specifically targeting BDS cofounder and one of the most prominent speakers on BDS, Mr. Omar Barghouti, who's been constantly targeted,[26] and most recently in an anti-BDS conference by the Minister of Interior Affairs and the Minister of Transportation, who called for the civil assassination of BDS cofounders.[27] And currently the state of Israel is banning Mr. Barghouti from travelling, from leaving the state of Israel, and trying to strip him of his civil rights. And the UN embassy and many other international human rights organizations issued statements urging the Israeli government to cease its intimidation of human rights defenders and protect them from attacks. Now clearly, we are concerned for the safety and liberty of Mr. Omar Barghouti and other BDS activists. And I think here the UN can play a very significant role. I will be completely honest with you, I'm not a great fan of the UN, but I have recently attended a Commission on the Status of Women at the UN in New York earlier this March, and today maybe more than ever I can understand the importance of advocating to UN venues and all kinds of commissions in order to advance—first of all, like I said, increase awareness among people and, you know, UN venues and events bring a lot of attention from stakeholders, from organizations, either based in the U.S. or around the globe. And I think it's extremely important to create global activist solidarity around these issues and litigate and lobby at UN venues as well.

Now, the U.S. role has always been very extremely supportive of Israel, asking no questions about the legitimacy of the acts of Israel or even trying to question the constant violation of international law and human rights and human conventions. I think today more than ever, the U.S. plays an extremely significant role in protecting Israel, unfortunately. But more and more we see more efforts trying to bring more visibility. Today, Palestine is recognized by the UN. Recently, during the Commission on the Status of Women, there was a paper on the rights of Palestinian women. Currently, Aswat and many other feminist and human rights organizations are working on drafting a shadow report for CEDAW (the UN Convention on the Elimination of all forms of Discrimination Against Women) and are involved in many other reports. So, I think it is important to be more active or engaged in these platforms. But at the same time, it's important to know that—I don't know to what extent it can change the policies of the UN but, yes, changing opinions of activists, academics, organizations, unions, student bodies, universities, professors are also organizing to be in more solidarity with Palestine. Whether the U.S. will continue to veto decisions to try and make Israel comply with international law, we haven't seen it during the Obama administration. I don't think we will expect to see it during Hillary or Trump if they get elected. We might see a shift in policy if Bernie Sanders is elected. This is my two cents about the issue.

KC: Yeah, yeah for sure. Well, we actually—I'm going to bring another caller on here who has a question about an experimental school in Israel. Mike, welcome to *A Public Affair*.

MIKE: Yes, thanks Karma. First, I just wanted to make a quick comment. You mentioned that the U.S. embassy is in Tel Aviv, and it's a minor technicality, but I think it has some significance, the fact that the U.S. doesn't recognize Jerusalem as the capital of Israel but keeps—or maintains the embassy in Tel Aviv.[28] My second question is about, I believe it's a school known as Neve Shalom where Israelis—Israeli Arabs attend together. And as I understand it it's been working fairly successfully. So, I guess my question is, do you think it would be more advantageous to try experiments like Neve Shalom. And I can take my answers off the air and thanks for an interesting program.

KC: Thanks a lot for the call, Mike. So, Ghadir, two questions there. One is related to why it is that the U.S. doesn't recognize Jerusalem as the official capital of Israel. And then the second part about what could be the possibility of these alternative kinds of schools that seem to be working bringing people together.

GS: Mhm, absolutely. So, thank so much Mike for your two questions. First of all, all embassies are based in Tel Aviv, I think whether this means that all countries don't recognize Jerusalem as the capital of Israel—I don't think to what extent this is true. But I think that some of the candidates expressed—and I particularly remember hearing Trump pledging to move the embassy to Jerusalem. But beyond that, I think that the Neve Shalom model as a school is an excellent model. Unfortunately, this is a private effort by civil society to organize and try to provide a model that, yes, Palestinians and Israelis can live together peacefully or not peacefully, this is obviously not the question. I think—and the Neve Shalom model was duplicated to other three models that have been working for the past decade if not more. The effort is a very private effort. I think in order for us to—you know, there was a lot of coexistence, now we call them normalization projects, or attempts to bring Arabs and Israelis together. I think these efforts should be government efforts which are systematic.

I live in a so-called mixed city where Palestinians and Israelis live side by side in the same vicinity, but the municipality, the local authorities, the government doesn't invest any effort to bring the two communities together. Because I live in a mixed city, I went to an Israeli kindergarten for two years, but then, you know, the municipality and the local authority did not afford—or allocate any resources to creating joint schools in my city, or any other city for that matter. And therefore, the next twelve years of my life I was in a Palestinian school, I had absolutely no interaction with my Israeli counterparts or neighbors, and the second meeting we had was at university where, you know, where obviously each one of us was already an adult and forming his own political and social opinions. So, I think the Neve Shalom model is an excellent model, I think it works, but I think it works in a bubble. Because when you step outside of Neve Shalom, you see the true face of segregation, separation.

As a mother, I also sent my son to a mixed kindergarten where he was called a dirty Arab and a Palestinian terrorist. For us, it was the reality that, you know, I wanted my son to show the other side, I wanted him to learn about other cultures. But when he was going to first grade, there is nothing available, and I can either send him to an Israeli school where he will learn Israeli heritage, holidays, religion, and language. Or I can send him to an Arab school where he'll be completely alienated from anything Israeli. So—and this is a mixed city, so imagine people living in either Arab villages or Israeli-Jewish villages or settlements, if you want. They have absolutely no interaction with the Palestinians, and all they know about us is what they see on television. So, I think the state of Israel at large and even the local municipalities are not investing in any effort, of course, other than normalization efforts to have—you know, allow Arabs to be in the Israeli parliament, to have an Arab singer singing in the Eurovision, to have someone, you know, an Arab doctor lighting something at the Jewish Independence Day. Of course, we are against all these normalization efforts which aim to serve a fig leaf to the international community, to portray a false image of liberal and democratic Israel. A lot of people think about Israel and occupation and think that Israel is a democracy. I've been living in Israel for more than forty years, I know that Israel discriminates against its Palestinian minority. And, actually, very little—little by little, aspiring to keep us in our own ghettoes and separate us from whatever progress, processes are happening in the Israeli community. So, I agree, we should have more of these efforts, but these efforts should come from the government and not from individuals because individuals remain in their own bubble and they will remain a small program.

KC: I wanted to make sure, as we're running out of the hour here, Ghadir, to expand a bit on the concept of pinkwashing, specifically because your work with Aswat centers the experiences of Palestinian gay women. And this term *pinkwashing* gets thrown out a lot, and I think people have maybe some basic understanding of it. But you've talked about it as both an external and an internal strategy, and I wonder if you could just take a moment to really clarify what that term means and how it works in these two ways.

GS: Well, first of all, I would like to—if we don't get to talk about everything, I would like to draw the listeners' attention to a piece I published, a testimony, actually, that I published at *Kohl: A Journal for Body and Gender Research*, in the first volume, titled "Pinkwashing: Israel's International Strategy and Internal Agenda," where I talk about the experience of Aswat in pinkwashing. Obviously pinkwashing, as I said earlier, is an internal agenda aiming to portray Israel as liberal and gay friendly compared with its neighboring countries. And as a counterpoint of this false picture of Israel, the pinkwashing campaign also aims to paint a racist and false image of the homophobic, backward, and barbaric Arab Palestinian. And I think it's very important for some of the few minutes we have left to talk about Aswat's work and activism, not just in the context of pinkwashing, but in the context of queer and feminism, if I may.

KC: Please.

GS: We started as a membership-based organization in 2002–2003 and became a feminist queer movement uniting feminism, queerness, and resistance to all forms of oppression into one monumental struggle. And I think by uniting our struggle and making these connections visible to groups, whether locally or globally, we have, you know, as Palestinian feminist queer women, we have brought a lot of attention and visibility and ultimately acts of solidarity to Palestine and not just queer Palestinians. And I think it's extremely important for us to make the intersectionality of this struggle visible to others. Because from the very first steps, Aswat believes that we should fight and struggle for our rights as Palestinian queer women, first as Palestinians, an indigenous minority living inside Israel, suffering systematic discrimination in policies and practices. As women, in the context of conflict and the geopolitical challenges facing our feminist movement. And, finally, as queers in the context of homonationalism, homophobia, and pinkwashing. And I think that Aswat's unique insight into our struggle as Palestinian feminist queers and our relationship of interdependency, it affirms that our struggle as Palestinian queer feminists is not merely related but rather it's very much dependent on one another. And I think this is, you know, extremely important because it builds a lot of regional and, even more, global attention to promote the rights of all Palestinians and not just queer Palestinians.

Of course, we have done a lot to promote our own movement and our own journey. A lot of people ask, "So, what do you do within Palestinian society?" So, for more than a decade of work and activism, Aswat has raised the bar in our own communities. We have inspired the feminist Palestinian movement and paved the way for other Palestinian queer groups and activists to become an integral part of the feminist agenda and discourse here in Palestine. We have formed solid commitments and partnerships with activists in our communities. We are actively educating our agenda and working closely with human rights organizations to advocate for policy change through the different venues that are available to us. And yes, the queer international has affected our struggle very, very—very greatly in the past couple of years. Academics and activists like Judith Butler, Karma Chávez [KC: *laughing*], Jasbir Puar, Sarah Schulman, and many others have allowed us access into universities, academic venues. Also, Katherine Franke has been active on Palestine. So, I think through these brilliant feminist academics and activists, as a women-led organization, they have paved the way through their acts of solidarity, through their academic work, through their endorsement of BDS to really break the silence of Palestinians and allow the queer Palestinian movement to be in solidarity and in active solidarity with a lot of movements in the U.S. like Black Lives Matter. There was a lot of solidarity going on between Ferguson and Palestine. Today we can see that Jewish Voice for Peace are very powerful on BDS and campaigning for BDS. So, I think through these partners and through all efforts that are going on in universities and other venues, we are making the bonds more visible and actually learning more of how essential it is to be supportive and in active solidarity with other struggles.

KC: And you mention a lot there that a lot of these are cultural workers and academics. If someone is listening right now in Madison and they're not one of those folks, what can the average person outside of the university who's not a cultural worker do to show solidarity with the Palestinian struggle? Whether that's connecting through the queer feminist piece or more broadly.

GS: Well, I think everyone can connect, whether you are in the academy or whether you are an activist, or you are part of a student union or a work union. I think that everyone can, first of all, increase awareness and learn more about the conflict and not confine their education to CNN and Fox News and other outlets that completely portray a false picture of the struggle. I think a lot of people came on solidarity delegations to learn more about the reality in Palestine, and a lot of people said that seeing is believing, and they could not believe what they saw here. I think a lot of statements in support of Palestine in general and queer Palestinians are being circulated and issued that are extremely powerful in supporting organizations endorsing BDS in light of the massive attempts by governments to criminalize BDS. I think there's a great deal to be done to organize events and bring more awareness by bringing activists, whether from feminist or queer organizations to engage more people in Q & A about Palestine, engage in debate to advocate for the rights of Palestinians, for the rights of BDS. There are numerous things that people can do in terms of just showing their involvement and solidarity with Palestinians.

You, Karma, have done a great deal by visiting here and talking to activists in the feminist and queer organizations and making the linkage with your own struggle and constantly keeping in touch with our struggle and making the linkage visible. I think this is extremely important. And from where you sit, you know better what to do in order to promote a greater understanding among fellow Americans in your surroundings. These are only some of the examples I can think about. And you can always log in to our website at www.aswatgroup.org or our Facebook page and other social media in order to learn more about our struggle and be actively engaged in our work and activism.

KC: Well, and I was going to, yeah, ask you about resources. Because definitely aswatgroup.org and if you add "/en," that takes you directly to the English website. Are there other—we have just about a minute left—are there other resources you would direct people to if they're just trying to learn about these issues?

GS: Obviously, BDS, that's the bdsmovement.org, is one of the main sources for information about BDS activism, BDS successes, some of the challenges we're facing right now, especially with governments, especially the state of Israel trying to target human rights defenders and activists. There's a lot of attention to be given to the specific targeting of Mr. Omar Barghouti, one of the cofounders and one of the most prominent speakers on BDS. I would urge listeners to join solidarity campaigns and statements to urge the state of Israel to stop intimidating human rights defenders. Of course, PACBI (Palestinian Academic and Cultural Boycott of Israel), BNC (Palestinian BDS National Committee), BDS, No to Pinkwashing, and Pinkwatchers, a lot of the queer activists here in Palestine are promoting a lot of attention to pinkwashing. Of course, Al Qaws for Sexual and Gender Diversity in Palestinian Society are being extremely active on these issues and others. You can also log on to their website and learn more about their activism in the queer Palestinian movement and their specific attention to pinkwashing and contribution to BDS. So, there's a lot of resources available. And of course, you can join e-lists of BDS and PACBI and get daily updates. You can also log into Jewish Voice for Peace, JVP, because they're doing excellent work on BDS and hopefully pinkwashing as well. So, there are many ways to get involved, just find your passion and the most effective way for you to be active on Palestine and bringing more visibility to the issue of Palestine.

KC: Well, we're going to have to leave it right here. Thanks, Ghadir Shafie for being here today.

GS: Thank you so much Karma for your work and activism on Palestine and thank you to the listeners and to the people who called and asked questions.

KC: For sure. Again today, our guest Ghadir Shafie from Aswat—Palestinian Gay Women.

NOTES

1. Palestinian Civil Society, "Palestinian Civil Society Call for BDS," *BDS*, July 9, 2005, https://bdsmovement.net/call.

2. "UW-Madison Union of Graduate Student Workers (TAA) Endorses BDS Movement," press release, May 19, 2016, http://taa-madison.org/taa-endorses-bds-movement/.

3. Ryan Teague Beckwith, "Read Hillary Clinton's Speech to AIPAC," *Time*, March 21, 2016, http://time.com/4265947/hillary-clinton-aipac-speech-transcript/.

4. Alan Rappeport, "Donald Trump Calls Himself 'Lifelong Supporter' of Israel," *New York Times*, March 21, 2016, https://www.nytimes.com/politics/first-draft/2016/03/21/donald-trump-calls-himself-lifelong-supporter-of-israel/.

5. Jason Horowitz and Maggie Haberman, "A Split Over Israel Threatens the Democrats' Hopes for Unity," *New York Times*, May 25, 2016, https://www.nytimes.com/2016/05/26/us/politics/bernie-sanders-israel-democratic-convention.html.

6. "Palestinians Say They Number 12.1 Million Worldwide," *Times of Israel*, May 12, 2015, https://www.timesofisrael.com/palestinians-say-they-number-12-1-million-worldwide/.

7. Palestinian Central Bureau of Statistics, *On the 68th Anniversary of the Palestinian Nakba*, May 15, 2016, http://www.pcbs.gov.ps/post.aspx?lang=en&ItemID=1661.

8. Palestinian Central Bureau of Statistics, *On the 68th Anniversary*.

9. It is not exactly 12 percent. The percentage depends on which statistics used. Twelve percent of 12 million is approximately 1.5 million. As of April 2018, the Arab population of Israel was approximately 1.9 million. "Vital Statistics: Latest Population Statistics for Israel," Jewish Virtual Library, accessed July 1, 2018, https://www.jewishvirtuallibrary.org/latest-population-statistics-for-israel.

10. Peter Beaumont, "Israel Brands Palestinian-Led Boycott Movement a 'Strategic Threat,'" *Guardian*, June 3, 2015, https://www.theguardian.com/world/2015/jun/03/israel-brands-palestinian-boycott-strategic-threat-netanyahu.

11. According to its website, "Breaking the Silence is an organization of veteran combatants who have served in the Israeli military since the start of the Second Intifada and have taken it upon themselves to expose the Israeli public to the reality of everyday life in the Occupied Territories." See https://www.breakingthesilence.org.il/about/organization. Breaking the Silence is viewed by some in Israel as a threat to the state. See "'Breaking the Silence': Israeli Whistleblowing NGO under Pressure for Exposing IDF Abuses," *RT News*, December 21, 2015, https://www.rt.com/news/326706-breaking-silence-israel-ngo/.

12. "The Discriminatory Laws Database," Adalah, last modified September 29, 2017, https://www.adalah.org/en/content/view/7771.

13. The concept of *homonationalism* is introduced in Jasbir K. Puar, *Terrorist Assemblages: Homonationalism in Queer Times* (Durham, NC: Duke University Press, 2007). In a later essay, Puar defines *homonationalism* as "a facet of modernity and a historical shift marked by the entrance of (some) homosexual bodies as worthy of protection by nation-states, a constitutive and fundamental reorientation of the relationship between the state, capitalism, and sexuality." See Puar, "Rethinking Homonationalism," *International Journal of Middle Eastern Studies* 45 (2013): 337.

14. "Education: Primary and Secondary," Israel Ministry of Foreign Affairs, accessed July 1, 2018, http://www.mfa.gov.il/mfa/aboutisrael/education/pages/education-%20primary%20and%20secondary.aspx.

15. Human Rights Watch, *Second Class: Discrimination against Palestinian Arab Children in Israel's Schools*, September 2001, https://www.hrw.org/reports/2001/israel2/ISRAEL0901-01.htm.

16. Slightly different than what Shafie said, at this time, one-third less was spent on Arabs versus Jews. See Organisation for Economic Co-Operation and Development, *OECD Reviews of Labour Market and Social Policies: Israel* (Paris: OECD, 2010): 25.

17. This precise statistic could not be found, but in 2016, government figures indicated that the "average Jewish student receives 78 to 88 percent more funding than the average Arab student." Yardena Schwartz, "The Two-School Solution," *Foreign Policy*, May 18, 2016, https://foreignpolicy.com/2016/05/18/the-two-school-solution-israeli-arab-children-education-integration/.

18. This is true for the overwhelming majority, though a tiny percentage do serve. See Jane Corbin, "Israel's Arab Soldiers Who Fight for the Jewish State," *BBC News*, November 8, 2016, https://www.bbc.com/news/world-middle-east-37895021.

19. Adalah, *The Inequality Report: The Palestinian Arab Minority in Israel*, March 2011, https://www.adalah.org/uploads/oldfiles/upfiles/2011/Adalah_The_Inequality_Report_March_2011.pdf.

20. Adalah, "Widening Use of Military Service as a Condition for University and Employment Benefits Discriminates against Arab Citizens of Israel," September 19, 2010, https://www.adalah.org/en/content/view/7889.

21. Judah Ari Gross, "Eisenkot's 'Revolution': A GI Bill of Rights for the Israel Defense Forces," *Times of Israel*, August 12, 2016, https://www.timesofisrael.com/eisenkots-revolution-a-gi-bill-of-rights-for-the-israel-defense-forces/.

22. See her own research on this: Ghadir Shafie, "Pinkwashing: Israel's International Strategy and Internal Agenda," *Kohl: A Journal for Body and Gender Research* 1, no. 1 (2015): 82–86.

23. Mordechai Kedar, a Middle East scholar from Bar-Ilan University in Israel, called for the rape of mothers and sisters of would-be suicide bombers as the only possible deterrent for such terrorism. Calls for assassination of Palestinian mothers were not discovered. Or Kashti, "Israeli Professor's 'Rape as Terror Deterrent' Statement Draws Ire," *Haaretz*, July 22, 2014, https://www.haaretz.com/.premium-prof-s-words-on-stopping-terror-draws-ire-1.5256331.

24. There was one instance where the Minister of Justice, Ayelet Shaked, called for this, but it is a stretch to say she "constantly" does it. Ali Abunimah, "Israeli Lawmaker's Call for Genocide of Palestinians Gets Thousands of Facebook Likes," *Electronic Intifada*, July 7, 2014, https://electronicintifada.net/blogs/ali-abunimah/israeli-lawmakers-call-genocide-palestinians-gets-thousands-facebook-likes.

25. Abunimah, "Israeli Lawmaker's Call."

26. Dalia Hatuqa, "Israel Imposes Travel Ban on Boycott Movement Leader," *Al Jazeera*, May 10, 2016, https://www.aljazeera.com/news/2016/05/israel-imposes-travel-ban-boycott-movement-leader-160510152536984.html.

27. Amnesty International, "Israeli Government Must Cease Intimidation of Human Rights Defenders, Protect Them from Attacks," April 12, 2016, https://www.amnestyusa.org/press-releases/israeli-government-must-cease-intimidation-of-human-rights-defenders-protect-them-from-attacks/.

28. On December 6, 2017, Donald Trump recognized Jerusalem as the capital of Israel and announced plans to move the U.S. embassy. See Mark Landler, "Trump Recognizes Jerusalem as Israel's Capital and Orders U.S. Embassy to Move," *New York Times*, December 6, 2017, https://www.nytimes.com/2017/12/06/world/middleeast/trump-jerusalem-israel-capital.html. On May 14, 2018, the new U.S. embassy opened in Jerusalem. See Ruth Eglash, "Under Banner of Peace, U.S. Opens Embassy in Jerusalem. Sixty Miles Away, Dozens of Palestinians are Killed," *Washington Post*, May 14, 2018, https://www.washingtonpost.com/world/middle_east/jerusalem-gears-up-to-embrace-the-new-us-embassy/2018/05/14/1d6707dc-5558-11e8-a6d4-ca1d035642ce_story.html?utm_term=.644940faeac9.

JOHAYNA SAIFI

"Akka, Israel," June 17, 2015

https://www.wortfm.org/johayna-saifi/

KARMA CHÁVEZ: Often when we hear about Palestine/Israel and the ongoing occupation and Palestinian struggle, we hear of the Gaza Strip, and sometimes the West Bank. We rarely hear about Palestinian society within the borders of Israel as defined in 1948. Palestinian citizens of Israel comprise about 1.7 million people or just over 20 percent of the population of Israel.[1] While Palestinian citizens of Israel have many of the same rights as Jewish citizens, more than fifty laws exist in Israel that privilege Jewish citizens,[2] schools for Palestinians are underfunded compared to Jewish schools,[3] and several communities founded by Arabs in Israel are unrecognized by the state and so do not have basic services like water and hospitals.[4] Moreover, in some cities that once possessed a Palestinian majority, processes of displacement have happened over many years, such as what has happened in the northern coastal city of Acco, the name Israelis give the city,[5] or Akka, the name that Palestinians use.[6] Originally designated part of what would be an Arab state[7] in 1922,[8] in 1948 more than three-quarters of Akka's Palestinian population[9] was displaced in the war by the Israelis. In the 1990s, Jews from the former Soviet Union settled in the city,[10] and Palestinians currently comprise about one-third of the city,[11] though with increasing development of the old city, longtime Palestinian residents are encouraged to move out to be replaced by Jewish residents using a variety of means.[12]

When I visited Palestine/Israel last month, I had the opportunity to take a walking tour of the city of Akka thanks to my friend Ayelet who introduced me to today's guest, Johayna Saifi. Johayna is a lifelong Palestinian citizen of Akka, and her vast knowledge of the city and the broader Palestinian struggle is beyond impressive. I felt like the story of Akka tells a bigger story about life in Israel for Palestinians, and so I invited Johayna to share with us today.

Johayna Saifi is a community activist, known by every single person we met during our walking tour. She is also the director of a nonprofit organization called Hirakuna. Hirakuna is a forum of ten civil society organizations specializing in community volunteerism and leadership in the Palestinian society in Israel. "Hirakuna's mission is to enable safe spaces and create opportunities for the empowerment of young people to take active responsibility and become socially involved in their communities and beyond," with a specific focus on Palestinian society in Israel.[13]

Johayna Saifi, welcome to *A Public Affair*.

JOHAYNA SAIFI: Hi, Karma, hello.

KC: It's really good to have you here, and thanks so much for joining us. Did I get anything right or wrong there in that introduction?

JS: Your introduction was great, that's fine.

KC: So, will you tell us a little bit about yourself and how you grew up and how you got into the kind of work you do now?

JS: I was born in Akka, in the city of Akka, and as I know, as I remember myself, I was involved in life here and very much rooted, very much rooted in Akka and have a strong belonging to this city. And as I grew as a child, you know in the old city here, I saw all the difficulties that my family and people around went through during all the years. And then, as I started being more and more involved and asking more questions about what's happening around, I started realizing and understanding a few things about the policies and about how the system is working in Israel and the situation and the conditions that Palestinians in general are going through here. So, it's linked, as you said in your introduction, the situation of Palestinians in Akka is very similar to the situation of, or the conditions of Palestinians in other places. But, we are talking about uniqueness about this city, and I think it's part of the sophisticated policy of Israel to treat each place and each city with different methods, so it will be divided, and it will be separated between Palestinians, that will be separated in their struggles. But, at the end, in general, I think we are talking about the same policy, about results that are serving a policy of expelling Palestinians and Judaizing the land. Judaizing Palestine in general, but I'm talking now about—we are supposed to talk more about the situation of Akka, that is also going through the Judaization process and colonization, during all these years.

KC: So, I wonder, maybe for people who aren't entirely—I mean, it's a very complicated situation over there, and there's a lot of nuance. Particularly I think, one of the ways or one of the things I guess I didn't know so much when I got there was the different sort of categorizations of Palestinians, both within Israel, in West Bank/Gaza, as well as refugees. Can you talk about those existing separations that have occurred since 1948 among Palestinians?

JS: I think that the main idea is to try to divide Palestinians in general, between Gaza and between West Bank and Palestinians in the diaspora. And usually people are not aware of Palestinians that are in Israel, we are talking about 20 percent of the people here, of the citizens. Most people don't even know about that, that Palestinians are living here. So, when we are talking about inside Israel, it seems that all the citizens here are equal, and they are living by the same laws that Jews are living by in this state, but it's not true. Palestinians here, they are not living under a military occupation like the West Bank, but we are talking about another method of oppression that Palestinians are going through, by taking their land, stealing their land if you want, about creating a lot of racist laws, about getting the space—if we can talk about democratic space—making it smaller and smaller all the time. For example, two days ago,[14] the Minister of Culture, Miri Regev, she decided to cut the budget for Al Midan Theater, which is a Palestinian theater in Haifa.[15] After they decided to cut support for one of the shows there, they decided after that they are going to cut the budget from the whole theater.[16] In general, we are talking about really small budgets that the theaters are getting from the Ministry, it's not the same budget that Jewish theaters or organizations are taking, but now they decided to cut it because they prepared a show that is talking about one of the political prisoners' stories.

KC: Will you talk a little bit about maybe some of the disparities? That's a really concrete example, will you talk about things like education or other kinds of cultural activities where there's a disparity between, say, budget for Jewish schools and budget for Palestinian schools? Or it doesn't have to be education but other instances similar to the theater story.

JS: Yeah, we can talk about educational organizations, we can talk about schools, we can talk about community centers. All these kinds of activities and programs are not allowed for Palestinians in Israel. And if we do have some organizations or some budget for these kinds of activities, it's much smaller than budgets that the Jews are getting here. We are not getting the percentage that we are supposed to get as citizens that pay taxes in this state. And we have numbers, I don't remember numbers now, but we have all these numbers now from the ministries that are publishing these numbers, and they are talking very clearly about Jewish schools or community centers et cetera, and not for Palestinians.

Again, as an example, I live in Akka. Akka used to be a Palestinian city. Since '48, or during '48, most of the people were expelled during the Nakba, and since then, since '48 until now, Israel is working very hard to bring Jews from all over the world all the time so they can keep a higher percentage of Jews than Palestinians. Now we are talking about 32 percent of Palestinians[17] living in the city and the rest are Jews,[18] while 25 percent of the Jews are Russians, they came from Russia.[19] And until now you can see all the time, every year, you can see new programs and plans to encourage Jews to come and live in Akka[20] and get different privileges for moving to this city.[21]

And living in this city, I can see the differences with my own eyes between how many schools Jewish students have and how many schools Palestinians have. Most of the Palestinian students, and I'm talking about, you know, children, I'm talking about elementary school, they are sending their children to schools in other cities and other villages, not in Akka, because they don't have enough places. We have just two elementary schools, and we have one high school in Akka for Arabs, it's of course separated schools for Jews and Arabs. And we have just two schools, so most of the families that can, economically, send their children to other cities, because it costs a lot of money, so they send their children because they don't have enough places here to study. So even basic education, it's not available for all the citizens here.

And then if you talk, again, about community centers, you can see that in the new part of the city, or the city outside the walls, you can see that in each neighborhood there is a community center and there is a sports center, et cetera. But when we are talking about the Palestinian society, you cannot see these options. So, we are talking about people in general, and I'm taking Akka as an example, but I can talk also about other villages and cities. And you just talked a little bit at the beginning about unrecognized villages, they don't even have water, hospitals, any other basic services in their villages.

KC: Can we talk about that just for a moment? We'll come back and talk about Akka, but what does it mean to say that a village, a place where people have made community, made their homes, is "unrecognized"? Or doesn't have these services? How does that work? It doesn't compute very well.

JS: Yeah, you know, I think there are some things that exist just in Israel. It doesn't exist in other places in the world. To say "unrecognized village," that means that people don't have any basic conditions for life. We can talk about not having welfare services, not having health services, not having educational services—not anything.[22] Like they are not existing in any place. And now we are talking about a new plan, there is a new plan now to demolish one of the villages, Umm al-Hiran, and building on this land and expelling all the people that live in this village in the Negev, in the Naqab, and building a Jewish village called Hiran and bringing Jews to live in this village.[23] Now, when we are talking about demolishing, that means that all the families don't have even a place to live in, but meanwhile they are going to build a Jewish village, and we saw it in other examples, that they are getting all the services and beyond all the services that they can get. So, you can see in very clear ways that people don't have the chance to live. We are talking about women that suddenly they are realizing that they are sick. And it's not suddenly, it's after a few or many years because they couldn't see doctors, okay? They realize that they have cancer, or they have other diseases. We are talking about people that are dying because until the emergency services come—if they come—it's too late. So, we are talking about really basic needs of people that they cannot find any response to this need.

KC: And so, the basic idea here—if I'm understanding this correctly, and correct me if I'm wrong—is that the state of Israel doesn't recognize these cities, and so people live there, then, in the eyes of the state, illegally. And because they're illegal, that means they have the right to demolish their homes, not provide services, et cetera because technically they don't legally belong there within the state law. Is that how they rationalize this?

JS: Exactly. In other places, for example in villages in the Triangle area, or in other places, people are not allowed to build on their own land.[24] They have papers that they own this land, but they are not allowed to build on this land.[25] Since '48 until now, the state didn't give any permissions for building.[26] So people, you know, they need to live. People since '48 until now, some of them they have families and the children become, they want their own apartment and et cetera. So, people started building because they didn't have any other option, the state didn't give any permissions for building. So, they started building, and after they build, the building is illegal in the eyes of the state. So, the state has the permission to come and demolish this house. So that's what I started talking about at the beginning. We are talking about different methods—also in Akka but also for Palestinians in general—to take their property, to take their land, to take control of their houses.

And to use legal weapons. They are using legal—and I'm saying legal, you know, in an ironic way, because they are using the law that they created to take the property of people and to push the people to the corner, to make them leave. To make them leave as if it's their choice, but it's not really their choice. The same in Akka, in Akka tough laws and tough conditions, poverty and expelling people from their homes, and at the end they are trying to push the people to leave their houses. In my understanding, if they had the ability to put the people—as they did with the refugees in '48—and put them on boats and send them to Lebanon or Syria or other places in the world, that would be easier for them. But now they cannot do it because they want to save the picture that it's a democracy. So, they are using "legal" ways to push the people out of these cities and villages. And the idea is to have less and less Palestinians living here.

KC: Yeah. So, I want to return to a little bit about Akka because Akka is this beautiful place, and I wonder if you could talk a bit about what Akka was like pre-1948, what was the economy like? And then how that's changed over the last seventy years.

JS: Akka, it's very beautiful, and it's a very ancient city, it's existed for more than 5,000 years. So, it's very important on the historical side, but it's also very important for Palestinians and Arabs in general because it used to be a very central city, it was very strong in the economy, in the culture, in education, and in all points of life. People came to study here, at schools. It used to be a center for people that came from different places. People came from Lebanon and Syria, and they had open borders, open economy here, and we can still see the sites that show the importance of this city on the economic side, but people came here, and all the time it was a touristic and very important city.

And now the authorities here they realized the importance of the city, but since '48 the historical sites were very neglected. Like if you walk in the neighborhood, in the streets of the old city, you can see that the houses were not renovated, were not taken care of, and it was also forbidden by the law, people couldn't make any renovations to their houses by the law. But you can see also that people used to be—it's a seaside city—so you can see that most of the people were fishing. Most of the men here used to work as fishermen. The economical [*sic*] situation was good because of that, also, but now after '48 they created very tough laws and they forbid fishing in different areas and different zones in the sea. And they didn't create new opportunities for jobs for the people. So, most of the people here, they are unemployed, they are not working. We are talking about a high percentage of poverty in the city.

Most of the people now are trying to develop the touristic side, like coffee shops and restaurants, but it's very difficult because of the bureaucracy here, for Palestinians of course it becomes very hard. But when we are talking about this investment or to develop this part of the touristic side, you can see also that the plan of the state is to encourage Jewish investors to come and invest in these places.[27] One of the examples, three of the important historical sites of the city, Hammam al-Danham, it's a Turkish word, —we have two hammams, hammam al-Shuni and hammam al-Dan and another Turkish bath. They want to sell these historical sites and build boutique hotels.[28]

The plan is to build boutique hotels, and usually they are talking to Jewish investors, not Palestinian investors. But as a result, they are selling these sites, they also want to expel families. In this concrete plan, we are talking about expelling thirty-seven Palestinian families that live around these sites that they want to expel, for building boutique hotels. And we know that, we succeeded, the residents, the people that live in these neighborhoods, they succeeded in postponing the selling of these sites, but I'm not sure about what they are planning for in the future. So, the plan is to make the whole city a touristic place with boutique hotels and taking out all the Palestinian families that live there. And they're making it a touristic city, but not with the people that live there.

KC: So, the old city, the old city part of Akka historically was all Palestinian, is that correct?

JS: Yeah, yeah.

KC: And so now what percentage of the old city is Palestinian?

JS: Now we are talking about, let's say that all the people that live in the old city they are Palestinians[29] now except we have a Zionist organization now called Ayalim[30] that they started bringing young students and giving them scholarships—Jewish young students—and giving them scholarships to live in the old city.[31] So they are also taking the houses of the, that used to belong to Palestinian families,[32] and they are living in these neighborhoods. We are talking now about twenty students,[33] we are talking about eight thousand Palestinians that live in the old city,[34] but I am sure there are already many owners, many Jewish owners, that already bought houses in the old city.[35] And this is a little bit problematic for the conditions of the houses because most of the properties, most of the houses in the old city used to belong to Palestinian refugees.[36] Most of the people, most of the Palestinians that used to live in Akka were expelled during the Nakba. They are refugees now. And most of the people that live in Akka, they came from, they were also internal—we call them internal refugees, they came from villages that were demolished during the Nakba and the cities, like Haifa and other cities. So that means that they lost their properties in the villages or the cities that they used to live in, and they cannot take it back. By law. There is a law called the Absentees Law that people that couldn't prove[37] that they were living in their own house in '48, they lost their property, and that the state is now taking responsibility or control of the properties.[38] So by this law, most of the families here except a few families that kept or stayed in their own houses in Akka—and this is the uniqueness of Akka, of the situation of Akka, that most of the people lost their houses, lost their properties, and they are renting their houses from the state.[39] Okay? So the state is responsible for these buildings, and the state has the power to do whatever they think they can do with these properties.[40] Plus there is a law, the renters are renting these houses by a law called the Protective Renters—it's supposed to give them some privilege, it's supposed to be easier for these people,[41] but still we are talking about very tough laws for the people, we are talking about the people that cannot even pay the rent,[42] we are talking about another issue. This protective—the law of protective renters is working just for three generations. So now we are talking about the fourth generation, families now have—Palestinian families have the fourth generation after the Nakba now, so that means that they don't have any solutions.[43] Or any solutions where to go after that.

And on the other hand, outside the walls, in the new part of the city, there are new neighborhoods that Palestinians are not allowed to buy or rent houses, by law. These neighborhoods are new neighborhoods that they built, and it's just for Jews. Palestinians cannot buy or rent houses. Okay? And even in other neighborhoods that it's not forbidden, let's say, they are not welcome. We are talking about a very racist sphere that most of the people here doesn't feel that they are welcome in their own city. If they want to leave the old city, for example, and live in the new part of the city, they are not welcome there. So, it's very problematic, and it's very—and people need to go through a struggle each day in all levels of life, so they can stay in their own homeland and keep their life here. And again, about all levels of life, we can talk about families and thinking about education for their children, if we talk about people that want to find places to work and opportunities for jobs, if we talk about developing, I don't know, activities or developing projects, everything is very controlled. Everything is very difficult to work with. The state is very, let's say, narrow. Everything is very difficult to act in.

KC: Well it's very narrow and it's very—there are so many layers of restriction it sounds like, to me.

JS: Yeah.

KC: So, one of the things I wanted to go back to that you were talking about that I know is very, again very counterintuitive, but that's why I want to highlight it, was this point you made about renovations. And so, the old city is, well, old, that's why it's called the old city. And as you said, you know, a lot of these historic sites, these buildings were very run down. But if a Palestinian resident of one of these buildings wanted to renovate, it's not legal for them to renovate?

JS: In the last sense— in the '70s[44] the state created a body called the Company for the Developing of the Old City of Akko, of Akka, and it's the only body that has the permission to make renovations in the old city. So, it's their own decision, they decide when to do renovations and for whom they will make the renovation. But again, it's very manipulative, because, again, they can choose the timing and they can choose the cost that they want to demand from the people for the renovations.[45] Usually most of the people don't have this money for the renovations. Some cases that we checked and tried to understand, they are asking for a huge amount of money that is not even close to realistic for the renovation that they are making. And two years ago, or three years ago, we went to the Israeli Parliament and we asked for their intervention in this work because it's totally wild, they are doing whatever they want to do, and they are asking for the money that they want to ask for. There are no criteria, there is no place to negotiate. People cannot say, "Yes, I'm accepting this," or "No I'm not accepting this." They are coming like facts, and they are demanding money for the renovation, and, as I said, most of the people don't have the money to pay because it's really very expensive what they are demanding. And again, by the law, because some people couldn't pay for the renovation, the law sells their houses. So, you can see, again, different ways, different methods that at the end the result will be that people are losing their houses.

KC: So, just to clarify really quick with what you just said, so you can't renovate your house except with this one state approved company, this one developer. This developer charges exorbitant rates to renovate, which the people can't afford, and then when they don't renovate, they're now out of code and so they're kicked out of their home.

JS: Yeah, exactly. For many years, even, they didn't make any renovations. For many years people were in really—until now, you can see that some houses are in very bad conditions. And we had a few houses that were collapsed a few years ago because they were not renovated. Because we are talking really about very old buildings, and it's very close to the sea, so it needs to be renovated all the time. And people are not allowed to make any renovations. Example: if a family even wants to fix their window, or I don't know—even small renovations, I'm not talking about changing the basic things in the house, I'm talking about small things that they are fixing because of the daily life you can do it, in your house you can change things, you can fix things sometimes. So even that, it's not allowed by the law. And people can be charged for these small renovations and each charge or each renovation, even a small one, that means that people are supposed to pay money as a fine for doing that. So, it doesn't matter what these families needed to do, just you know, to try to survive, to live their life. I'm not talking about making extreme, or now they want to make a really extreme renovation. I'm talking about basic needs. To live in these houses during many years, families cannot stay in the same situation. Even if they go and—

KC: I was going to say, we actually have a caller on the air who has a question here, so I think we'll take it. Barbara, you're on the air.

BARBARA: Yeah, hi, thanks. I tuned in late, so I don't know if this was covered in the beginning, but about six years ago my family and I were in Akka, we were visiting relatives up in the Galilee, and we took a trip there, and we went to both Haifa and Akka. And one of the things that I noticed was that it seemed to me that the old city is basically seen as prime real estate. And so, a lot of this pressure of preventing Palestinians from staying there seems to be aimed at building, you know, luxury things for people that can afford—for Jews, basically, that can afford to live there. And I was wondering if she could comment about how much of a motivation she feels that is because we saw examples where they were advertising right there, you know, this big new fancy building is going up in this old neighborhood and now leasing and stuff. Because it's so beautiful there, it is right by the sea, it seems to me that that's part of the pressure, and I'll take my answer off the air, thank you.

KC: Thanks, Barbara. I mean I think this is an interesting point, Johayna. I mean, so on the one hand, is this a bigger project of the sort of Judaization of Akka? Or is this capitalist vultures coming in to take over this very beautiful place as they do everywhere?

JS: Yeah, I think this is one of the—it's a very good question, thank you for that. It's one of the dangerous situations in a city like Akka because you can see the combination of the capitalism, of the economic interests, as we can see it in all (or in many) places in the world. But it's a combination of political and national interests with the economical [*sic*] interests. So, it's true. What is happening in Akka today is not unique just for Akka. We can see it in many older cities in the world. But what is happening here is that after they are taking these houses and these properties and these buildings, these historical buildings, from Palestinians, they are giving or selling these buildings to Jews. And they *do* have identity after that. It's not just an economical interest.

KC: Yeah, and so it's all the more sinister because it's similar to what's happening elsewhere but then it becomes part of this bigger sort of nation-building project.

JS: Yeah, and some of the projects, again the example of the hammam that they want to build into a boutique hotel there—again, it's part of the gentrification process that is going on in the world. I can give you another example of a Jewish investor called—there's a hotel called the Efendi Hotel, and we are talking about a boutique hotel, very expensive hotel, very beautiful hotel in the old city. But the presence of this hotel makes everything in the neighborhood and around very expensive. The rent for the people becomes much more expensive. Even if people go to the grocery it becomes much more expensive because it's part of the gentrification. If you have a boutique hotel that you can pay big money there, everything becomes very expensive, and it's a process of, again, pushing the poor people that are living there to leave because they cannot afford anymore life in such a neighborhood. But the other example of the hammam[46] that they want to build as a boutique hotel,[47] it used to be in the property of the Islamic Committee. And the state is renting this site, it's a historical site, it was written by UNESCO in 2001[48] as Historical World Heritage[49] and is rented by the Islamic Committee to the state.[50] And the state wants to sell it, although it's rented! They don't have—they don't own the place. So, although they don't own the place and they are renting this place, they are having plans to build it as a boutique hotel.[51]

And we are talking about a public place, we are talking about a historical place that's supposed to stay public, supposed to be open for all the people that can come and see and enjoy the building, the type of building, and the beautiful place. But instead of that it becomes a very expensive boutique hotel that only very rich people can come and visit. And of course, they give a lot of privilege to Jewish investors to come and invest in this kind of project. It's very difficult, for example, also for Palestinian families and people, investors for example, to buy houses or properties here. The bureaucracy becomes very complicated and very difficult. So, it's true, it's part of the whole capitalism system that is going, and that we can see in other places. But here it's linked or connected to a political interest of killing or expelling all the Palestinians that live here.

KC: Yeah. Well as you can see they just clicked the music on so that means we're out of time. Johayna Saifi, thank you so much!

JS: Thank you Karma, and to you listeners.

NOTES

1. As'ad Ghanem, "Israel's Second-Class Citizens: Arabs in Israel and the Struggle for Equal Rights," *Foreign Affairs* 95, no. 4 (July/August 2016): 30–37.

2. "The Discriminatory Laws Database," Adalah, last modified September 9, 2017, accessed June 16, 2018, https://www.adalah.org/en/content/view/7771.

3. Or Kashti, "For Jews and Arabs, Israel's School System Remains Separate and Unequal," *Haaretz*, July 7, 2016, https://www.haaretz.com/israel-news/.premium-for-jews-and-arabs-israels-school-system-remains-separate-and-unequal-1.5406700.

4. Jillian Kestler-D'Amours, "Israel: No Place for Bedouin," *Al Jazeera*, June 29, 2011, https://www.aljazeera.com/indepth/opinion/2011/06/20116238174269364.html.

5. "Acco," Nefesh B'Nefesh, accessed June 18, 2018, http://www.nbn.org.il/aliyahpedia/community-housing-aliyahpedia/community-profiles/acco/.

6. Eyad Barghouti, "Akka: A Palestinian Priority," *Palestine Remembered*, February 2, 2009, http://www.palestineremembered.com/Acre/Acre/Story12400.html.

7. "Akka," Zochrot, accessed June 18, 2018, https://zochrot.org/en/village/49425.

8. 1947, in fact, not 1922—there was no state plan in 1922. See Zochrot, "Akka."

9. World Heritage Sites in Israel, ed., *Wikipedians* (Mainz, Germany: PediaPress, 2018), 16.

10. Efrat Elisha, "Geographical Distribution of the Soviet-Jewish New Immigrants in Israel," *GeoJournal* 24, no. 4 (1991): 360.

11. Meirav Moran, "No Mosque in Plans for Expansion of Israeli City of Acre, which is One-Third Arab," *Haaretz*, November 30, 2017, https://www.haaretz.com/israel-news/no-mosque-in-plans-for-expansion-of-acre-which-is-one-third-arab-1.5627306.

12. Harriet Sherwood, "Israel's Historic City of Acre Faces Tourist and Settler Tensions," *Guardian*, June 24, 2012, https://www.theguardian.com/world/2012/jun/24/israel-historic-city-acre-tensions.

13. "Hirakuna," Dafna Fund, accessed June 26, 2018 from: http://www.dafnafund.org.il/en/what-do-we-do/grantmaking/

14. It was June 16, 2015. See Yair Ashkenazi, "Culture Ministry Halts Funding to Haifa's Al-Midan Theater," *Haaretz*, June 16, 2015, https://www.haaretz.com/.premium-culture-ministry-halts-funding-to-haifa-s-al-midan-theater-1.5372247.

15. Ashkenazi, "Culture Ministry Halts Funding."

16. Diaa Hadid, "Play Set in Israeli Prison Imperils Arab Theater," *New York Times*, June 13, 2015, https://www.nytimes.com/2015/06/14/world/play-set-in-israeli-prison-imperils-arab-theater.html.

17. Sources say, "a third," so "about 32 percent" is accurate. See World Heritage Sites, *Wikipedians*, 16.

18. World Heritage Sites, *Wikipedians*, 16.

19. This number could not be confirmed.

20. Amy Tiebel, "Orthodox Israelis Moving into Arab Areas of Mixed Cities," *Times of Israel*, October 4, 2012, https://www.timesofisrael.com/settler-movement-moves-to-jewish-arab-cities-in-israel/.

21. It was difficult to find information about specific privileges, but one could argue that allowing people to build a Jewish-only apartment building is a privilege. See Jack Khoury, "Appeal against Acre Housing for Religious Jews Fails," *Haaretz*, April 24, 2012, https://www.haaretz.com/court-upholds-acre-orthodox-only-housing-project-1.5216451.

22. U.S. Department of State, Bureau of Democracy, Human Rights and Labor, *Country Reports on Human Rights Practices for 2011: Israel*, May 24, 2012, https://2009-2017.state.gov/documents/organization/190656.pdf.

23. Edo Konrad, "Israel is Razing a Bedouin Village to Build a Jewish-Only Town on Its Ruins," *+972*, August 10, 2017, https://972mag.com/israel-is-razing-a-bedouin-village-to-build-a-jewish-only-town-on-its-ruins/129192/.

24. Amjad Iraqi, "Israel's Housing Policy for Arabs is Designed to Fail," *+972*, February 2, 2016, https://972mag.com/israels-housing-policy-for-arabs-is-designed-to-fail/116599/.

25. This is definitely the case in general, although some Palestinian citizens have managed to build. Nir Hasson, "Only 7% of Jerusalem Building Permits go to Palestinian Neighborhoods—Israel News," *Haaretz*, December 7, 2015, https://www.haaretz.com/israel-news/.premium-only-7-of-jlem-building-permits-go-to-palestinian-neighborhoods-1.5432437.

26. This statement is overwhelmingly accurate, but not 100 percent true. See Iraqi, "Israel's Housing Policy."

27. Sherwood, "Israel's Historic City."

28. As a general statement, this is accurate. Fact checking this claim did not reveal anything about the selling of those particular Turkish bathhouses, nor could mention of those Turkish bathhouses in the English press be found. See Sherwood, "Israel's Historic City."

29. Sherwood, "Israel's Historic City."

30. Avigayil Kadesh, "Volunteers Get Free College, Cheap Digs," Israel Ministry of Foreign Affairs, May 7, 2014, http://mfa.gov.il/MFA/IsraelExperience/People/Pages/Israelis-get-free-college,-cheap-digs-in-exchange-for-volunteering.aspx.

31. Kadesh, "Volunteers Get Free College."

32. "Acre Facing the New and Old Colonizers," *Tarabut-Hithrabut*, January 25, 2012, http://www.tarabut.info/en/articles/article/Colonizing-Acre/.

33. It's two-dozen, so 24, not 20. See Kadesh, "Volunteers Get Free College."

34. Joseph Algazy May, "And the Walls Came Tumbling Down," *Haaretz*, May 9, 2004, https://www.haaretz.com/1.4831098.

35. Fact checking did not reveal anything about Jews buying houses in the old city. Much of the land is state owned, though.

36. "Acre Facing the New and Old Colonizers."

37. The law says nothing about "proof." See "Absentees' Property Law," Adalah, accessed June 18, 2018, https://www.adalah.org/en/law/view/538.

38. "Absentees' Property Law."

39. "Acre Facing the New and Old Colonizers."

40. Jenny Nyman, "Palestinians of Acre Face Growing Israeli Push to Evict Them," *Middle East Eye*, December 9, 2016, http://www.middleeasteye.net/in-depth/features/old-city-acre-judaisation-gentrification-1509989529.

41. Rasha Assaf and Aleef Sabbagh, The Arab Association for Human Rights, *Acre: A City of Development and Neglect*, 2014, http://www.arabhra.org/uploads/userfiles/files/HRA%20Report%20_Acre_%20A%20City%20of%20Development%20and%20Neglect_.pdf.

42. Nyman, "Palestinians of Acre Face."

43. Assaf and Sabbagh, *Acre: A City of Development and Neglect*.

44. It was 1967. See "About the Old Acre Development Company Ltd.," Akko, accessed June 18, 2018 from: http://www.akko.org.il/en/About-the-Old-Acre-Development-Company.

45. Jack Khoury, "A Renovation on Shaky Ground," *Haaretz*, January 3, 2012, https://www.haaretz.com/1.5158136.

46. It is unclear if the Khan al Umdan is a hammam. It seems like it is next to a Turkish bath. See Khoury, "Renovation."

47. Sarah Irving, "New Campaign to Save Historic Palestinian Building," *Electronic Intifada*, October 28, 2013, https://electronicintifada.net/blogs/sarah-irving/new-campaign-save-historic-palestinian-building.

48. Irving, "New Campaign."

49. The term is *UNESCO World Heritage Site*. See Virág Gulyás, "Israel's Top 10 UNESCO World Heritage Sites," *Culture Trip*, May 8, 2018, https://theculturetrip.com/middle-east/israel/articles/living-ancient-history-israel-s-top-10-unesco-world-heritage-sites/.

50. Assaf and Sabbagh, *Acre: A City of Development and Neglect*.

51. It is not entirely accurate to say the plans are current, as a court threw out the plan in 2014. See "Hotel Proposal for UNESCO World Heritage Site Thrown Out by Court," *Middle East Monitor*, March 10, 2016, https://www.middleeastmonitor.com/20140310-hotel-proposal-for-unesco-world-heritage-site-thrown-out-by-court/.

CHARLOTTE SILVER
"One Year after Operation Protective Edge," July 22, 2015

https://www.wortfm.org/gaza-one-year-after-operation/

Joined by WORT High School Intern Amanda Zhang

KARMA CHÁVEZ: As you know, I am doing a series on Palestine this summer after my trip to the West Bank in May. I did not get to go to the Gaza strip, the 139-square-mile region on the coast and just north of Egypt. Last summer, the Israeli military launched a fifty-one-day offensive on the Gaza strip called Operation Protective Edge. In June of last year, three Israeli boys living on illegal settlements in the West Bank went missing. The Israeli government blamed Hamas for disappearing and killing the boys, and on July 7, began attacking Gaza, where Hamas has a political stronghold, in retaliation.[1]

AMANDA ZHANG: By the time Operation Protective Edge ended on August 26, over 2,100 Palestinians had been killed, including more than 1,500 civilians and over 500 children, and over 10,000 wounded.[2] With more than seven thousand homes destroyed and ten thousand more severely damaged by Israeli bombing, approximately 30 percent of the 1.8 million residents of Gaza were internally displaced, with hundreds of thousands needing emergency food assistance and seeking shelter in UN-run schools.[3] The Institute for Middle East Understanding reports that the attacks destroyed civilian infrastructure, including its electrical grid, nearly five hundred businesses or workshops were severely damaged, and agricultural and fishing sectors were also horribly impacted.[4]

One year later, things in Gaza are still very difficult. Many promises of international aid and support have not come through, the rebuilding process is thus much slower than anticipated, and an Israeli lockdown on all land and sea borders makes accessing basic necessities virtually impossible.[5] Our guest today just returned from Gaza. Charlotte Silver is an independent journalist based in Oakland, California. She has been reporting from Palestine and Israel since 2010. She writes for the *Electronic Intifada, Al Jazeera English, The Nation* and other publications. Follow her on Twitter @CharESilver.

KC: In a July 8 piece on Gaza one year later, Silver wrote of the ongoing situation in Gaza, that in addition to the struggles of rebuilding lives and infrastructure, "the Israeli military and naval forces have fired into Gaza and on Palestinian fisherman at least 739 times since last August. Fishermen are fired on within six nautical miles of Gaza's shore more than once a day, on average, as are Palestinians farmers and residents near to the boundary. In recent months, 23 airstrikes have been carried out on Gaza; and Israeli military vehicles have made 23 incursions into the border area."[6]

Charlotte Silver, welcome to *A Public Affair*.

CHARLOTTE SILVER: Thank you so much, I'm so happy to be here.

AZ: Hi Charlotte, thanks for joining us. Could you tell us how you started working in Palestine, just as a brief background?

CS: I—my work with Palestine started mainly as a student, a college student. I was active in a young divestment group called Students Confronting Apartheid by Israel at Stanford, which was founded in 2005, the same year that the call for BDS was launched. And I also, while I was working in that group, I was also studying the history of modern Palestine and Zionism in classes. So, I was reading a lot about Palestine, I was reading a lot about the development of a sort of Jewish nationalism under the banner of Zionism in Europe and how it focused into a state-building project. And it wasn't until after I went to Palestine that I began working as a journalist. And I first visited the West Bank in 2010 and was working as a journalist and an editor of a local English publication there. And I can't emphasize enough how after looking at Palestine, reading about Palestine, thinking about Palestine for so many years, but not actually being in Palestine, how dramatically your understanding of what is at stake and what the conflict consists of changes when you see it.

And so, for two years I lived in the West Bank and reported from there. And during—and I also reported from 1948 Israel, Jerusalem, but never was I able to go to Gaza. Gaza's extremely difficult to enter as a freelance journalist, although that has changed in the past year. And, so—but the West Bank has remained very open to internationals and foreigners whereas Gaza is still completely cut off except for a very few exceptions. And so, this past summer I was able to go to Gaza as a journalist and it was—it was an extremely important place to *see* and not just read about in the media. And it emphasizes the destruction and the power of Israel's blockade on Gaza, not just in terms of its devastation to the people of Gaza, preventing people from getting basic necessities like fuel and reconstruction materials, as you mentioned in the introduction, but also communication with the outside world.

KC: Will you—and so, before we move to mentioning Gaza, I was wondering if you could just expand a little bit on some of the specific things that really shaped your viewpoint, actually spending extended time in the West Bank and why that was so important for you to really understand what's going on?

CS: Well, I think for one there's this—there's this kind of understanding when you read about and when you're kind of forced to write about Israel and Palestine that they're these two separate entities. And they're kind of—they're in conversation with one another. And when you go there, the sort of fluidity of the two spaces is very poignant. And the repression of Palestinians in the West Bank is not confined to what usually makes the news, which is tear gassing shot at protestors or people being regularly killed and injured by the military, which is a very important aspect and very brutal aspect of the occupation. But it's also things like a daily commute from Ramallah and Jerusalem, which is occupied and annexed by Israel, consists of, you know, up to two hours sitting in traffic or standing in a cage trying to cross the checkpoint. Things like, you know, you can drive through the Jordan Valley and it looks maybe demilitarized but 90 percent of that space is controlled by the Israeli military,[7] meaning that the people who live there, the thousands of people who live there who have traditionally always maintained agricultural livelihoods, cannot access the land, cannot access the water to irrigate the land.[8] Their livelihoods have been completely eliminated by this invisible control by the Israeli military. And seeing how it's sort of—being there and seeing that and seeing how there's this sort of necessity to try to survive amid this sort of very easy to maintain occupation, you see—it drives home the point of how entrenched the current situation is and how it's not just a matter of removing settlements or removing the settlers to reach a solution.

KC: Well let's actually talk a little bit, just to—the question of settlers is part of what, at least, the Israeli government—the disappearance of these three settlers is what they used as a part of the rationale for last summer's fifty-one-day war. Will you talk about how the Israeli government made this connection and used it as a rationale for last summer's war?

CS: The missing three teens was a sort of convenient hook for the Israeli government to whip up a national frenzy of fear and also retribution, revenge. And, as has been documented already, the three boys who went missing were found, had been killed—kidnapped and killed very soon after they went missing,[9] but that information was kept under gag order by the Israeli government[10] while the Israeli military proceeded to raid the entire West

Bank.[11] Raid villages, raid cities, raid cities that, you know, maybe were in Area A and had enjoyed some sort of freedom from direct military presence and turned the area upside down. I spoke with people—I wasn't there last year, but when I went this summer, I spoke to people who were there, and they spoke of how it was a wakeup call, really, for how quickly things can change.

The West Bank has been—you know, relative to Gaza, the West Bank has enjoyed a sort of muted—sort of a low level, constant level of violence. I don't want to undermine the kind of violence that Palestinians living in the West Bank endure, both at the hands of settlers, civilian settlers, and the military. But it's this constant drone that maintains a kind of status—that's sort of the status quo, it's not these surges and crises like in the Gaza Strip, as we see. And it was just interesting to speak with people in the West Bank to hear how they—last summer was sort of a wakeup call to how fragile this kind of quiet is, and how easily Israel can just turn everything upside down and create a true state of crisis for Palestinians there. But this was all—this was all on the heels of Hamas and Fatah creating a unity government that had been condoned by the U.S. government, that the Israeli government wasn't happy about. They weren't happy that there was this reconciliation going on between Hamas and Fatah because it disrupts Israel's long and successful strategy of divide and conquer in Palestine—

KC: And of course, these are the two political groups of—in Palestine, the two predominant political groups, Fatah and Hamas.

CS: Right, I'm sorry, so Fatah is the political party that occupies the Palestinian Authority in the West Bank and Hamas rules Gaza. And the separation occurred after Hamas was democratically elected in both the West Bank and Gaza in 2006 and then P.A. (Palestinian Authority) maintained control in the West Bank and then Hamas maintained control in Gaza.[12]

KC: And so, thinking about this sort of precarity of the situation that people experienced after living under this low level of intensity—is it the view of most Palestinians that these missing settlers was just kind of a ruse? Or what are the real reasons that the Israeli military attacked last summer?

CS: Right, so, the settlers—no reason to believe that the settlers were not kidnapped by Palestinians, they were, but there's no link to any political movement, any political party. Hamas had nothing to do with it, there would be no plausible explanation why Hamas would kidnap settlers, which would clearly disrupt the unity government they have just achieved.[13] So—but this was sort of a way of whipping up frenzy and allowing the Israeli government, with the help of the U.S. government, [John] Kerry in particular, of blaming

Hamas for committing this act, which they described as a terrorist act. And that is what precipitated, eventually, airstrikes on Gaza that, as you said, began on July 7. And it wasn't until the next day that there were retaliatory rockets fired from Gaza. And so that sort of marks the beginning of the war.

And then, after it was very clear that it couldn't have been the children, the reason to attack Gaza that was just—as the war became so wide scale, so expansive, Israel shifted its explanation to that it was trying to destroy tunnels,[14] the tunnels that Palestinians had built as their only access to outside of the completely sealed off Gaza Strip.[15] And so Israel described these as terror tunnels, that they were using them to import weapons[16] and also conduct terror acts in Israel.[17] I'm using the word "terror" in scare quotes, over here. And, you know, on the ground it didn't—this didn't translate to what Israel was targeting, who they were targeting, and how they were conducting this war. There was nothing precise or discriminate about this attack, this fifty-one days of attack. And that's evident by the fact that seventeen thousand homes and buildings were destroyed. Seventeen thousand.[18] I've heard some statistics that 20 percent of Gaza was actually ruined.[19] And this includes, you know, the count of structures that were destroyed doesn't include the amount of agricultural land that was destroyed. I mean, agricultural land of Gaza lies mostly at the border areas,[20] and so they're the first to get scorched, destroyed. I spoke with many farmers who, though they tried to maintain their fields throughout the war, as it's their only means of income, eventually had to escape to somewhere safer. And they returned to their homes—maybe their homes weren't destroyed but their land was. I mean, that represents a huge cost, a huge loss of earnings, a huge cost to repair.

And, you know, this is not—this is not evident of a specific mission on the part of Israel to destroy tunnels, or whatever excuse they gave. It represents the way Israel considers Gaza, which is—it is a place that contains only enemies. And, you know, this is evident in the way colonels and officers and politicians speak of Gaza. You know, it's not Hamas, it's all Palestinians in Gaza. And, you know, the way—I went to Khuza'a, for example, which was completely blacked out from media, from medical care for almost ten days at the end of July. And almost every single house in Khuza'a was occupied, was directly targeted by either ground invasion or airstrikes. And the commander who, Ofer Winter [in Kuhza'a], who directed that operation,[21] is on record of saying, "Every single house here is the home of terrorists."[22] And so this is the—this is the mentality of the Israeli military going into Gaza, and that's why the statistics bear this out. Over 70 percent of those who were killed were civilians.

KC: We actually have a caller on the line here, Charlotte, so I'm going to bring him on the air really quick here. So, Phil, you're on the air?

PHIL: Yes, thank you. I think of the Israeli-Palestinian situation as something akin to the apartheid government in South Africa before liberation. Or something akin to the fascists in Germany who sought to, basically, displace everybody from Eastern Europe so that the German people could have a wider homeland. The territoriality of the Israelis, and American support for it, is completely misdefined for me. I *can't* understand how our government can claim any honor in its diplomacy with this kind of position. So, I'm wondering about the one-state, two-state solution and if your guest could speak to that. Ali Abunimah stipulated that a two-state solution is a failed solution.[23] It's ultimately going to keep people on different sides and there will continue to be warring between them. Whereas, if you institute a one-state solution, you basically meld them together and they can learn to coexist. There will be friendship, but there's no end to the killing that exists as it does now, with the Palestinians in Gaza and West Bank. The deprivation of the Palestinians by the Israelis. Could your guest speak to that please?

KC: Thanks a lot for the question, Phil. Charlotte, what's your view on this or what's, maybe, the predominant view of the people you talk to about the one-state, two-state?

CS: Well I have to say that I don't hear—I don't find a consensus among Palestinians for the one-state or the two-state. Among people in Gaza, their hopes are much simpler and much smaller scale than a master solution to the entire conflict, right? Their needs are so acute that they're not thinking about this in the abstract. They're thinking about this in the, "How am I going to get out of Gaza to go to college next year?" or "How am I going to get out of Gaza to save my children from the next war?" And I think that it's important to remember that these conversations about one-state and two-state solution are important to have because I think that they elucidate realities on the ground, but they are still abstractions from the more acute needs that every Palestinian faces and the fact that—you know these—each family, each person, each city has to try and overcome whatever obstacle, whatever imposition the occupation is putting on them at that moment.

I don't—I—to me it seems like the reality is that there is one state ruling the land of historic Palestine that is now several different political zones. And that state is Israel. And so, it does seem like it is a more plausible solution to create—to have that state, whatever that state would be called or look like—be one that's based on equality for all the people living under it. And not based on a religious nationalistic identity. But I will say that in terms of explaining the territoriality of Israel, you know, like, it's Israel as it was created in 1948, the borders that the 1947 Partition Plan established, and that Israel cleansed of nearly a million Palestinians to create a majority. And that state depends on the resources of the area around it. And so, its attachment to the West Bank and Gaza is not just about the, sort of, fringe religious settlers that we hear a lot about in the news that are portrayed as sort of marginal and not representative of a political majority. That their control over that land is necessary for Israel, 1948 Israel, to operate as a unified state, to maintain an agricultural industry, to water the lawns, to give people water as much as they want. All of the water that enters Israel is coming from resources that lie outside of its borders.[24] So I think that it's important to know that there are very strong material interests keeping the occupation in place, not the kind of religious conflict that I think a lot of times overshadows these reasons.

AZ: Let's talk about the destruction that occurred last summer. So, we know that the Israeli military killed over 2,000 Palestinians, including over 500 children. Could you explain—how were the majority of these people killed?

CS: The majority of the people killed were killed in their homes,[25] were actually crushed to death.[26] Israel—the main target of Israel's air strikes were residential buildings.[27] And they would excuse it by saying there was maybe one Hamas or Islamic jihad operative militant in it.[28] And they would use that as an excuse to demolish an entire building. And Israel did—Israel often sort of counts their use of warnings—leaflets, text messages to residential areas warning them of an imminent attack so that those people can flee, go somewhere else. And from people I spoke to and from reports I read, it is true that Israel would maybe litter some leaflets and text messages. But in reality, no one could get this text message and know where to go. Many times, these notifications were delivered amidst an area-wide air strike. So, if one person gets a text message that their building is going to be targeted, there's no safe building to go to. And so most people—these were useless for them, they didn't provide any kind of protection or any kind of sufficient warning. And a lot of people felt like it would be safer for them to stay in their homes than try to get onto the streets and flee en masse to somewhere that supposedly could be safer. But, remember, Israel targeted—they targeted medical facilities,[29] UN shelters that were holding people who had fled areas that had been warned of attack, those places were hit also.[30] And so once someone hears of these attacks, no one feels like they can go there and find any kind of real security or safety.

KC: We have a couple more callers waiting on the line hear, Charlotte, so I'm going to take the first one and let you respond, and then I'll take the second one. So, our first question comes from Thomas, you're on the air.

THOMAS: The comment I wanted to make is two things. Number one, Israel, with the help of the American Jews and the American people is committing genocide of the Palestinians. This has been going on for sixty years, and until the politicians stop—and the president and all the military stop kissing the Israeli butt—it will continue. And I predict that within five years there will be no Palestine because it will be exterminated. The people will be exterminated, and the land will be taken over by Israel. And nobody seems to want to say that, either on a local program like this or on the news, they're always defending Israel. "Oh, Israel did this, but they had to do it because there was little couple of people there running around with guns." And so that's my comment, and I understand, I've listened to many people speak about Palestine and Gaza, but it won't change. And unless the Palestinians get enough weapons to overthrow the Israelis, it'll never happen. So, I would like you to comment on this or say why nobody wants to talk about this. And also, I think it's important that anybody who's voting this year—don't vote for candidates that support U.S.-backed foreign relations in Israel. Because they should not be—they are a terrorist nation just like we call Iran, or we call ISIS. There's really no difference, and nobody wants to talk about it. And thank you for the program, because I like listening to people regarding this subject, thank you.

KC: Well thanks so much for the call Thomas. A lot of points there that are important. It's sort of a pessimistic view, maybe, compared to others. Do you have a response to that Charlotte?

CS: Well, I—I agree that, you know, the media's coverage of Israel and Palestine and the atrocities committed against Palestinians doesn't really seem to help. I think that there is hope that after every atrocity, after every war, that things are going to start changing. The idea that this time Israel went too far. And I think people felt that way last summer. Not only was it one of the most expensive and brutal attacks on Palestinians, in recent history, but it was covered extremely well by the media. Better than usually. I mean, not only by foreign media, local journalists were doing an incredible job of covering what was happening on the ground inside Gaza through online publications and also Twitter and social media. There was more information, more images, more video footage of what the war looked like than ever before. And I think that that is very important for people to understand, the brutality of these attacks on the civilian population.

I don't—I don't know what's going to happen, how things are going to change. I don't think that in five years there's going to be no more Palestine, you know, there's a lot of discussion and focus on the rubble and the destruction from last year in Gaza, that Gaza's on the verge of collapse. There's a lot of language that describes Gaza as in crisis and sort of destroyed. And I think it's really important to also realize and know that Gaza is more than that. It is a society that functions, you know, with a huge disadvantage, and handicap, and obstacles, but people are there living. They're not just huddled in rubble, they're also trying to survive, and it's not something that, if you see, you're going to think it's going to not exist in five years. You're going to think this is going to exist forever, whether or not Israel likes it. And the point of Israel's regime is not necessarily total destruction but total control. And it has achieved that in Gaza, and it has achieved that in the West Bank, whether through constant surveillance, whether through the ability to enter, raid whenever they want. Palestinians are completely in the hands of Israel in terms of its economy and in terms of its safety. And so, I think that that has been achieved and that is the state of things right now.

KC: We're going to—a lot of people are interested in what you have to say today, Charlotte Silver, so we're going to keep going through some calls here. Our next caller has a question about the psychological effects on children, so Barb, you're on the air.

BARB: Hi, thanks for taking my call. I haven't been to Gaza, but a group that I work with, Madison-Rafah Sister City Project, we have sent people there, so we're somewhat familiar with the situation. I just wanted to mention—to reinforce the first idea, that this is repeated over and over, this type of military assault. It's either at a high level like it was last year and five years before that in Operation Cast Lead, or it's at a constant daily low level; there's drones, there's shootings, there's bombings, there's attacks. It's a constant presence, and it disrupts, particularly, the lives of children. And we've recently been contacted by partners in Rafah that want us to help them raise funds for a psychological counseling project for some children with disabilities. And I guess my question is twofold: when you were there, did you have any firsthand experience either with children or people who try to deal with them? Because it's estimated, I think by the UN, that there's something like 400,000 children in Gaza who suffer from various forms of PTSD, and it has caused them a lot of difficulties.[31] And the second, maybe more broader question, given that—I agree with her that we're not looking at a five-year extermination, we're looking at a long-term struggle, but if you saw or discussed with people, what do they feel is the role of outside assistance? Because the society is extremely dependent on various forms of aid. And we ourselves here are constantly being asked to do sort of targeted projects, whether it's children or water, whatever. And I was just curious if in your—if you looked at any of that. And I'll take my answer off the air.

KC: Thanks a lot, Barb. Do you have responses to those questions about what's going on with regard to psychological questions for children, Charlotte?

CS: Yeah, I mean, I don't think that you could say anybody in Gaza is not traumatized by three wars—massive wars—in six years. And the children are, of course, the most acutely affected by what they saw last summer. I did visit a number of attempts to nurture these children in areas that were targeted, like Khuza'a, Beit Hanoun. And these are pretty modest attempts to bring children together to sort of play games, have fun, and also talk about what happened last summer. Talk about the losses they experienced and what they saw. And from people I spoke to, from the people who were working with these kids, they talked about the huge improvement in their—in them, in their behavior and their demeanor. You know, a year ago these children were coming in unable to speak, most of them—many of them. And when I saw them they were shy but laughing, having fun, enjoying the games, and this speaks to children's ability to—they are resilient, but they're not—the war isn't over in Gaza and the anxiety that is constant is there.

And, you know, I think that it's important to recognize the trauma in adults as well and the desperation in adults as well. After the war, people in Gaza tried to escape by the sea.[32] They tried to escape through Egypt on boats to go to Europe, and many of them died.[33] And this speaks to the kind of desperation that the blockade creates. The inability for nearly two million people to live in an area that's smaller than New York City. I can't emphasize enough the maddening effect of that. And every single young person I spoke to—and the majority of Gaza are young people—every single person is trying to figure out how they can get out. And it's heartbreaking to listen to them trying to figure out a way to get out knowing that ultimately, it's out of their hands. And so, I want to emphasize that the trauma's not confined to children, even though they are the most tragic cases in a lot of ways. It's something that persists beyond war and pervades society in Gaza.

And then in terms of outside assistance, you know Gaza—I think 80 percent of Gaza's population are dependent on international aid for food, for the most basic of needs.[34] Forty-three percent of Gaza's population are unemployed.[35] The World Bank recently estimated—warned that the economy's on the verge of collapse.[36] I mean, it has collapsed, and it's being kept on life support by the international community. So, I don't think that you can question the necessity of that, but I also think that Gaza's problem is not just a humanitarian crisis, it's a political crisis. And I think that the international community does a disservice to that when they focus exclusively on these crises, like the war. You know, they choose to condemn Israel's action, and even when they do that they force a sort of false symmetry between Israel and Hamas, presenting it as actually a war, where two sides are committing wrongs. And if only this war could be fought fairly, then they'd be okay with it. And so, you know, we saw that with the recent UN report, we saw that with Amnesty International in particular sort of seeming to bend over backwards to condemn Hamas's tactics in the war[37] when, in reality, we really can't compare it to Israel. And if you do, you know, at least the figures, Hamas killed—not Hamas, the Palestinian different factions killed a total of seventy-two people, Israelis, last summer.[38] Only 8 percent of those were civilians.[39] And if you compare that to the devastation among Palestinian populations, 70 percent were civilians.[40] And this is—this is even with Gaza's homemade rockets, you know, low—inferior technology. Israel has one of the largest arsenals, most sophisticated arsenals in the world, you know, it has a booming industry of exporting its military wares, and yet these are the statistics that it ends up with.

KC: We got about ten minutes left in the show here. We have one more caller on the line here who has a comment or question about the sort of emergence of the good relations we currently have with the U.S. and Israel, but they haven't always been that way. So, Michael, you're on the air.

MICHAEL: Yes, I guess basically what I wanted to point out is it hasn't always been this monolith of the U.S. and Israel being inseparable. There've been a lot of incidents, most of which have been covered up, or not subject to public discussion. The most obvious and the best-known one would be the attack on the USS *Liberty* in 1967 in which thirty-four American sailors were killed. The Israelis claim that it was a complete mistake.[41] But any attempt to seriously discuss the issue is stymied by either accusations of anti-Semitism[42] or invoking the sacred cloak of national security.[43] Another example, also not very well-known, is the document that was found by the Iranians when they occupied the U.S. embassy. They found a document written by the C.I.A. describing the Israeli intelligence and police forces, and that report was replete with instances of dirty tricks played by Israel against American citizens and government officials, primarily in the hope of either blackmailing them or getting them to compromise positions.[44] And then another well-known incident would be Jonathan Pollard, a very, from what I've read, apparently unstable[45] and grandiose individual who spied for

Israel throughout his position in the office of naval intelligence.[46] My point being that the relations have not been smooth sailing, necessarily, between the U.S. and Israel, that there have been a lot of fairly serious breaches of security and other ruptures caused by Israel, but they never see the light of day, whether because of claims of national security or because of allegations of anti-Semitism if you bring them up. So, interested in what your guest would have to say on that, and thank you for taking my call. Take care!

KC: Thanks a lot, Michael. Charlotte, what do you have to say about the sort of past problems the U.S. and Israel have had, and maybe that points to future opportunities.

CS: Well, you know, I don't think that political—I don't think that geopolitical relations are based on friendship and love, I think they're based on geopolitical strategy. And the lens you have to look at, all maneuvering in the Middle East and understanding of—that's one of the reasons why Palestine is in such a desperate situation, it doesn't have a foothold in any sort of geopolitical strategy, it's sort of on its own. And so, all states that actually do wield some sort of power aren't using it to protect Palestine or to bolster Palestine's position in negotiations with Israel, in relation to the U.S. And I think that that's also important to consider going forward as people sort of predict a bipartisan rift among—between Democrats and Republicans regarding Israel. I mean, there's definitely been a rhetorical shift, Democrats have opened up an avenue of criticizing Israel, whereas Republicans have doubled down on defending all Israeli militancy.

But, in fact, all of this—this rhetoric is not backed by any sort of material shift, and the U.S. is prepared to give Israel more military aid sort of as a consolation to the Iranian—U.S.-Iran deal. And, you know, I think that the U.S.-Iran deal is a good example of how the U.S. conducts its foreign policy, which is not on the basis of humanitarianism. It doesn't pick its allies on their human rights records, even though it likes to pretend like it does. The U.S. had very specific reasons why it wanted to reach a resolution with Iran that did not have to do—they weren't concerned about the crippling economic sanctions that had been imposed on Iran. And so that's sort of—I don't think we can expect the U.S. to change its policy based on concerns over Israel's human rights record. And we can see that by the various allies that it maintains in the region.

AZ: And with just a couple minutes left we'd like to turn our attention toward the local efforts in rebuilding Gaza. Could you tell us about the kinds of local efforts people are engaged in for themselves in Gaza in terms of political or educational institutions?

CS: Well, rebuilding in Gaza is controlled by the crossings, which are controlled by Israel, and so the ability to get material and to start repairing some of the buildings is controlled by how much is allowed in through one crossing, Kerem Shalom, which Israel effectively controls. Some materials have entered through Rafah as well, through Egypt—through the Egyptian side. And last month Egypt had opened the crossing more than it had in over a year. So, more building supplies are entering, but it's such a slow pace that it will take around twenty years for all of the damaged buildings to be rebuilt. But, you know, societies, and cities, and states need building materials for more reasons than just devastation by war.

Gaza's entire infrastructure is completely—is in ruins because it hasn't been able to get the necessary materials to repair electricity grids, sewage infrastructure, water infrastructure. So, the ability for people inside Gaza to overcome that blockade is very minimal. But you do see—but people also have no choice. So, you do see people moving back into some of their homes that were partially destroyed. Some money has reached people whose homes were partially damaged, so those homes have been able to have some repairs done to it. I visited this neighborhood close to the old city in Gaza City that has been—that a resident, a painter who lived there decided he wanted to paint in all sorts of bright colors. Most of Gaza's buildings are cement, they're unpainted, especially in the poor neighborhoods, and he decided to take it upon himself to start painting the walls of this small little neighborhood bright colors like yellow and pink and blue, these bright Mediterranean colors. And decorate the area with pots of plants. It, you know, I couldn't—I saw pictures of it, but when I went there it was incredible to see, and it did do something to the people. Everyone there was participating, were just painting pots or painting walls, and everyone was very pleased with what they had done without any sort of help from the outside. But that's one end.

KC: Yeah. But it's a hopeful story. Unfortunately, we're going to have to end our show today there, which is never a bad place, I guess, to be hopeful. But we could talk for several hours about what's going on, what needs to be done. But thank you so much, Charlotte Silver, for being with us today.

CS: Thanks so much for having me.

KC: Again, our guest today is independent journalist Charlotte Silver talking with us about Gaza, one year after the fifty-one-day war. In fact, she just returned last week from Gaza, so we appreciate you taking the time. Also want to say thanks to you, Amanda, for being here today.

AZ: Thanks so much, Karma.

NOTES

1. From Karma: I would have worded this differently now. "Political stronghold" implies that Hamas was not elected by the people of Gaza, which they were.

2. 2,251 Palestinians died, including 1,462 civilians, of which 551 were children. 11,231 Palestinians were injured. "Key Figures on the 2014 Hostilities," United Nations Office for the Coordination of Humanitarian Affairs, June 23, 2015, https://www.ochaopt.org/content/key-figures-2014-hostilities.

3. "Key Figures." In actuality, 18,000 housing units were fully or partially destroyed. Twenty-eight percent of Gazans were internally displaced at the height of hostilities.

4. In its roundup of data from the 2014 attacks on Gaza, the IMEU reported that Israel bombed Gaza's only power plant, which led to the shutting down of its water treatment plant. Israeli bombs also severely damaged Gaza's water and sewage systems, and one of the effects of this was that raw sewage went into the Mediterranean Sea, which had a detrimental impact on fishers. "The 2014 Israeli Attack on Gaza ('Operation Protective Edge') One Year Later," Institute for Middle East Understanding, July 8, 2015, https://imeu.org/article/2014-israeli-attack-on-gaza-one-year-later.

5. "2014 Israeli Attack on Gaza."

6. Charlotte Silver, "One Year Later, Gaza Rebuilding Blocked," *Electronic Intifada*, July 8, 2015, https://electronicintifada.net/blogs/charlotte-silver/one-year-later-gaza-rebuilding-blocked.

7. "OPT: A Precarious Existence in the Jordan Valley," *ReliefWeb*, December 31, 2012, https://reliefweb.int/report/occupied-palestinian-territory/opt-precarious-existence-jordan-valley.

8. MA'AN Development Center, *The Status of Palestinian Agriculture in the Jordan Valley*, 2012, http://www.maan-ctr.org/old/pdfs/FSReport/spotlight/Spotlight10.pdf. It is likely not 100 percent of Palestinians there that face this problem, though it is fair to say thousands do experience these restrictions.

9. David Horovitz and Mitch Ginsburg, "What Happened on the Night of the Kidnapping," *Times of Israel*, June 30, 2014, https://www.timesofisrael.com/what-happened-on-the-night-of-the-kidnapping/.

10. Noam Sheizaf, "How the Public was Manipulated into Believing the Teens Were Alive," *+972*, July 2, 2014, https://972mag.com/how-the-public-was-manipulated-into-believing-the-teens-were-alive/92865/.

11. Max Blumenthal, "Netanyahu Government Knew Teens Were Dead as it Whipped up Racist Frenzy," *Electronic Intifada*, July 8, 2014, https://electronicintifada.net/content/netanyahu-government-knew-teens-were-dead-it-whipped-racist-frenzy/13533.

12. "Palestinian Territories Profile," *BBC News*, December 7, 2017, https://www.bbc.com/news/world-middle-east-14630174.

13. This claim is disputed. Israeli government reports say the Qawasmehs, who were indicted for the kidnapping, have ties to Hamas. See Isabel Kershner, "New Light on Hamas Role in Killings of Teenagers That Fueled Gaza War," *New York Times*, September 4, 2014, https://www.nytimes.com/2014/09/05/world/middleeast/killing-of-3-israeli-teenagers-loosely-tied-to-hamas-court-documents-show.html?mtrref=nymag.com&assetType=nyt_now. A Hamas official did confirm their group was tied to the kidnapping. See "Hamas Admits to Kidnapping and Killing Israeli Teens," *NPR*, August 22, 2014, https://www.npr.org/2014/08/22/342318367/hamas-finally-admits-to-kidnapping-and-killing-israeli-teens. At the same time, there is significant reporting saying that the Hamas leadership, as a political movement, did not order the kidnappings. See Jodi Rudoren, "Palestinian Gets 3 Life Sentences in Killing of Israeli Teenagers," *New York Times*, January 6, 2015, https://www.nytimes.com/2015/01/07/world/middleeast/palestinian-sentenced-in-killing-of-kidnapped-israel-teenagers.html.

14. It is a matter of interpretation to say that Israel shifted its justifications, but Israel did use tunnels as a justification for war, though it stated the kidnapping was the catalyst. See James Verini, "Gaza's Tunnels, Now Used to Attack Israel, Began as Economic Lifelines," *National Geographic*, July 21, 2014, https://news.nationalgeographic.com/news/2014/07/140721-gaza-strip-tunnels-israel-hamas-palestinians/.

15. This statement is essentially accurate, although it is important to note that Israel allows a tiny number of Gazans out of the border crossings. See Bilge Nesibe Kotan, "Hamas: We Don't Like the Tunnels but We Need Them," *TRT World*, August 17, 2017, https://www.trtworld.com/magazine/hamas-we-don-t-like-the-tunnels-but-we-need-them-6755/amp.

16. This does not seem to be a justification for the 2014 war. Israel focused on the tunnels as a means to attack, not as a means to import weapons. See "Behind the Headlines: Hamas' Terror Tunnels," Israel Ministry of Foreign Affairs, July 22, 2014, http://mfa.gov.il/MFA/ForeignPolicy/Issues/Pages/Hamas-terror-tunnels.aspx.

17. "Behind the Headlines."

18. "War Left Four Million Tons of Rubble in Gaza, Says Environmental Group," *Haaretz*, September 16, 2016, https://www.haaretz.com/report-war-left-4m-tons-of-rubble-in-gaza-1.5301847.

19. Max Blumenthal, "How Long Before Israel Begins Another Operation in the Gaza Strip?," *Nation*, July 16, 2015, https://www.thenation.com/article/how-long-before-israel-begins-another-operation-in-the-gaza-strip/.

20. The UN puts the number at 35 percent. See Lena Odgaard, "Palestinians Reclaim Gaza 'Buffer Zone,'" *Al Jazeera*, May 5, 2014, https://www.aljazeera.com/news/middleeast/2014/03/palestinians-reclaim-gaza-buffer-zone-20143281519860884.html.

21. Not exactly wrong, but the Givati Brigade was the "main" force involved, though not the only brigade. See "The Ghosts of Gaza: Israel's Soldier Suicides," *Daily Beast*, October 28, 2014, https://www.thedailybeast.com/the-ghosts-of-gaza-israels-soldier-suicides; Simone Wilson, "What Really Happened in the Battle of Khuzaa, Gaza?," *Jewish Journal*, September 4, 2014, http://jewishjournal.com/cover_story/132997/.

22. Record of this quotation or something like it could not be found.

23. Ali Abunimah, *One Country: A Bold Proposal to End the Israeli-Palestinian Impasse* (New York: Metropolitan Books, 2006).

24. It is not totally true to say that Israel does not have its own freshwater. Eighty-five percent of Israel's freshwater does come from the West Bank, but some of the remaining 15 percent is in Israel. See Ben Ehrenreich, "Drip, Jordan: Israel's Water War with Palestine," *Harper's Magazine*, December 2011, https://harpers.org/archive/2011/12/drip-jordan/; United Nations Economic and Social Commission for Western Asia and Bundesanstalt für Geowissenschaften und Rohstoffe, "Chapter 19: Western Aquifer Basin," in *Inventory of Shared Water Resources in Western Asia*, 2013, https://waterinventory.org/groundwater/western-aquifer-basin; "Palestine: Water Resources," Fanack Water, last modified April 13, 2017, https://water.fanack.com/palestine/water-resources/.

25. As mentioned above, the total number of Palestinian casualties was 2,251 dead. An AP investigation found that at least 844 Palestinians were killed in strikes on their homes. While that is a significant number, it is not the majority. The AP investigation only focused on airstrikes, and not artillery—and artillery strikes could have hit homes and may have killed enough that it comes to a majority, but there are no hard statistics for the number of people killed by artillery in their homes. See "Majority of Palestinians Killed by Israeli Airstrikes Were Civilians," *Al Jazeera America*, February 13, 2015, http://america.aljazeera.com/articles/2015/2/13/majority-of-palestinians-killed-by-israeli-airstrikes-were-civilians.html.

26. There is no data on the number of people crushed to death versus being ripped apart by bombs.

27. No corroborating evidence could be found to indicate that residential buildings were the "main target" of the war, but it is a fair statement to make. Strikes on homes killed 844 people, as noted above, and artillery certainly struck many residential buildings.

28. "Rights Group: Israeli Bombing of Gaza Homes Was Policy," *Al Jazeera*, January 28, 2015, https://www.aljazeera.com/news/2015/01/rights-group-israeli-bombing-gaza-homes-policy-150128042200506.html; Yaakov Lapin, "IAF Destroys Homes of All Hamas Commanders, Kills Senior Members," *Jerusalem Post*, July 9, 2014, https://www.jpost.com/Operation-Protective-Edge/IAF-targets-Hamas-naval-commander-Palestinians-say-4-killed-in-strike-361947.

29. "Israel/Gaza: Attacks on Medical Facilities and Civilians Add to War Crime Allegations," Amnesty International, July 21, 2014, https://www.amnesty.org/en/latest/news/2014/07/israelgaza-attacks-medical-facilities-and-civilians-add-war-crime-allegations/.

30. Marilyn Garson, "Opinion: In 2014, Schools Offered Precious Shelter for Gaza's Civilians," *Haaretz*, July 26, 2017, https://www.haaretz.com/opinion/.premium-when-israel-bombed-7-school-shelters-in-gaza-1.5434233.

31. "10 Bodies Found in Rubble as Life Slowly Returns to Gaza Streets," *Ma'an News Agency*, August 7, 2014, http://www.maannews.com/Content.aspx?id=718676.

32. Renee Lewis, "Palestinian Migrants Fleeing Gaza Strip Drown in Mediterranean Sea," *Al Jazeera America*, September 14, 2014, http://america.aljazeera.com/articles/2014/9/14/gaza-migrants-boat.html.

33. Charlotte Silver, "Hundreds, Many from Gaza, Murdered at Sea by Smugglers," *Electronic Intifada*, September 17, 2014, https://electronicintifada.net/blogs/charlotte-silver/hundreds-many-gaza-murdered-sea-smugglers.

34. "Occupied Palestinian Territory and Israel," Oxfam International, accessed July 1, 2018, https://oxf.am/2FOAYy8.

35. Nidal al-Mughrabi, "Child Labor Rises in Gaza amid Soaring Unemployment," *Reuters*, March 30, 2016, https://www.reuters.com/article/us-palestinians-gaza-child-labour/child-labor-rises-in-gaza-amid-soaring-unemployment-idUSKCN0WW0YA.

36. "Gaza's Economy 'On Verge of Collapse' says World Bank," *Reuters*, May 22, 2015, https://www.reuters.com/article/gaza-economy-collapse/gazas-economy-on-verge-of-collapse-says-world-bank-idUSL5N0YD29920150522.

37. Paul Alster, "Hamas Guilty of War Crimes in Gaza Clash, Amnesty International Charges," *Fox News World*, March 30, 2015, http://www.foxnews.com/world/2015/03/30/hamas-guilty-war-crimes-in-gaza-clash-amnesty-internatl-charges.html.

38. Jack Moore, "Palestinian Factions Committed 'War Crimes' in Gaza Conflict, Says Amnesty," *Newsweek World*, March 25, 2015, http://www.newsweek.com/palestinian-factions-committed-war-crimes-gaza-conflict-says-amnesty-316732.

39. Technically, the number is 9 percent, since six civilians were killed. See *State of Israel, The 2014 Gaza Conflict: Factual and Legal Aspects*, May 2015, http://mfa.gov.il/ProtectiveEdge/Documents/2014GazaConflictFullReport.pdf.

40. William Booth, "The UN Says 7 in 10 Palestinians Killed in Gaza Were Civilians. Israel Disagrees." *Washington Post*, August 29, 2014, https://www.washingtonpost.com/world/middle_east/the-un-says-7-in-10-palestinians-killed-in-gaza-were-civilians-israel-disagrees/2014/08/29/44edc598-2faa-11e4-9b98–848790384093_story.html?utm_term=.d96852a14e85.

41. John Crewsdon, "New Revelations in Attack on American Spy Ship," *Chicago Tribune*, October 2, 2007, http://www.chicagotribune.com/chi-liberty_tuesoct02-story.html.

42. "West Haven I-95 Billboard on USS Liberty is Anti-Israel, Critics Charge," *New Haven Register*, March 25, 2016, https://www.nhregister.com/connecticut/article/West-Haven-I-95-billboard-on-USS-Liberty-is-11331509.php.

43. Miriam Pensack, "Fifty Years Later, NSA Keeps Details of Israel's USS Liberty Attack Secret," *Intercept*, June 6, 2017, https://theintercept.com/2017/06/06/fifty-years-later-nsa-keeps-details-of-israels-uss-liberty-attack-secret/.

44. Scott Armstrong, "Israelis Have Spied on U.S., Secret Papers Show," *Washington Post*, February 1, 1982, https://www.washingtonpost.com/archive/politics/1982/02/01/israelis-have-spied-on-us-secret-papers-show/163a965f-6e66-4c25-a609-077f47fb7a8a/?utm_term=.ee7969d2bd82.

45. Steven Erlanger, "Israeli Found Spy's Data Irresistible," *New York Times*, March 3, 2006, https://www.nytimes.com/2006/03/03/world/middleeast/israeli-found-spys-data-irresistible.html.

46. Adam Taylor, "A Small Selection of the Very Negative Things U.S. Officials Have Said about Jonathan Pollard," *Washington Post*, July 24, 2015, https://www.washingtonpost.com/news/worldviews/wp/2014/04/01/a-small-selection-of-the-very-negative-things-u-s-officials-have-said-about-jonathan-pollard/?utm_term=.1f56e8dd4d80.

DAVID LLOYD
"The American Studies Association and the U.S. Campaign for the Academic and Cultural Boycott of Israel," December 18, 2013

https://www.wortfm.org/israeli-academic-and-cultural-boycott/

KARMA CHÁVEZ: This week the American Studies Association, an academic organization of roughly five thousand academics, voted overwhelmingly in support of a resolution to endorse and "honor the call of Palestinian civil society for a boycott of Israeli academic institutions." The resolution also indicated that the "ASA supports the protected rights of students and scholars everywhere to engage in research and public speaking about Israel-Palestine and in support of the boycott, divestment, and sanctions (BDS) movement."[1] The vote was controversial, and numerous scholars and pundits weighed in before and after the vote in outlets ranging from the *New York Times* to the *Chronicle of Higher Education* to university papers around the globe. Other organizations, including the Asian American Studies Association and the Native American and Indigenous Studies Association, have also endorsed a boycott.

The votes to endorse boycott represent for some a breaking of a taboo on critiquing Israel, which may now have broader implications for the liberation of Palestinian people, and for others, reflect an attack on the academic freedom of Israeli academics, many who are in alliance with Palestinians. The move to boycott Israeli academic and cultural institutions is a part of the larger BDS movement, and in 2004 Palestinian intellectuals and academics created the Palestinian Campaign for the Academic and Cultural Boycott of Israel. "In July 2004, the Campaign issued a statement of principles, or what became known as the PACBI Call, addressed to colleagues in the international community urging them to comprehensively and consistently boycott all

Israeli academic and cultural institutions until Israel withdraws from all the lands occupied in 1967, including East Jerusalem; removes all its colonies in those lands; agrees to United Nations resolutions relevant to the restitution of Palestinian refugees rights; and dismantles its system of apartheid."[2] The U.S. Campaign for the Academic and Cultural Boycott of Israel started in response to the Palestinian call, and focuses specifically on the boycott of Israeli academic and cultural institutions.

To talk us through the complicated issues surrounding the academic and cultural boycott, and to answer some tough questions about it, I have invited a member of the U.S. Campaign's organizing collective, Professor David Lloyd. Lloyd is distinguished professor of English at the University of California–Riverside. Lloyd is recognized as a leader in the boycott movement, and in addition to his numerous academic books that include *Anomalous States: Irish Writing and the Postcolonial Moment* (1993), *Ireland After History* (2000), and *Irish Times: Temporalities of Modernity* (2008), he is the author of numerous articles and statements regarding the Israeli occupation and the importance of boycott as a nonviolent strategy.

David, welcome to *A Public Affair*.

DAVID LLOYD: Thank you so much, I'm very glad to be here, it's an exciting time.

KC: Indeed, it is. And I guess I want to start out by saying that—full disclosure that I'm both an endorser of the campaign for academic and cultural boycott, and I'm also a member of the American Studies Association, so I'm not a disinterested party in this conversation. Nonetheless, I want to make sure to ask you some of the hard questions and also give listeners a chance to do that. So, I guess let me start out by asking, did I get anything wrong in that introduction about sort of the evolution of this movement?

DL: No, I'm not always great on exact dates, but I think that's a pretty good summary. The USACBI, as we call it, the U.S. Campaign for the Academic and Cultural Boycott of Israel did start up, it's perhaps worth emphasizing, in the wake[3] of Israel's assault on Gaza in December 2008 and January 2009,[4] in which about 1,400 Palestinians were killed, most of them civilians or policemen,[5] which under most regimes are civilians,[6] but also the destruction of at least twenty-three academic institutions or facilities,[7] including the American University[8] and the UN[9] facility that was bombarded with white phosphorous. So, in the face of that kind of astonishingly disproportionate brutality, and on the other hand, the absolute lockstep of the U.S. Congress and the new Obama administration in supporting Israel, we felt that it was time that we really pushed for a civil society movement in this country that would support the Palestinian call for boycott, divestment, and sanctions. Because we felt that if the political process is completely blocked in this way, and we know the power of the pro-Israeli lobbies and the interest, that goes far beyond that of the United States and its military, of maintaining Israel as a kind of garrison in the Middle East, in the face of that, only a civil society movement in which ordinary citizens, and in our case academics, get involved, has any chance of shifting the kind of deadlock that the peace process has reached, and we can talk a bit more about that, too. So, we started USACBI at that point, and there were—I think, if I remember right—about thirty of us who signed on in the beginning, and we're now approaching one thousand. When we set up, the Israeli NGOs who monitor what they think of as anti-Israeli activities said, "Oh well, we'll take them seriously when they reach 500." Well, we're now pretty much twice that number. So, I think that is actually why the media are going haywire now that American Studies and Native American and Indigenous Studies, as you said, and Asian American Studies have all come out for the boycott.

KC: So, I want to back up just a minute on this, because I think we do get a very kind of particular perspective with mainstream media in the U.S. So the situation in Israel-Palestine is often referred to as a conflict, we often get a depiction of these being equal parties in sort of an equal conflict, so I wonder if we could back up a bit and talk about the BDS movement and how and why it got started as a broader thing and then move into this conversation.

DL: Yes, as I understand it, although there have been calls for boycott previously, the current boycott movement emerged out of Palestinian society after the Second Intifada, which was, in most people's account, a complete disaster for Palestinian society. And it had included things like suicide bombings, which did nothing but harm to the Palestinian cause, frankly. And of course, it had also in many respects simply accentuated the ways in which the Palestinian Authority, Mahmoud Abbas's leadership in the West Bank, really has ceased to represent the interests of Palestinians. So, I think it's important to recognize the BDS movement, which is supported by at least 170 civil society organizations, is itself trying to find a way around a deadlock, a deadlock in the struggle against Israel but also a deadlock in their own political process. So, the people who kind of—you know, we get a lot of vitriolic hate mail, and people often suggest that BDS is, you know, Hamas or BDS is Fatah, I mean that's so obviously wrong, this is a movement that's precisely emerged as a way that Palestinian civil society can begin to move around its own stymied political structure and come up with inventive nonviolent ways to engage in the struggle for human rights and justice.

KC: And when you say that there are 170 different civil society organizations and groups that support BDS in Palestine, who are we talking about? What are the kinds of groups that are involved here?

DL: Well, we're talking about the major trade union organizations, we're talking about teachers' unions, we're talking about women's groups—there's a very high preponderance of women's organizations in the BDS movement—we're talking about student movements, and we're talking about various kinds of NGOs and other movements that do really basic, fundamental infrastructure work for Palestinian welfare. So, it's a very broad range of constituents of what we would normally think of as civil society. And in addition, churches, mosques are also involved, so religious organizations. So, it's pretty much the whole swathe of Palestinian civil society. And although the Palestinian Authority and Mahmoud Abbas don't themselves endorse it, they certainly have not tried to prevent it. It has pretty much a space to move as it were within Palestinian society.

KC: Well that's an interesting point of course because that's been—for those who are opposed to the boycott that's been one of their rallying cries, to side with Abbas, to say, "He doesn't support boycotts."

DL: Yes, that's been spread around. Frankly, it doesn't really matter very much, as you and your listeners probably know, Mahmoud Abbas is no longer the elected representative of the Palestinians and the scheduled elections were not held. Many Palestinians—and, I can't speak for Palestinians—but many Palestinians regard the Palestinian Authority as a kind of collaborationist regime. And certainly, the whole point of the Oslo Agreement and the establishment of the Palestinian Authority back in 1993 seems to have been designed to do what the Israeli political theorist Neve Gordon calls "outsourcing the occupation."[10] In other words, the Palestinian Authority, under very strict control by the Israeli military, runs the police force, controls and moderates Palestinian resistance. The Palestinian Authority itself has been responsible for a sort of neoliberal regime in, particularly, Ramallah. Which, as you probably know, has had quite a lot of economic growth recently.[11] But it's an economic growth—it's fueled very largely by foreign NGO investment and so forth, and it's pretty fragile and based upon huge amounts of debt,[12] with which we are all too familiar in this country. So, the Palestinian Authority in many people's view has had a very corrupting influence on Palestinian society,[13] and also its own interests, if one analyzes it, is in—actually in maintaining its control over the very tiny portion of Palestinian land that it actually controls, which is about 8 percent in total of the occupied West Bank.[14] But, you know, that's a lucrative business to be in, it gives them considerable power on a small scale. And it is in their interest to push not for the rights and entitlements of *all* Palestinians but only really for the Palestinians under their control.

And I think that brings us to say what it is that is important about BDS is that it is a movement that seeks the rights of *all* Palestinians. Not just those under occupation, which is what a divestment campaign alone might focus on, but also Palestinians in Israel who don't have equal rights with Jewish Israelis. And for the Palestinian diaspora. So, the three points are all very important to note.

KC: Well, and I think, I think this is such an important conversation because we—you're pointing to the complexity of the situation in Palestine and the—whether it's conflict or just distinctions between civil society and the political authority, I think is important. And of course, one of the voices that also enters this in terms of civil society is the academics who in 2004, then, come onto this movement to call for an academic and cultural boycott. So, do you know the history of how academics came to make this call?

DL: Yes, you mean Palestinian academics?

KC: Yeah, I'm sorry, yeah.

DL: Yes, yes. Well, I know it in brief form. The movement for the academic and cultural boycott was a slightly later emergence in 2005, and in my understanding, they recognized that in the case of South Africa—and the divestment struggle in South Africa is a very important model on which BDS is being built—that divestment campaign focused not only on academic targets but also on sports and cultural exchanges with South Africa. The reason for that is that, like Israel, South Africa was an apartheid regime in which its civil population wanted to believe that it was a normal part of the world of Western democracies. And the impact of the sports boycott was not economic, it was really sending a message, if you like, to South African civil society that it was not and could not be considered a normal part of the Western democratic framework insofar as it was based on apartheid. And I think the logic was that, by the same token, Israeli universities, which are deeply embedded in the maintenance of the occupation in all kinds of ways, that these institutions were also bound up with Israel's sense of prestige. And through their connections with academics all around the world, particularly in the U.S. and Europe, were really a kind of normalizing factor. They presented the idea of Israel as a normal democratic state, as they always say, "the only democratic state in the Middle East," which is of course nonsense. But that they were part of the whole apparatus, both of maintaining the occupation and of normalizing relations with the U.S. And so any BDS campaign that's focused solely on economic targets within Israel would miss a very important constitutive part of how the occupation and discrimination within Israel, itself, are normalized.

KC: And so, how then—so you have the Palestinian move to do this in 2004–2005, and then a couple of years later, when the U.S. campaign sort of answers this call. How did you personally get involved with the movement?

DL: Well, I don't want to talk too much about myself because, although you very kindly said I was a leading member of the academic boycott campaign, it really is a movement without leaders. And that became very, very apparent in American Studies where the people who spoke so overwhelmingly at the open meeting that was held on the Saturday evening of the conference were largely people who had not known each other before. People who had come from all parts of the United States to this national conference and who found themselves picked at random at this open meeting suddenly speaking out for Palestinian human rights and for the boycott resolution. And I think everybody who was at it was surprised by how widespread the sense of the justice of the boycott campaign was. So, I can tell you briefly that for me it was a long process of learning. As a child—I grew up in Ireland, and as a child in Ireland, you know, I got the same pro-Israeli propaganda as everybody else in Europe did, and was very supportive of Israel in the '67 war and so forth. But very gradually I began to learn about what conditions of life were for the Palestinians. And began to get more interested in Palestine and over the years joined in demonstrations in favor of Palestine, organized things at my university, you know, talks by people who were coming back. But it was really only after the 2006 invasion of Lebanon and the horrific bombings of civilians there that I began to feel uncomfortable with just having an occasional talk at my university and so forth. And then, as I said, when Operation Cast Lead took place, and there was *no* pushback whatsoever,[15] despite the fact that it was self-evident that Israel was committing war crimes in the use of white phosphorous,[16] for example, or in the use of DIME, this experimental explosive that they used that scatters bombs in all directions in civilian areas.[17] That there was no pushback at all from the new Obama administration just felt to me the need to do something different, and that's how I got involved at the core of this movement.

KC: Sure, makes sense. So, David, I'd like to move us in a little bit to the ASA situation which you were just talking about. And, are you an ASA member, are you a longtime member?

DL: Oh yes, I'm a longtime ASA member, yeah. Since the mid-'90s, I think, I've been a member of the association.

KC: Okay. And I wonder if what we could talk about what the ASA resolution does, in concrete terms, because there's a lot of misinformation out there about the resolution.

DL: There is, and let me thank you for telling it very accurately in your own introduction. It is a call for a boycott of Israeli academic institutions. And it's often just called the academic boycott, which is where the misleading aspect starts. The misleading part is when people say this is a boycott of Israeli academics. The Palestinian call has always been perfectly clear about this. It does not impose any kind of political litmus test on Israeli academics, so that the AAUP, the American Association of University Professors, has been saying that at least the ASA boycott is watered down, it doesn't go after individuals. That's false, that's misleading. Never has the Palestinian call for the boycott been directed at individual Israeli professors. Their academic freedom is completely respected, that is, they can research, they can publish their research, they can travel to conferences and speak at conferences. All those individual academic rights are respected, which is really the only thing that academic freedom covers. Individuals have academic freedom, institutions don't. So, I'm glad to have this opportunity to clear that misperception up from the start.

The boycott is directed toward institutions. And what it basically means is that we withdraw our consent from collaborating with institutions that serve or represent the Israeli state, that are engaged in research, for example, and teachings that support the occupation, that maintain discriminatory facilities and so forth. And that we will not accept funding from them or enter into collaborative relationships that involve Israeli state funding. That includes, of course, not collaborating with academic institutions or their representatives who perform a function which is increasingly common now, which is to be kind of soft ambassadors for Israel. In other words, to try to present Israel in a light that normalizes or covers the brutality of the occupation and the discrimination and the siege of Gaza that it's engaged in. So, it's a withdrawal of our consent; it's like a strike where you withdraw your labor. In this case it's a withdrawal of consent to participate or collaborate with those institutions until such time as Israel meets the conditions that you outlined at the beginning.

KC: And so, for an individual academic institution, let's say a university comes out and says, "We denounce the Israeli state." What would that mean, I guess, in terms of the boycott?

DL: Well, let me give you a couple of concrete examples. At the moment, Cornell University is involved in a very elaborate collaboration on Long

Island[18] with Technion University.[19] Now Technion University, which is a very old university in Israel,[20] also it's a major technical university, it does things like developing the D9 bulldozer,[21] which is a modification of the ordinary Caterpillar bulldozer which is being used to demolish Palestinian houses[22] in acts of collective punishment.[23] And one could multiply the different military projects that Technion University is engaged in. And so, the collaboration that Cornell is engaged in with Technion probably presents itself as just being scientific research.[24] But, in fact, one of the things it's doing is integrating Technion into the American academic sphere. And so, there's a very active campaign in New York at the moment to try to get Cornell to suspend this collaboration, and that would be one example of the kinds of things we're asking universities to do. Because, when we talk about academic freedom, one thing that's not often enough said is that institutions don't have academic freedom. On the other hand, it is their duty as academic institutions to protect academic freedom. Technion, Hebrew University, Tel Aviv University—none of these Israeli universities have protected the full academic freedom, either of Palestinian citizens of Israel or of Palestinians living under the occupation where their academic freedoms are daily infringed. Just in every aspect of their life, it's almost impossible to actually engage in an ordinary academic life of research, expression of your opinions, and so forth. In some cases, students can't even get to their classes most of the time because of the whole regime of roadblocks and checkpoints and so forth that simply prevent them from getting from their homes to their universities. So, institutions are supposed to protect academic freedom, and these institutions are not.

There's another instance that I can give of something that would fall under the boycott, which is education abroad programs. If you look at the State Department website, you will see that students[25] who are of Palestinian descent, Arab descent, or Muslim descent are warned that if they try to enter Israel, they are likely to be subject at least to lengthy searches and interrogations, and possibly excluded.[26] Now that means that Israel has a blanket discriminatory policy that the State Department itself recognizes here, which adversely would affect *any* of our students at *any* of our campuses who happen to belong to any of those categories. It is, in other words, a very extreme form of racial and religious profiling. Now, we believe that on its face, such programs are therefore—education abroad programs that would take, you know, groups of students to Israel—are on their face discriminatory under our nondiscrimination policies, because some students would be allowed to enter, and other students would run the risk either of serious harassment or of exclusion. So, another thing that we would ask our institutions to do is actually to suspend those kinds of collaborations. You know, harmless as they seem, they're actually normalizing a deeply discriminatory policy which has to do with Israel's desire to reduce its Palestinian population, under what they call the "demographic threat" idea. That, you know, there are increasing numbers of Palestinians and they might one day outnumber the Jewish citizens of Israel. So that would be another example, so two very different kinds of collaboration that we feel are suspect.

KC: Well, and I think you maybe just answered my next question, but I want to pose it anyway, this kind of question of the U.S.'s endorsement of a blanket discrimination policy but further our unbridled support of Israel's military. So, I mean, the American Studies Association is the oldest and largest organization devoted to the study of American culture and history, so the question is how is it that an organization with that as its mission becomes the one to lead the way in an academic boycott?

DL: Well, first of all let me say that we didn't lead the way within the United States. The honor goes to the Asian American Studies Association, AASA.[27] But the situation is analogous in both cases. The Asian American Studies scholars pointed out that they have this experience of things like exclusion, of controls on immigration of Asian people, of internment, of racial discrimination throughout society. And they therefore feel a kind of kinship, if you like, with Palestinians suffering the same kinds of restrictions on their right to immigrate to Israel, on their right to return, in other words, to Israel. Because it's not an anti-immigrant policy in Israel, it's against the indigenous people who are there.

Which secondly makes it highly significant that yesterday the Native American and Indigenous Studies Association also joined the boycott movement because it points to something that's at the heart of American Studies' interest in this issue and its commitment to justice for Palestinians, which is that what Israel and the U.S. have in common—apart from huge military investments and huge military forces—is a history of settler colonialism. Now, I use that quite advisedly, that phrase "settler colonialism," because it's actually Israeli scholars who were in large part responsible for putting into circulation an analysis of Israel's history as settler colonial. And it's a fairly well-accepted sociological paradigm, there.[28] The largest part of the Jewish population that inhabits Israel has come from places like Europe and as a settler community. And the early Zionists were quite clear about that. They had no illusions that they were a settler population that was taking away the land of an indigenous population. And despite the fact that they tried, for ideological reasons, to circulate the idea that it was "a land without a people for a people without a land," they knew very well that there was an indigenous Arab population that was going to resist colonialism. And they planned from the start that this would be a settler colonial project protected by a very strong military force. In that respect, although the size of the area we're talking about is very different, it's not unlike the history of the expansion of the United States and the settlement of the frontiers slowly expanding westward and the deprivation of Native Americans of their land.

So, in recent years, probably the last two or three decades, American Studies has become, as an organization, more committed to the study of that history in the United States. And to understanding why it is that the United States would feel an affinity for, politically and culturally, and being willing to support a country like Israel. So, the analysis is that, you know, in a certain sense Israel is an aspect of the study of the United States because it has so many connections, so much support from successive administrations in this country. And therefore, you know, apart from the fact that everything that happens in Israel impacts our relation to the Middle East, which, as you probably know, is one of the most important areas for U.S. foreign policy at the moment—quite apart from that, we feel that, as American Studies scholars, understanding these *kinds* of histories also helps us to understand the kind of social movement that the Palestinians are organizing in order to resist their expropriation and dispossession. And that has its affinities with Native American struggles, with Chicano struggles, with African American struggles, as well as with Asian American struggles. And that's the sort of context out of which we understand the boycott movement.

KC: So building on that then, a common question then becomes if the situation with Israel is akin to the United States, or akin to maybe other terrible situations in the world, is Israel not then being unfairly targeted amidst a broader situation of inequity and oppression worldwide?

DL: Well, this question does come up all the time, and one can see where it comes from. The difference is that the usual example that comes up is why not boycott China? Well, the United States, when I last saw it, was not supporting China, not supporting its military, not supporting its occupation of Tibet. On the contrary, the U.S. policy at the moment seems to be much more about trying to encircle China and trying to make alliances with its neighbors to counteract China's expansion. But if we also take something like Darfur, and the question often goes, why are they not boycotting Sudan? One just has to recall that Colin Powell in the previous Bush administration condemned what was happening in Darfur, and the genocide. There has been no comparable condemnation of what Israel is doing, which amounts, in a certain respect, to a project of ethnic cleansing of Palestinians and of Bedouins. If you take, for example, the other one that comes up, why are they not boycotting North Korea? Well, all of the U.S. military is arrayed against North Korea. Only Israel is in breach of tens of UN resolutions and is protected every single time it's condemned by such resolutions by the U.S. veto. Only Israel gets three to four billion dollars in military aid,[29] quite apart from the aid it gets in kind, from the U.S. taxpayers. Only Israel gets away with consistently defying even the expressed policy of the United States[30] against the expansion of the illegal settlements, gets away with that time and again. So, the real question is why is Israel being singled out? Not why are we singling Israel out but why is the U.S. singling Israel out for its unrelenting support in the face of consistent reports—by Amnesty International, by Human Rights Watch, by the UN itself—that document over and over again the kinds of infringements of human rights, war crimes, and other injustices that Israel commits. So, as I said at the beginning, the boycott movement is designed precisely to try to make a space within American, and of course global, civil society for the criticism of Israel to take place and to change the political climate that is so unanimously supportive of Israel. And I think the evidence of the last week or so is that we're succeeding in that.

KC: I want to pick up on something you just said there near the end, which is, why is it that Israel's being singled out in the face of consistent reports of abuses by organizations that in other circumstances would be highly regarded by the U.S. government, we would take those claims as legitimate. This leads me into thinking about the question, of course, of anti-Semitism, which is what has come up a lot as people have been debating the endorsement of the boycott, suggesting that the boycott amounts to nothing more than anti-Semitic scapegoating. So, can you address that?

DL: Well frankly, I think that's become a pretty threadbare accusation, the more often it's recycled. And quite apart from the fact—and I honestly think that this is not even really something that should be necessary to invoke—quite apart from the fact that probably half of the people that I work with in USACBI, the Academic and Cultural Boycott Campaign, are themselves Jewish. And quite apart from the fact that there is an increasing number, even within Israel, of Jewish and Palestinian citizens of Israel who are part of a movement called Boycott from Within.[31] What I would really want to say is that the accusation that it's anti-Semitic to criticize a state is a very strange accusation. I mean, when I criticize, let's say, England for its behavior toward Ireland, which I have done quite frequently, no one ever accuses me of some insidious anti-Britishness. If I decide that I want to criticize China's occupation of Tibet, it's pretty rare that anybody will accuse me of being anti-Chinese in the general sense. So, it's an odd accusation to say that if you criticize a state and its policies you are actually attacking a whole people.

Now, the confusion arises because Zionism, which is the political theory that founds Israel, Zionism has always tried to argue that Israel is *the* sole state that represents the Jewish people in its entirety. And, frankly, a lot of Jews don't agree with that, but they're not consulted. And in my view, any doctrine or any political philosophy that tries to say that *every* member of a specific group *must* adhere unquestioningly in its support of a particular state that desires to be representative of that people is actually in and of itself quite racist. Because it's suggesting that everybody who belongs to a particular ethnic group, race, or religion must, in fact, adhere to one particular representation. And, you know, what Israel is doing, so far as I can comment on it, is really running in the face of long traditions of Jewish ethics and Jewish notions of the neighbor and Jewish notions of how one treats the other. And, in that respect, is itself infringing upon Jewish ethics and moral codes. So, I don't see that the accusation holds water whatsoever.

KC: I wanted to just read something from the Jewish Voice for Peace—what they had to say on this point. So, an organization, I believe based in New York City, that really focuses very much on this issue, they said in their statement that they released on Monday: "While Jewish Voice for Peace takes no position on academic boycotts, we do not believe that boycotts to pressure Israel to abide by international law are inherently anti-Semitic. Like the grape boycott by the United Farm Workers union and the Nestle boycott, such boycotts employ nonviolent tactics in the service of liberation. They are among the tools that Nelson Mandela and the African National Congress employed to topple apartheid in South Africa. In particular, the ASA resolution—the American Studies Association—was clearly a sensitively written and thoughtfully argued effort that targets Israel's policies, not Jewish people."[32]

DL: That's very well put. I mean I would say that there have been anti-Semitic boycotts, the most famous one the boycott in Germany of Jewish businesses. Those were anti-Semitic because they engaged in a boycott of people for who they were. Right? They targeted Jews as Jews. Nothing that any German Jew at the time could have done would have changed that identity in the eyes of the Nazis that they were Jewish and therefore alien and therefore susceptible to boycott. In the case of this boycott, we are targeting what people do, not what they are. We are targeting institutions in the state of Israel because of what it does over and over again, repeatedly, to Palestinians. And, ironically, it's not that we are targeting Israelis because they are Jewish, it's that Israel is targeting Palestinians for who they are. So, they are targeting all Palestinians, telling them that they cannot enter the country. They are targeting all Palestinians under forms of collective punishment with the roadblocks and so forth. They are punishing all Palestinians in Gaza because they are Palestinians, effectively. So that the real question is why is Israel subjecting a whole people to such conditions of occupation and discrimination and dispossession just because of who they are? Because their history should actually tell them that that itself is a deep injustice.

KC: Well, and I wanted to—we have about fifteen minutes left in the show, and the one issue that—I've had many conversations about the ASA resolution and the concept of boycott in the last several days, because I've been thinking about this ever since the ASA convention. So, I wanted to spend a little bit of time in the last few minutes, in the last fifteen minutes of the show, really turning back to this question of academic freedom, because it seems to me, in what I've been reading, this becomes a kind of lynchpin in many of the arguments that people are making. And one of the arguments that has come up a lot that I'm wondering if you can address is, so this is a boycott of institutions, as we said, not individuals. But where is the line between an individual who is paid by an Israeli institution, so in that way inevitably a representative of that institution—so where is the line between that individual and the institution that might support them and pay their way to go to a conference or to participate in a research study?

DL: Well, again I do encourage people to read the PACBI statement. And if you just Google PACBI you'll find this. They're really clear on this: All academics are employed by institutions who in the normal course of things will give them funding to attend conferences and so forth. That's one kind of relationship that we as professors have with our institutions. The Palestinian call for boycott of academic institutions does not target people for accepting, as part and parcel of their work as professors, money from their institutions to travel. However, there is a distinction between that and being paid specifically to travel for the purposes of representing the state. Now, that's usually something that administrators do. For example, it's as an administrator that you would go to set up a contract for study abroad program, for example. And we make this distinction every single day in our working lives as academics or as students. We know, for example, that one of our colleagues may be appointed a dean or a provost. We know, however, that functioning as a dean or a provost, they become a different kind of entity than when they're our colleague in the History or the English department. So, it's not a very hard distinction to make, it's one that we make all the time.

And I think it's important to emphasize that because when I—let's say I functioned as a dean for my university, I would be representing that university. If I went to a conference of deans, I wouldn't be speaking for myself anymore. Indeed, that's precisely what makes me a representative of the institution: I cease to speak as an individual, and I start to speak as a corporate entity. So that distinction is quite clear in every other sphere of academic life, and I'm not quite sure why scholars who should know this are having so much difficulty making a distinction between what it is to boycott an institution and its representatives and what it is to boycott individuals. We don't boycott an individual Israeli professor—or indeed a professor from anywhere—who happens to support Israel's policies, its occupation, or whatever. They're entitled to express their opinion. Benny Morris, the Israeli historian, would be quite entitled to come here on his own[33] and speak at a conference and recommend what he calls the "transfer" of Palestinians out of Israel,[34] if he wants to do that. If, on the other hand, he came at the behest of the Israeli consul to try to represent that as a political opinion of the Israeli state, that would be a rather different matter.

KC: So, the American Association of University Professors, this sort of large organization whose purpose is to advance academic freedom and shared governance, these kinds of values that are important to most of us as scholars, in the past has of course taken principled stands against governments. They supported the divestment campaign against South Africa, for example. But in this instance, they have indicated their disappointment with the American Studies Association and called the vote a "setback for the cause of academic freedom." How is an organization like the AAUP defining academic freedom in this instance, in your opinion?

DL: Well, it's actually quite interesting to look at the history of the AAUP because it's a very compromised history. Its 1940 statement on academic freedom, they actually encourage professors not to teach in their classroom controversial work.[35] The AAUP emerged as a compromise with academic institutions that were being increasingly corporatized, already then, as a way to make sure that faculty were not politicized, and particularly faculty on the left. So, it has a long history of seeking to moderate and to temper the exercise of academic freedom.[36] And of course it defines academic freedom very narrowly, as simply the right for individuals to engage in their political practice like, for example, boycott.[37] They're perfectly happy if individuals want to follow their conscience as they put it and do it. But that seems to me a remarkably narrow definition of what the exercise of academic freedom looks like because real academic freedom is, first of all, universal. And the AAUP statements have never once mentioned the actual and ongoing denial of academic freedom to Palestinians. They're always concerned about the hypothetical denial of academic freedom to Israeli scholars.[38] Which, as I keep saying over and over again, that's not what's being targeted by the boycott even though, with what has to be understood now as a malicious misunderstanding on the part of the AAUP, which has been corrected on this point so many times, they continue to argue as if it was an infringement of individual academic freedom.

And I would just say to the AAUP—frankly, the AAUP claims to represent something like fifty thousand scholars around the United States, but in so claiming I have yet to see the AAUP engage in the extraordinarily democratic process that the ASA engaged in. So, the ASA not only had this boycott resolution published and on the table since April, where people could read it, discuss it in the run-up to the conference, they facilitated an open meeting at the conference, at which an overwhelming majority of the speakers spoke for the boycott. Even with that endorsement from the open meeting in place, the national council deliberated, and against the usual practice which is that the national council is responsible for passing resolutions, they went to the whole membership. Now, one has to emphasize that here, an exception was made for the case of Palestine as always is. One is always demanded to engage, if you like, in a surplus of democracy in the case of Palestine. So, that being said, it's good that they put it out to the membership. It may be an anomaly procedurally, but they did it, and it's good. And an overwhelming majority of the voters—and it's the largest number of voters that have ever voted in the association's history on an issue like a resolution—that majority endorsed the boycott. So, we know that the boycott has been endorsed by our membership. The AAUP, as far as I know, has never put its policy on boycott to a membership vote, has never opened it up to democracy. So, I don't think they're really in a position to lecture an association that has obeyed its own procedures and then gone beyond them, in terms of democracy, on who should or should not be representing the position of academic freedom.

KC: I think what's interesting about what you've just said in describing the differences in being able to speak for your membership is key to think about in a broader context. because I think that kind of statement gets made a lot, like, "This group of people feels this way." And it might be the very elite of a particular university who doesn't want a certain speaker to come, as has happened a lot on this issue, probably most famously—not long ago

Judith Butler not allowed to speak at City University of New York, I could go on and on, down the list. And that brings me to this issue of the question of intimidation and backlash. As one example, Lawrence Summers, the former Harvard president, essentially called for boycott of the ASA. He noted in an interview, "My hope would be that responsible university leaders would become very reluctant to see their university funds used to finance faculty membership and faculty travel to an association that's showing itself not to be a scholarly one, but more of a political tool."[39] Can you talk a little bit about intimidation and backlash?

DL: Yes, I mean it is ironic, is it not? That these people who stake so much on condemning academic boycott in principle then turn around as soon as the institution turns against them and say that the association should be boycotted. I mean, the irony is glaring. But apart from the fact that this is coming from the extraordinarily discredited Larry Summers, I mean the man who thinks that women do not make good scientists and the man who brought us the financial crisis, I mean, honestly. But the backlash really has been quite predictable; my inbox is full of extremely nasty vicious messages that merely show that extreme Zionists outdo the Aryan Nation in the extremity of the kind of ugly language that they use, that is not just defending Israel, it's actually homophobic, it's Islamophobic, and in some cases it's completely racist. And anybody who doubts that can just go to the American Studies Association's Facebook page and see some examples of this kind of stuff. And it's totally typical.

And the other thing that, of course, more seriously, I think, this intimidation involves is often representations to the administration of any professor who supports the boycott or who criticizes Israel, which are designed to try to get them fired. It usually takes the form of language that includes things like, "You have brought your institution into disrepute." Which is actually an offense under the law, whereby someone who's employed by a corporation can lose their job. So, they're kind of fishing, in the hope that, you know, they can actually intimidate professors into keeping their mouths closed about this issue. And in some cases, they have actually gone directly after people's tenure. And all I can say is that, on an issue that has to do with justice and human rights, on an issue that has to do with nonviolent practice like this, coercion is not a very strong position. If you engage constantly in coercive attempts to silence people, it actually has the opposite effect, which is to bring publicity to what it is you're trying to suppress. And I think that part of the anger and the frustration on the part of supporters of Israel is that they're terribly used to having the monopoly on speech on this issue, and really not having to argue.

And now suddenly they're forced to actually defend Israel's practices. Which are, on the face of it, indefensible practices of discrimination, and it's very hard for them to do so. And I think this actually affects, particularly, liberal Zionists who would like to believe themselves to be, in every other aspect of their political lives, liberal or on the left, whatever. And yet find themselves defending practices that, frankly, constitute really something comparable to apartheid. And that's a very hard position to occupy if you want to be liberal. But it does lead—it leads to extraordinary contortions. I don't know if you've read Peter Beinart's latest piece in the *Daily Beast* where he describes the refusal to allow Palestinians to enter, or the demographic problem that Israel faces, as a problem of Israel's preferential immigration policies.[40] Now, it's an extraordinary thing to refer to the indigenous population of Palestine as if they were immigrants. And he tries to normalize it by comparing it to Britain[41] or Germany's immigration policies.[42] But that's not what it is. It's about actually trying to get rid of people who've always lived there. So, in terms of contortions and illogic that their responses get into really, really do indicate just how indefensible Israel's practices are.

KC: Well we're going to have to leave it right there, David. I want to thank you so much for being on the show, thanks for being here today.

DL: Thank you very much, it's very good to have this opportunity to speak publicly.

NOTES

1. "Boycott of Israeli Academic Institutions," American Studies Association, December 4, 2013, https://www.theasa.net/about/advocacy/resolutions-actions/resolutions/boycott-israeli-academic-institutions.

2. "Academic Boycott," *BDS*, accessed June 14, 2018, https://bdsmovement.net/academic-boycott.

3. "U.S. Campaign for Academic Boycott Gaining Strength," *BDS*, January 12, 2010, https://bdsmovement.net/news/us-campaign-academic-boycott-gaining-strength.

4. "IDF Operation in Gaza: Cast Lead," Israel Ministry of Foreign Affairs, last modified January 21, 2009, accessed June 14, 2018, http://mfa.gov.il/MFA/ForeignPolicy/Terrorism/Palestinian/Pages/Aerial_strike_weapon_development_center%20_Gaza_28-Dec-2008.aspx.

5. "Fatalities during Operation Cast Lead," B'Tselem, accessed June 14, 2018, https://www.btselem.org/statistics/fatalities/during-cast-lead/by-date-of-event.

6. United Nations Fact Finding Mission on Gaza, *Human Rights in Palestine and Other Occupied Territories*, September 15, 2009, http://image.guardian.co.uk/sys-files/Guardian/documents/2009/09/15/UNFFMGCReport.pdf. Note: the wording of "under most regimes" is a bit unclear, but it is true that under international law, police are civilians unless they are incorporated into a combatant force.

7. This number is incorrect: 14 higher education facilities were damaged. See "Tough Times for University Students in Gaza," *IRIN*, March 26, 2009, http://www.irinnews.org/news/2009/03/26/tough-times-university-students-gaza. However, 18 primary/secondary schools were

destroyed, and at least 280 were damaged during the assault. See Ali Abunimah, "Israeli TV Admits: No Rockets Were Ever Fired from UNRWA Schools in Gaza during 'Cast Lead,'" *Electronic Intifada*, October 25, 2012, https://electronicintifada.net/blogs/ali-abunimah/israeli-tv-admits-no-rockets-were-ever-fired-unrwa-schools-gaza-during-cast-lead.

8. There is no American University in Gaza. Lloyd means the American International School, which was destroyed. See Harriet Sherwood, "Childhood in Ruins," *Guardian*, December 16, 2009, https://www.theguardian.com/world/2009/dec/17/gaza-israel-invasion-children-traumatised.

9. Human Rights Watch, *Rain of Fire: Israel's Unlawful Use of White Phosphorus in Gaza*, March 25, 2009, https://www.hrw.org/report/2009/03/25/rain-fire/israels-unlawful-use-white-phosphorus-gaza.

10. Neve Gordon, *Israel's Occupation* (Berkeley: University of California Press, 2008).

11. Mohammed Assadi, "Ramallah Building Boom Symbolizes West Bank Growth," *Reuters*, August 2, 2010, https://ca.reuters.com/article/topNews/idCATRE67129P20100802?sp=true.

12. Hugh Naylor, "Ramallah is Booming, But Residents Wait for the Bubble to Burst," *National*, April 25, 2012, https://www.thenational.ae/world/mena/ramallah-is-booming-but-residents-wait-for-the-bubble-to-burst-1.597511.

13. "West Bank–Palestinians Shutter Shops, Block Roads to Protest Spiraling Prices," *Vos Iz Neias?*, September 10, 2012, https://www.vosizneias.com/113264/2012/09/10/west-bank-palestinians-shutter-shops-block-roads-with-burning-tires-to-protest-spiraling-prices/.

14. Palestinian Authority fully controls 18 percent of the West Bank. See Ehab Zahriyeh, "Maps: The Occupation of the West Bank," *Al Jazeera America*, July 4, 2014, http://america.aljazeera.com/multimedia/2014/7/west-bank-security.html.

15. It is arguable there was little pushback from powerful states, particularly the United States, but the UN did pushback, as did human rights groups.

16. Human Rights Watch, *Rain of Fire*.

17. DIME actually scatters in a limited range. It has never been proven conclusively that it was used in Gaza. Many people assert it was, but there is no conclusive proof. See "The Israeli Arsenal Deployed against Gaza During Operation Cast Lead," *Journal of Palestine Studies* 38, no. 3 (Spring 2009): 175–91; Jonathan Cook, "Is Gaza a Testing Ground for Experimental Weapons?," *Counter Currents*, January 14, 2009, https://www.countercurrents.org/cook140109A.htm.

18. The collaboration is on Roosevelt Island, not Long Island. See "Cornell Tech Campus Opens on Roosevelt Island, Marking Transformational Milestone for Tech in NYC," *Cornell Tech: News*, September 12, 2017, https://tech.cornell.edu/news/cornell-tech-campus-opens-on-roosevelt-island-marking-transformational-mile.

19. "Cornell Tech Campus Opens."

20. "Technion Overview," Technion–Israel Institute of Technology, accessed June 14, 2018, https://www.technion.ac.il/en/technion-israel-institute-of-technology/.

21. Shimrit Lee, "Top Israeli University Marketing Country's Arms Industry to the World," *+972*, March 9, 2017, https://972mag.com/top-israeli-university-marketing-countys-arms-industry-to-the-world/125720/.

22. Josh Nathan-Kazis and Larry Cohler-Esses, "Caterpillar Caught in Web of Middle East Politics," *Forward*, July 21, 2010, https://forward.com/news/129547/caterpillar-caught-in-web-of-middle-east-politics/.

23. "Home Demolition as Collective Punishment," B'Tselem, accessed June 14, 2018, https://www.btselem.org/topic/punitive_demolitions.

24. "Jacobs Technion-Cornell Institute," Cornell Tech, accessed June 14, 2018, https://tech.cornell.edu/jacobs-technion-cornell-institute/overview.

25. This information is not specific to students; it is to all travelers. See "Israel, the West Bank, and Gaza," U.S. Department of State, last modified May 14, 2018, accessed June 14, 2018, https://travel.state.gov/content/travel/en/international-travel/International-Travel-Country-Information-Pages/IsraeltheWestBankandGaza.html?wcmmode=disabled.

26. "Israel, the West Bank, and Gaza."

27. It's actually the Association for Asian American Studies, AAAS.

28. Uri Ram, "The Colonization Perspective in Israeli Sociology," in *The Israel/Palestine Question: A Reader*, ed. Ilan Pappé (London: Routledge, 2007), 53–79.

29. It is much closer to $3 billion than $4 billion. See U.S. Library of Congress, Congressional Research Service, *U.S. Foreign Aid to Israel*, by Jeremy M. Sharp, RL 33222 (April 10, 2018), https://fas.org/sgp/crs/mideast/RL33222.pdf.

30. "Settlements: Statements from U.S. Government Officials," Churches for Middle East Peace, accessed June 14, 2018, http://cmep.org/issues/settlements/statements-us-govt-officials/.

31. See: https://boycottisrael.info.

32. The statement from Jewish Voice for Peace is available at: https://portside.org/2014-01-09/israel-boycott-movement-and-controversy-differing-views#3.

33. "PACBI Guidelines for the International Academic Boycott of Israel," Palestinian Campaign for the Academic and Cultural Boycott of Israel, last modified July 31, 2014, accessed June 14, 2018, http://www.pacbi.org/etemplate.php?id=1108.

34. He endorses "transfer," or ethnic cleansing. As Lloyd states, insofar as that's his personal opinion as a scholar, he would not be boycotted. If he went as a representative of the Israeli embassy, then he would be. See "Survival of the Fittest (Cont.)," *Haaretz*, January 8, 2004, https://www.haaretz.com/1.5262428.

35. The original AAUP statement says teachers "should be careful not to introduce into their teaching controversial matter which has no relation to their subject." A clarifying statement introduced in 1970 says: "The intent of this statement is not to discourage what is 'controversial.' Controversy is at the heart of the free academic inquiry which the entire statement is designed to foster. The passage serves to underscore the need for teachers to avoid persistently intruding material which has no relation to their subject." See American Association of University Professors, *1940 Statement of Principles on Academic Freedom and Tenure*, accessed June 14, 2018, https://www.aaup.org/report/1940-statement-principles-academic-freedom-and-tenure#4.

36. Colleen Flaherty, "Accidental Activists," *Inside Higher Ed*, October 22, 2015, https://www.insidehighered.com/news/2015/10/22/new-book-details-founding-and-evolution-aaup.

37. American Association of University Professors, *1940 Statement of Principles*.

38. American Association of University Professors, *On Academic Boycotts*, accessed June 14, 2018, https://www.aaup.org/report/academic-boycotts.

39. Beth McMurtrie, "Scholars Debate Significance of American Studies Assn.'s Vote to Boycott Israel," *Chronicle of Higher Education*, December 16, 2013, https://www.chronicle.com/article/Scholars-Debate-Significance/143645.

40. Peter Beinart, "The Real Problem with the American Studies Association's Boycott of Israel," *Daily Beast*, December 17, 2013, https://www.thedailybeast.com/the-real-problem-with-the-american-studies-associations-boycott-of-israel.

41. He does not compare it to British immigration policy, but he does compare Israel's legitimacy to Britain's.

42. Beinart, "Real Problem."

KATHERINE FRANKE AND SARAH ROBERTS
"The Firing of Steven Salaita," September 3, 2014

https://soundcloud.com/wort-fm/a-public-affair-wednesday-september-3rd

KARMA CHÁVEZ: Last October Steven Salaita, a scholar of English and Native American Studies who writes and teaches about Arab Americans, Indigenous peoples, race and ethnicity, and literature, was hired as a faculty member with tenure in the American Indian Studies Department at the University of Illinois in Urbana-Champaign. He signed a letter of offer, resigned from his position at Virginia Tech, and had plans to move to Illinois. When Israel began its bombing of Gaza in early July, Salaita, like many critics of U.S. and Israel policy and action against Palestinians, took to social media to offer strident critique and air his frustration. As of late July, and despite some raised concerns about the apparent tone of Salaita's tweets, the University of Illinois defended Salaita's right to free speech and affirmed that he would be arriving on campus in the fall.

But as time went on, some of Salaita's 140-character reactions were apparently too controversial for the University of Illinois' comfort. In early August, reports emerged that University of Illinois Chancellor Phyllis Wise announced that Salaita would not be sent to the Board of Trustees to approve his hire, effectively rescinding his offer of employment. Normally, the Board of Trustees functions as a rubber stamp on such matters, and so defenders of free speech, academic freedom, and pro-Palestinian politics were furious about this flagrant violation of Salaita's rights, but also the veiled threat implied for other scholars who hold unpopular opinions. Yet, Chancellor Wise insisted that this was not about Salaita's opinions on Israel; rather, as she put it in a statement: "What we cannot and will not tolerate at the University of Illinois are personal and disrespectful words or actions that demean and abuse either viewpoints themselves or those who express them. We have a particular duty to our students to ensure that they live in a community of scholarship that challenges their assumptions about the world but that also respects their rights as individuals."[1] The American Association for University Professors has denounced the decision noting, "Aborting an appointment in this manner without having demonstrated cause has consistently been seen by the AAUP as tantamount to summary dismissal, an action categorically inimical to academic freedom and due process."[2]

So far, twenty-two faculty members, including myself and one of today's guests, Katherine Franke, have canceled lectures scheduled for UIUC's campus this academic year, and nearly four thousand have signed in support of boycotting UIUC for its unwillingness to defend free speech and academic freedom. Just yesterday the UI board noted that it would financially settle with Salaita as they don't want to hurt him financially, they just don't want him to teach there, and it seems there are conflicting reports about whether the board will in fact vote on his hire.

Clearly a lot is going on in this case, and to help us sort through the issues, I've invited two guests. The first is Columbia University Professor of Law Katherine M. Franke. Professor Franke is the director of the Center of Gender and Sexuality Law, she's been the recipient of a Guggenheim Fellowship, and is a well-known writer on issues of race, gender, and sexuality. Our second guest is Dr. Sarah Roberts, assistant professor of Information and Media Studies at Western University in Ontario, Canada. Dr. Roberts is a lifelong Madison resident and a recent alumna of the University of Illinois in Urbana-Champaign. She writes at the blog illusionofvolition.com. Both are supporters of what might be characterized as the Palestinian justice movement.

Katherine Franke and Sarah Roberts, welcome to *A Public Affair*.

KATHERINE FRANKE: Thanks so much for having me.

SARAH ROBERTS: Thank you so much for having us.

KC: I'm glad you're both here. So that was a rather long introduction because this is a rather complicated situation, but I want to start out by making sure that we have all the facts straight. What are the things that need to be added to the information I provided in my intro, points that need to be clarified, and the like. So, Sarah Roberts, would you mind starting out a little bit there on that?

SR: Yeah sure, Karma. I think that was a pretty comprehensive and straightforward trajectory of events. I guess the one thing that I would add into this mix—which, you know, on the one hand is complicated and on the other maybe not so—is that it's been revealed in recent days, through some Freedom of Information Act documents that in fact, although Chancellor Wise has made public overtures that her concerns had to do with civility,[3] there's been great pressure on the Chancellor from a relatively small pool of very wealthy donors at the University of Illinois. This is documented in some 280 pages of emails that just came out yesterday.[4] So in fact we do need to expand the conversation, then, into one that asks questions about what the role of donors and alumni might be in making governance decisions at the university. Certainly, they have played a significant role in this affair, but the chancellor herself and the Board of Trustees have not made it clear that that's where they were getting their orders from, and that needs to be acknowledged, I think, to have a fair and frank discussion.

KC: Well, and this—we actually lost Katherine for a moment, so we'll get her back on the line here momentarily—but I think that this is a really important question, or this is a really important piece of this, is who it was that was putting the pressure on. So, in part it's donors, but it's also part of this bigger conversation of what's going on within the context of Israel-Palestine. So, you know, could we talk a little bit about what some of those critiques were within those 280 pages that have been released of these emails to Chancellor Wise?

SR: Sure, I think it's no secret that Steven Salaita's an outspoken opponent of the Israeli state. And I make that distinction because it's one that he makes in his own scholarship. His criticism is levied against the practice of Zionism, which he views—as an indigenous scholar and as a comparative indigenous scholar—as a settler colonial project, right, so—

KC: Can we pause on that for a minute, Sarah? Because I think some people might not know what Comparative Indigenous Studies are or the concept of settler colonialism.

SR: So, what Steven Salaita's talking about in his many published works is the encroachment on indigenous Palestinian people in lands that are commonly called Israel now. And various land grabs and expulsions that have gone on since the founding of the state of Israel in 1948. And he and others try to draw comparisons with that practice and the sort of functional practice of how those movements take place at a state level with things that have gone on in other parts of the world, such as to indigenous populations in the lands that we now call the United States. So, I think it matters, too, that he was hired into an American Indian Studies program to do this kind of scholarship. All of this was very much above the board when the offer that was extended to him was made. There was a national search conducted, as there often is in an academic hiring process. I expect that there were a number of viable candidates, and a search committee within the American Indian Studies program at the University of Illinois selected Steven Salaita out of a pool of candidates. So, there was nothing unusual about the hiring process or practices that went on at the University of Illinois, and I think the point that you made at the top of the program that the going forward to the Board of Trustees is something of a perfunctory act at the University of Illinois is really critical. This goes to the issue of faculty governance, where faculty are making decisions internally and that goes through a system of approval within the university structure itself. And so, to have this holdup be at this high level of administration is highly irregular. I don't really know of another case that I can think of off the top of my head—there are some others, people have made bridges to some other cases, but this one is certainly the highest profile in recent years.

KC: Katherine, I'm glad we got you back on the phone here. So, what Sarah and I were talking about, you probably gather, is just kind of filling in some of the gaps of the narration that I provided at the beginning of the show to make sure we were all on the same page in terms of the facts of the case. Were there other things that you wanted to add to that set-up of what's happened?

KF: Well, I think the case is both about Professor Salaita and not at all about him. And it's in some ways an accident that he's the one who got wrapped up in what is a much larger and well-organized political campaign being waged on university campuses in the U.S., but not only, where there is an effort to purge the academy of scholars or scholarship that take a particular critical stance toward political Zionism. And it just so happened he was the one who became the target of this effort this summer, but it could easily have been many others of us, and there will be other cases as there have been cases that came before him. So, much of the way I've been trying to work on this case is to situate what's going on here to Professor Salaita, without minimizing at all how devastating it is to him and his family, but to situate it within a larger, very well-organized and well-oiled machine that has a particular strategy that we see absolutely working out at the University of Illinois Urbana-Champaign.

KC: Well, and as I said at the beginning—myself included—none of the three of us are disinterested in this conversation in the sense that not only do we have a political investment but probably each of us could be a target in different ways too, for things that we've said publicly. And so, I think it's important to talk about it in that context. Let's for a minute, before we go too much in that direction, let's pull back a bit to look at Salaita's case in particular—because I want to spend a moment talking about this question of civility and then talk about his Twitter activity, just so that everything's on the table there. So, when the chancellor made this statement of civility, how was she justifying that? How has that played out in the public discourse that she's put out or that her supporters have put out? Sarah, as an alumn[a], if you want to talk about that.

SR: Yeah, thanks Karma. Well this notion of civility is an interesting one. I think the reason that so many scholars have taken issue with it is because that's a very slippery concept. One person's civility is another person's truth-telling—incivility, right? Or, you know, can civility be used as a mechanism to silence? And I think in this case that's actually what's going on. What's interesting is that nowhere in the very limited public statements that the chancellor and the Board of Trustees have made is there any kind of aspersion being cast on Salaita's scholarship, one, or his classroom activity, two. In fact, he's got the kind of record in the classroom, based on student evaluations and so on, that put many of us to shame and we ought to wish we would have. So there really was no suggestion that anything he had done, either in the framework of his scholarship or in the framework of his role as a professor in the classroom, was out of order. But I think many of us find that suspicious. I think many of us do believe, in fact, that the tone—which at times was harsh and incensed, because Salaita was referring to, of course, the massacre that was being undertaken in Gaza toward civilians when he was tweeting—I think many of us suspect that in fact it was the subject matter of his tweets that got him in hot water. If he had just simply presented his discontent with the Gaza massacre, would that have been adequate to allow his employment to go forward? We'll never know. But in a way this notion of civility is being deployed as a silencing mechanism. And I think that is the aspect that is chilling, not only just to employed professors, those of us without tenure, but those in the graduate student pipeline who are coming up into the professoriate and have this to contend with. The other piece too, Karma, that I think we ought to get on the table is the role that social media is playing in this controversy.

KC: Yeah, definitely.

SR: Right, so it's important, and I think it matters, that Salaita's being punished for activity on Twitter that he was undertaking, not in his public role as a professor at Virginia Tech or a professor at the University of Illinois, but as a citizen expressing a viewpoint—an informed viewpoint, I might add, one that's supported by many, many years of scholarship and numerous publications. So, he's not just talking out of turn on this, he's actually quite learned. And as you pointed out, again, in your intro, we're talking about a medium in which speech is broken down into 140 characters. So, the room to fully articulate complex viewpoints is not always there. Furthermore, he was often in dialogue with other people, yet we see the tweets pulled out and isolated, without context, without the background on Salaita's scholarship and point of view or perspective. So, there are a lot of issues at play. I think many professors are now asking themselves, "Do I need to go look at my Twitter feed and maybe scrub it if I'm going on the job market? Do I need to silence myself?" There's certainly a chilling effect there for people like us in this role. And I think even people who don't agree with Salaita politically have come out in support of his right to speak his mind on this matter, so that matters, too.

KC: Well, Corey Robin, who was one of the early ones to break the story, he's an academic and a commentator, he had—on August 6th when he put the first blog post out, he said on his blog, "I have no doubt that an easily rattled administrator would find my public writings on Israel-Palestine to have crossed a line. If you're in favor of Salaita being punished you should be in favor of me being punished, and not just me. On Twitter many of us—not just on this issue but a variety of issues, and not just on the left but also on the right—speak in a way that can jar or shock a tender sensibility. We swear, we accuse, we say no, and thunder. That's the medium. Though I never really thought twice about it, it's fairly chilling to think that a university official might now be combing through my tweets to see if I had said anything that might warrant me being deemed ineligible for a job."[5] And so, I think that really speaks to that point, the nature of the medium being evaluated in this way. So, the question is, if our Twitter accounts and our Facebook pages can prevent us from getting jobs, should we—I think Sarah, as you put it when we were talking before the show—should we get credit, then, for that as part of our job? Which, of course, currently we don't, as academics, for that.

KF: Well, if I could add something to this, I agree with all that you both have said on this question and the relevance or perils of the kinds of things we say on social media. But I think it's also important to recognize that this turn to civility has been a well-orchestrated and thought-through strategy that has come out of the David Project[6] and several other right-wing, pro-Israeli organizations in the U.S. to frame any criticism of Israeli state policy as "uncivil," as creating a kind of intolerance toward Jews in particular, and conflating criticism of Israel with anti-Semitism. They used to come to my classrooms and sit—people from the David Project—not just mine, but others at Columbia and other universities, and tape our classes and then play them on the internet with annotations of how anti-Semitic they were. Or critique the ways in which we were talking about complex issues. They don't come to my classes as much anymore, but they turned to this strategy of talking about the kinds of things Professor Salaita has put in his scholarship as being "uncivil." And, first of all it's interesting to note that what Chancellor Wise's letter did was basically come right out of the playbook of the David Project in reframing this issue as a matter of civility and incivility. But the second thing I want to emphasize is that civility is an odd norm in an academic context. Part of what we do, as professors, as academics, is unsettle comfortable notions across as wide a range of ideas as we possibly can. Part of what we do is create discomfort. And we don't always do so in a civil way. We do so with rigor, we do so with care, but civility would never be what I would turn to as a guiding principle in an educational context, whether in the classroom or in our scholarship. So, it's an inappropriate norm, I think, to invoke as the basis for a criticism and then a justification for the termination of Professor Salaita.

SR: I think that, yeah, I think Katherine is raising really what is the crux of the issue for so many around this concept of civility. In the chancellor's own letter, she admonished those who might seek to, as she put it, "demean viewpoints." But I think many scholars are perplexed by what in practice that would look like. In fact, many of us are actively engaged in demeaning viewpoints on a daily basis, but we simply call that rigorous or vigorous debate or wrestling with or engaging with concepts in dialogue. So that seems to actually be somewhat antithetical to the project of scholarship. And also has pedagogical implications too, as Katherine was pointing out, that that is unclear as to how that would be implemented in the classroom setting when civility seems to be a stand-in for not taking issue with any viewpoint.

KC: I think it's also, just to throw out, I know Katherine in some of the other work you've done on this and obviously Sarah, as an alumna of Illinois—it's interesting that some of this is happening on this campus. Of course, this is the home of the very controversial college mascot and a history of a particular kind of policing. I don't know if either of you want to take that point in relation to this now using civility as a measure of the academy.

KF: Well, when I was doing some research for a letter I wrote on behalf of Constitutional law professors to the chancellor about a month ago, I was noodling around on the University of Illinois's website, and it turns out they have a web-based archive, a digitized archive, that their librarians have put together that documents threats to academic freedom on their campus.[7] And it profiles two really important cases, one is of McCarthy-based anticommunist purges of the university in the '50s. And the second had to do with the firing of a biologist on campus in the '60s who advocated for premarital sex. He was thought to be way over the line in terms of what an academic could be talking about in a civilized university, if you will.[8] So, I think this incident's going to have to appear on their website as the next iteration of threats to academic freedom on this campus. But, you know, this is not unique to the University of Illinois, we all have that at all of our universities, these low moments where we hopefully learn something rather than repeat them.

KC: Sarah, I don't know if you want to add anything to that point?

SR: Well, I think one thing that feels painfully ironic in connecting the kind of climate that is present at the University of Illinois regarding the unfortunate mascot, it's interesting to point out Salaita was joining the American Indian Studies program there. And so, language of civility and behaving civilly, when levied against people who are part of Indigenous Studies and American Indian Studies is particularly problematic given the history that we have in this country around the "civilizing" forces that have been unleashed upon Native populations. So, I find that language disturbing and pretty unexamined on the part of the chancellor in that regard.

KC: I wonder if—so one of the things about this situation, too, that I think is important to kind of broaden out—so, it is about Salaita, but it's more broad—is thinking about the distinction between what we might call our Constitutional right to free speech and academic freedom, and how that plays out. And I've heard one argument that says, "Is this not a kind of *Duck Dynasty* situation?"[9] So, you know, you can say whatever you want, but then there may be repercussions in terms of your job, you may lose money, that kind of thing. How does one respond to that kind of argument within this context of academic freedom? Katherine Franke?

KF: Well, *Duck Dynasty* was a program on television, and what's happening here is at a public university. So, we have a First Amendment to protect free speech, and particularly in a university context, that doesn't protect private speech the way that the outrageous things one might say on television might be a matter of concern. So, the fact that this is a public university matters because it means that the First Amendment applies in a way that it wouldn't apply to a television show. But more than that, what this is, is viewpoint discrimination. So, anybody who would have said things that were pro-Israeli—and Cary Nelson, who is another member of the faculty at the University of Illinois at Urbana-Champaign who has been quite critical of the call for cultural and academic boycotts of Israel, and quite defensive of certain forms of political Zionism, has not been fired, he's not been disciplined, he's not been called on the carpet by the university.[10] It's those who have had a particular viewpoint about Israel, and it's one that's critical of Israel. So, the Constitution is quite clear on this question that a *state* entity, like the University of Illinois, cannot discriminate against particular viewpoints or people who express particular viewpoints. And the analogy to *Duck Dynasty* just doesn't hold because the First Amendment doesn't apply there. That's your Constitutional Law 101 class.

KC: No, I appreciate that, that's great. Well, and, this is I think interesting, the reach of this, right, because I do think there is a lot of confusion about where we do and don't have free speech rights.

KF: That's right, so if I were fired from Columbia University for something I said, I would not have a Constitutional claim the same way that Professor Salaita does. I would have other claims having to do with my employment but not under the Constitution.

KC: And so, this is really where we see that distinction between the public and the private that you're drawing.

KF: Exactly, yeah.

KC: I want to spend some time moving in this direction of the broader conversation, the Israel-Palestine conversation that you were touching on, talking about Cary Nelson. And I also want to be able to talk at some point about the American Association of University Professors. And so, I guess I wonder if—some listeners are familiar with what's been going on for the past year or so with—well I guess it's been about a year and half—with calls for the academic and cultural boycott of Israel and Israel's state policies. So, most famously of course, the American Studies Association last December voted to uphold the boycott which has been called for by members of Palestinian civil society. Other organizations have considered resolutions and the like, so I wonder if—I'm not sure which one of you prefers to take this question—to talk a bit about this trajectory and how this issue has been building over the last eighteen months or two years.

KF: Well, it has gained enormous support in the academic community because there's such vibrant intellectual exchanges between Israeli academics and universities and academics and universities in the United States and Canada. And there are a number of us in the academy here who are troubled by our collaborations with Israeli state institutions. And more importantly than that, Palestinian civil society organizations have asked us—as a matter of solidarity with their cause if we're sympathetic to it—to boycott Israeli state institutions as part of our academic work. And it's an important thing to note, and there's a bit of confusion about this, is that the boycott is not of Israeli academics but of Israeli academic institutions that are state funded. So,

I can co-write a paper, or have speak at a conference of mine at Columbia, a colleague from Tel Aviv University or Hebrew University, I'm just not going to go to Hebrew University and give a talk or teach for a semester.

KC: Sarah, did you want to add to that?

SR: Yeah, well I think that you're absolutely right to make the connection between this case and the broader context of what's been going on in the BDS movement and in academia, because I don't believe they're unrelated at all. In fact, I think that the desire on the part of some to stop or to rescind the employment of Steven Salaita, who's an outspoken critic of the state of Israel, is absolutely predicated on these issues. I think that although this is a terrible situation for Steven Salaita personally, who has actually been rendered without an income by the uncivil action of the University of Illinois, I do think it speaks to a larger story of a shift in public sentiment in the United States and also in Canada, as Katherine pointed out, to people actually rejecting the status quo around unquestioned and uncritical support of the state of Israel. So, in that regard it may be actually something of a positive when we think about it that way. And that's one of the ways that I've been trying to contextualize it for myself and trying to get to grips with what's happening. It may be that these kinds of moves are going to intensify in the face of the growing, mounting movement to reject support for the state of Israel. It's not an accident that this has come right on the heels, for example, of this encroachment into Gaza. So yeah, I very much think these things are connected, and I think it speaks to a larger battle being waged. A philosophical battle, a cultural one that's going on within the United States and North America, broadly speaking. And also, in Europe, right. But I can mostly speak to the American context.

KF: You know, there was a decision made by the Palestinians after the Second Intifada, to turn to a call for boycott, divestment, and sanctions as an alternative to violence. The Second Intifada was very violent, and the Palestinians suffered enormous casualties, and they realized that they needed to come up with a different tactic for opposing the occupation and the threats to their sovereignty in the region. And so, they turned to the international community and they said, "Would you support us through this particular tactic, boycott, divestment, and sanctions?" So, it's important to situate that call in relationship to the local politics of seeing that as an alternative to suicide bombing and other forms of violence that they realized were not getting them where they wanted. But I do think for those of us over on this side of the political movement in the U.S. and in Canada, but also in Europe, BDS, or the boycott, is just a tactic. And I think there's some confusion or some people are conflating this tactic with a larger politics. You can choose to adopt this tactic, we can abandon it when it doesn't work anymore, but it's not a goal in itself. And it shouldn't be seen as a litmus test for whether one's work, whether one's thinking, whether one's politic is consonant with rights to sovereignty and self-determination for Palestinians. And I worry a little bit sometimes when the educational and cultural boycott is discussed, that it becomes a test for one's political correctness, and I think we ought to back off a little bit from that. The South Africans didn't view it that way, and I know that the Palestinians don't either.

KC: Building on this point, I want to talk about the question of anti-Semitism, and I want to talk about common responses. So, I want to read a quotation from a UIUC student that was part of this 280 pages of material, one of the seventy people who wrote to the chancellor, urging her not to hire Salaita. And then also throw out an example from a friend of mine. This student writes, "As a Jew, I do not feel comfortable knowing that the University of Illinois allows and supports this sort of behavior. I am currently an incoming senior, and this is not the first time I've felt anti-Semitism at the University of Illinois. This is by far the most extreme and hurtful case."[11] So, a student there, and then related to that I have a good friend, a colleague who is opposed to the academic boycott, he's Jewish, our politics differ generally on this issue. But this friend doesn't think it's right that the chancellor in this situation did what she did. But at the same time, he said to me very frankly that he's not sure how he would feel about how someone like Salaita would interact with him as a Jewish colleague, given that he still views some of what Salaita said as anti-Semitic. And I'm not a Jewish person myself, so I'm not going to deny one's experience of that, but how do we deal with these kinds of very real concerns in situations like this and critiques of Israel more broadly. Katherine, maybe you'd like to start.

KF: Well, part of being a grown-up is working and living with people who hold very different views than your own, and often views that you find almost intolerable. And I can tell you, I have colleagues at Columbia who are homophobic—I'm a lesbian—who are sexist—I'm a woman—and hold other views that I find abhorrent. And the solution to that isn't for me to ask that they be fired and for us to purge the academic setting of people who hold views that I think need to evolve in certain ways. What we do instead is we engage each other as scholars, with reasoned arguments and with evidence in defense of our positions and perhaps in criticism of theirs. Now, I'm not conceding that Steven Salaita's texts, or his own views are anti-Semitic. But what we often do is find ourselves in an academic setting confronted by people who hold views very different from our own. And the fact that students would feel uncomfortable at the thought that there would be someone in his educational environment who holds views very different from his own about political Zionism or about the merits of certain actions of Israel isn't enough of an argument to have him fired. Now, I think these tweets, some of them were ambiguous in their meaning, as complex statements like those that can take up 140 characters might be. And the right thing to do is to turn to his work, turn to him and say, "What did you mean by this?" Not fire him and purge him and those ideas from this environment.

SR: Well, I was just going to say I couldn't agree more with that analysis. And again, I also don't concede that we have evidence at all that Salaita holds anti-Semitic, meaning anti-Jewish, views. I think that he holds anti-Zionist views, and he would be the first to say that. Which, in his mind and in the mind of many, are two very different things. But again, yes, as Katherine has pointed out, we work with people all the time from whom we differ greatly, on many issues; politically, the way we live our life, who we are, and so on. And we also find ourselves in the classroom, as students and also as professors, in that same kind of environment. And so, part of the pedagogical experience of at the university level is being confronted with ideas that may be new or, as Katherine said earlier, may be unsettling, but in the classroom—a colleague of mine from the University of California often says to students, "Bring the evidence." So, bring your challenging viewpoint but bring the evidence to support it. And that's the way we contend with it in the classroom, that's the way that Salaita has always done it, and that's the way that it should've been done in this case too.

KC: We have a caller on the air actually, so I'm going to put her through. Molly, you have a question about how this is different from other academic hiring, is that correct?

MOLLY: Yes, I do. So specifically, I'm just wondering how this case is different from the case of James Kilgore[12] in Illinois and also Ward Churchill,[13] who of course blamed American foreign policy for the 9/11 attacks and compared the victims to those Germans complicit in keeping quiet during the Nazi occupation of Germany. So how is this case more significant, and how does it up the ante in terms of violations of academic freedom? And I'll hang up and listen, thanks.

KC: Thanks Molly. I don't know which of you is more comfortable, or if one of you is comfortable taking that question.

KF: Sarah, do you want to start off?

KC: Sarah, do you want to start?

SR: Well, I'm no expert on those other two cases, I must admit, but I will say that there's a whole lot to unpack in them, and we start getting into the realm of conversations about the way in which labor is structured at the university level in this contemporary moment so that now we're dealing with issues of tenure versus with issues of people who are considered adjuncts. Again, I think it's important to point out in Salaita's case, too, that the concept of tenure is under attack here, too. He was hired in with tenure, he had tenure at Virginia Tech. So that's one way in which it differs greatly. One other way, at least kind of from cursory knowledge of the Churchill case, is that there's been no aspersions cast upon his scholarship. No one has brought his scholarship into play and suggested that there was something problematic with that. It's solely about his speech as an individual, in fact outside of the classroom, so I think that's one way in which his situation may differ from the other two that were invoked, and I'll pass it over to Katherine.

KC: Katherine did you have something to add there?

KF: Well, Professor Churchill was fired, I'd say pretty close to the aftermath of 9/11 at a time when sentiments in the United States were so overwhelmingly pointing in one direction of sympathy for the victims of the 9/11 attacks and a sense of—almost a frenzy of nationalism—that made his comments seem all the more outrageous and intolerable. But many of the organizations I associate myself with, including the Center for Constitutional Rights,[14] got involved in his defense. I think it was wrong to terminate him because his comments were outrageous. I don't think that they were evil, I'm not even sure what the standard would be for comments such as his (**SR:** Uncivil?) that would justify—yeah, uncivil right? But we'd have to think a little bit harder, the three of us here, about what appropriate standards one would want to apply for public comments outside of the classroom made by a professor that were not just outrageous but offensive in some way, but not hate speech. So, I think that this case shares a similarity with some of these other cases, but I would say it's different in the sense that it's not *sui generis*, it doesn't stand by itself, it's part of what is a well-organized campaign to go after tenuring decisions, publication decisions, hiring decisions, and then to fire people who take—academics who take a particularly critical stance in their scholarship and/or their comments outside of the academic context toward the state of Israel. And, Sarah, I just want to reiterate something that she said earlier, that it's so important to note that criticism of the state of Israel is not the same thing as anti-Semitism.

KC: Yeah, thank you again for that clarification. We actually have another caller on the line here who I think wants to talk a bit about these comparisons. Howard, are you on the air? Hey Howard, you're on the air.

CALLER: It's not Howard actually. What I wanted to say is actually I would've hoped that you would've had somebody taking the other side of the issue. But, you know, Salaita's a person who said Zionists made anti-Semitism honorable, and in the wake of kidnapping Israeli children, said he wished all West Bank settlers would disappear. I think it's—I think that your guests would have to admit that if he'd made similar statements about African Americans or Asian Americans, something like "African American leaders make racism honorable" or "Asian Americans make racism against Asians honorable," there would be no public outcry, and for that reason I think it's clear that the campaign in his defense is much more about politics than it is about academic freedom. There's the pro-Palestinian perspective is very, very well-represented in academics, there are many academics in tenured positions that are quite outspoken in defense of the Palestinian cause, so I think this is a sort of opportunistic thing on the part of Salaita's defenders to just advance the BDS movement and pro-Palestinian politics.

KC: Thanks for your comments. Katherine or Sarah would you like to respond to that?

SR: Well, I just would make a brief comment to say that from my personal point of view, I would've much rather given up this opportunity to advance BDS to allow a man to take up the position that he was hired for at the University of Illinois.

KC: Katherine did you want to add to that?

KF: Yeah, a couple other things. First of all, the claim that the academy is populated with a lot of Palestinian sympathizers is, I think, factually untrue. We're a minority, and because of these campaigns to censor us, it makes it seem that there are more of us than there are. But I can assure you that on campuses like mine, we are a very small minority of people who don't only understand ourselves as being Palestinian sympathizers, but as people who want to think critically about the kinds of issues that Professor Salaita's raising in his scholarship, which is how do we understand notions of belonging and dispossession and indigeneity and exile in a complicated place like Israel? It's a hugely complicated problem, and there aren't right answers to these difficult questions. And the fact that we want to question what seems to be a kind of orthodoxy around who belongs there, and who is right, itself gets framed as a kind of incivility and intolerance. So, I wanted to get you with the idea that there are a lot of us, I don't think we feel that way at all.

And the second thing is, that was a nice lawyerly trick, lawyerly switch that Howard made saying, well, if these were Black people or Asians or other minorities who were being criticized in lieu of Israelis or the Israeli state, we wouldn't stand for it. And I think while it's an attractive move, it doesn't really work because there's an underlying context that generated the comments that Professor Salaita made that have to do with settlements, that have to do with settlers taking land or settling in land that's on the other side of the Green Line.[15] There are ways in which Zionism, in particular extreme forms of Zionism, have generated responses that are sometimes troubling but understandable in a particular political context that you can't just pick up and then drop in an African American context and say, "See, that wouldn't work here." So, part of the problem is Twitter has so few characters that it's hard to make a nuanced argument, but I think rather than firing the guy, let's see what he was trying to talk about and then evaluate the merits of it.

SR: I might point out, too, that this particular tweet that's gotten so much traction, that was just invoked by your last caller, is one worthy of unpacking. The anti-Semitism that Salaita mentioned in that tweet was in quotes, it was in quotes for a reason, it was in quotes because Salaita, like many others, takes issue with the conflation of anti-Semitism and anti-Zionism. In his work he goes to great lengths to articulate exactly what he means by that position. Now, we've talked about Corey Robin before, Corey Robin being a political scholar in his own right, but he's also been doing a lot of writing on this case, and he has a piece on his blog that listeners could seek out or maybe we can link to somehow where he actually unpacks a lot of these tweets, connects it to Salaita's scholarship, and makes the very case that I think Katherine was just making, too.[16]

KC: Cool. We only have about three/four minutes left of the show here, but we have a couple callers on the line, I'm going to first put on Walid.

WALID: Yeah, thanks Karma, I'll keep this really short because you and your guests have made the argument that I wanted to make about the real problem with confusing criticism of Israel with being anti-Israel or, certainly even worse, anti-Semitic, and just the notion that in Salaita's tweets it's—the sort of arguments he uses, the way he references himself as being quote-unquote "anti-Semitic," given his other tweets and his other writing, is consistent with an argument that there's a rhetorical battle going on to suggest that being critical of Israel is anti-Semitic when it's actually very different, they're very different concepts. So, I just wanted to kind of add to that conversation.

KC: Cool, thanks so much, really appreciate the call.

SR: And Karma, if I could just say again, something that Katherine has said all along that is so important is, why can't this debate be happening where it's supposed to be happening, which is at the University of Illinois, itself? Where this rich kind of debate could have taken place, but we've now lost that opportunity seemingly.

KC: Right, right. And I think we have one other caller who is on hold here, so is it Rukamin?

RUKAMIN: Yup. Thank you again, I think this is a very interesting and a very needed conversation. Because if somehow saying anything about Israel is anti-Semitic, then we can guess what Constitutional law that you just broke. And Israel wouldn't exist without acting as America's little mini-me, and we participate in the existence of Israel, which is really detrimental, I think personally. And that's my comment.

KC: Thank you, thank you so much for calling in. Did either of you want to respond to that? We have about a minute and a half left.

KF: Well, I often get criticized for, "Why am I picking on Israel? There are plenty of bad things happening in the world? Why be so tough on Israel?" And, if you know my wider work, you know I'm tough on a lot of places, this isn't the only human rights violation in the world that I give my scholarly and other attention to. But I do think, as your caller said, there is a special relationship between the United States and American citizens and the state of Israel and Israeli citizens. Were it not for an enormous foreign policy budget and subsidies and military subsidies, Israel would not exist. And in that sense, it's really the fifty-second state, in so many ways. So, I think we have an obligation as Americans to think critically about American foreign policy, American domestic policy, and Israeli foreign and domestic policy because these are our tax dollars at work. And we have a particularly tight relationship with this country more than any other country on the globe—partly out of recognition of the horror of World War II and the reason why Israel was founded as a Jewish state, but also because of the contemporary funding of the Israeli military and the maintenance of the occupation.

KC: Well, we're going to have to leave it right there because we are out of time for the hour, our guests today, Katherine Franke and Sarah Roberts. Katherine and Sarah, thanks so much for being here today.

SR: Thanks, Karma. I encourage your readers to just seek out the volumes of information from other scholars online about this.

KC: Excellent, yeah, there's a lot of information online, and definitely we'll keep following this case, Steven Salaita.

NOTES

1. Statement of Chancellor Phyllis M. Wise. Reproduced in full at Christine Des Garennes, "Updated: Wise Explains Salaita Decision, Gets Support from Trustees," *News-Gazette*, August 23, 2014, http://www.news-gazette.com/news/local/2014-08-23/updated-wise-explains-salaita-decision-gets-support-trustees.html.

2. "AAUP takes UIUC to Task for Apparent Summary Dismissal," *AAUP Updates*, August 29, 2014, https://www.aaup.org/news/aaup-takes-uiuc-task-apparent-summary-dismissal#.WzEnu6knZMU.

3. Charlotte Silver, "Civility and Its Discontents: Dissident Academic Steven Salaita Takes a Stand in Defense of Incivility," *In These Times*, November 10, 2015, http://inthesetimes.com/article/18588/civility-and-its-discontents.

4. Christine Des Garennes, "Salaita Prompted Donors' Fury," *News-Gazette*, September 2, 2014, http://www.news-gazette.com/news/local/2014-09-02/salaita-prompted-donors-fury.html.

5. Corey Robin, "Another Anti-Zionist Professor Punished for his Views (Updated)," *Crooked Timber*, August 6, 2014, http://crookedtimber.org/2014/08/06/another-anti-zionist-professor-punished-for-his-views/.

6. The David Project describes its mission as empowering "student leaders to build mutually beneficial and enduring partnerships with diverse student organizations so that the pro-Israel community is integrated and valued on campus." See https://www.davidproject.org/mission/.

7. "The University of Illinois in the Cold War Era 1945–1975: Academic Freedom of Speech," University Library, University of Illinois at Urbana-Champaign, last modified December 8, 2015, https://guides.library.illinois.edu/c.php?g=348250&p=2346778.

8. "University of Illinois in the Cold War Era."

9. See: Brian Lowry, "'Duck Dynasty' Suspension: Free Speech Doesn't Mean Consequence-Free Speech," *Variety*, December 19, 2013, https://variety.com/2013/tv/columns/duck-dynasty-suspension-free-speech-doesnt-mean-consequence-free-speech-1200977229/.

10. Cary Nelson, a UIUC professor, emerged as the central antagonist in the Salaita case. He had long been considered one of the strongest proponents of academic freedom, including serving as president of the American Association of University Professors from 2006–2012, and yet, he was a fierce and public defender of UIUC's decision to fire* Salaita. Because Nelson has also been a longtime opponent of the BDS movement and then chose to support Chancellor Wise in what seemed to many as a contradictory stance, Nelson was critiqued by his peers (and not institutions) for what critics have called his "blindspot" on Israel and his double standard on academic freedom when it comes to Palestine. Colleen Flaherty, "In a Hurricane," *Inside Higher Ed*, August 15, 2014, https://www.insidehighered.com/news/2014/08/15/cary-nelson-faces-backlash-over-his-views-controversial-scholar. In the wake of Salaita's firing, Nelson publicly took "a Zionist identity." Cary Nelson, "Am I a Zionist?," Opinion, *Jerusalem Post*, October 25, 2014, https://www.jpost.com/Opinion/Am-I-a-Zionist-379801. *Although to some, it is controversial to say that Salaita was fired, I believe that is the appropriate word (Salaita also makes a case for that in his interview in this collection). As John K. Wilson put it, "One thing should be clear: Salaita was fired. I've been turned down for jobs before, and it never included receiving a job offer, accepting that offer, moving halfway across the country, and being scheduled to teach classes." John K. Wilson, "Fighting the Twitter Police," *Inside Higher Ed*, August 8, 2014, https://www.insidehighered.com/views/2014/08/08/essay-criticizing-u-illinois-blocking-controversial-faculty-hire.

11. Scott Jaschik, "The Emails on Salaita," *Inside Higher Ed*, August 25, 2014, https://www.insidehighered.com/news/2014/08/25/u-illinois-officials-defend-decision-deny-job-scholar-documents-show-lobbying.

12. James Kilgore was an adjunct (contingent) faculty member at the University of Illinois–Urbana-Champaign who was blocked from his teaching after his radical activist past and criminal conviction came to light. He was later reinstated. See Jodi S. Cohen and Michelle Manchir, "U. of I. Clears Way for Convicted Radical to Teach Again," *Chicago Tribune*, November 14, 2014, https://www.chicagotribune.com/news/ct-james-kilgore-decision-met-20141113-story.html; Colleen

Flaherty, "A Second Chance?," *Inside Higher Ed*, November 10, 2014, https://www.insidehighered.com/news/2014/11/10/u-illinois-board-receives-report-recommending-reappointment-ex-convict.

13. Ward Churchill was a tenured professor and chair of the Ethnic Studies Department at the University of Colorado–Boulder who drew attention for an essay referring to some victims of the September 11, 2001, terrorist attacks as "little Eichmanns." The negative attention led to assessments of his scholarship, and Churchill was accused of fraud and plagiarism, which led to his termination. See Anthony Cotton, "Fired Colorado Professor Ward Churchill Loses High Court Appeal," *Denver Post*, September 10, 2012, https://www.denverpost.com/2012/09/10/fired-colorado-professor-ward-churchill-loses-high-court-appeal/; Kirk Johnson and Katharine Q. Seelye, "Jury Says Professor Was Wrongly Fired," *New York Times*, April 2, 2009, https://www.nytimes.com/2009/04/03/us/03churchill.html?hp&_r=0.

14. "The Center for Constitutional Rights is dedicated to advancing and protecting the rights guaranteed by the United States Constitution and the Universal Declaration of Human Rights. CCR is committed to the creative use of law as a positive force for social change." See "What We Do," Center for Constitutional Rights, last modified February 29, 2016, https://ccrjustice.org/home/what-we-do.

15. The Green Line refers to Israel's pre-1967 borders.

16. Corey Robin's extensive writing about the Salaita case can be found at coreyrobin.com/tag/steven-salaita.

STEVEN SALAITA
"Uncivil Rites," October 21, 2015

https://www.wortfm.org/pledge-edition-uncivil-rites-with-steven-salaita/

KARMA CHÁVEZ: Last summer, Israel engaged in a bombardment of the Gaza Strip called Operation Protective Edge. Citing the disappearance of three settlers in the West Bank as the impetus, Israel's fifty-day campaign killed more than two thousand Palestinians, including five hundred children.[1] Steven Salaita, a Jordanian-Palestinian-Nicaraguan American with Appalachian roots and a renowned Indigenous Studies scholar was just a little over a month away from starting his new tenured position as an associate professor of American Indian Studies at University of Illinois at Urbana-Champaign when the bombing started. He'd resigned his position at Virginia Tech, his wife had resigned her job, and they were ready to make the move west. Throughout this time, Salaita, an avid contributor on social media, aired his frustrations with the bombardment in 140-character bites on Twitter. These many, many tweets ranged from contemplative and witty, to acerbic and angry.

Salaita was no stranger to being a target for his viewpoints on Palestine, and so he was likely not surprised when Zionist donors to UIUC initially shared their concerns to Illinois Board of Trustee members and then Chancellor Phyllis Wise. As should be expected, in early July, the administration showed its support for Salaita's right to free speech. But in early August, something changed.

Salaita was approved at every level of the UIUC to take his tenured position in American Indian Studies to begin in August 2014. Although UIUC originally supported Salaita, in early August UIUC Chancellor Phyllis Wise notified Salaita that she would not be sending his name to the Board for a vote due to his lack of civility and alleged promotion of anti-Semitism.[2] Eventually, under pressure, she sent his name to the Board of Trustees, a step usually regarded as a rubber stamp in hiring decisions. The Board denied his hire in an 8–1 vote,[3] a move viewed by proponents of free speech, academic freedom, and shared faculty governance as a gross overstep.[4]

For the last year, this case has been the subject of immense controversy as UIUC was subject to censure by the American Association of University Professors,[5] and more than five thousand faculty have continued to boycott the institution until it reinstates Salaita's offer.[6] While academics have taken various positions on this ongoing case, the firing of Salaita (and I am persuaded that this is the correct term to use) brings up sobering questions about free speech, academic freedom, shared faculty governance, the place of Indigenous and Ethnic Studies, and the state of the university.

These subjects and more are covered in Salaita's new book, *Uncivil Rites: Palestine and the Limits of Academic Freedom*, just out from Haymarket Books. In this book, Salaita details what he and his family have gone through, the political stakes of speaking out on Palestine, the weakening protections for faculty at universities, and much, much more. As Morehouse professor Marc Lamont Hill put it, "*Uncivil Rites* is Steven Salaita's most important work to date. Using his unjust dismissal from University of Illinois as the backdrop, Salaita exposes the intellectual, moral, and political contradictions of the 21st century neo-liberal university. He also spotlights the dangers of conflating anti-Zionism with anti-Semitism, resistance with terrorism, and righteous outrage with incivility. This book only reinforces Salaita's well-deserved reputation as one of the most honest, courageous, and incisive scholars of our generation."[7]

Steven Salaita is currently Edward Said Chair of American Studies at the American University in Beirut. He is author of several books, including *Anti-Arab Racism in the USA: Where it Comes from and What it Means for Politics* (2006)—Winner of 2007 Gustavus Myers Center for the Study of Bigotry and Human Rights' "Outstanding Book" Award; *The Holy Land in Transit: Colonialism and the Quest for Canaan* (2006); *Arab American Literary Fictions Cultures and Politics* (2007); and *The Uncultured Wars* (2008).

Steven Salaita, welcome to *A Public Affair*.

STEVEN SALAITA: Thank you for having me.

KC: So, Steve, first of all, how is life transitioning to Beirut? And how are you liking your position there?

SS: It's definitely been an interesting transition, but you know, it's—it's been about as well as one could expect. I love my students and colleagues here at AUB, and life in Beirut is always interesting and exciting. It's quite the change, but being in the classroom has a universal feeling about it as well.

KC: And are most of your students local there or are these U.S.-based students?

SS: The majority of them are Lebanese, but they come from all over the Arab world, and there are a decent amount of European students and also Lebanese students from the diaspora.

KC: And so, I want people to get to know—so it's good to hear you're back in the classroom, I know you love the classroom, and you are a teacher who gets rave reviews. But you're also a scholar who gets rave reviews and not just this icon you've become over the last year. And so, I wonder if you'd talk a little bit about your research agenda and how it's grown since getting your PhD in Native American literature from the University of Oklahoma a decade ago.

SS: Sure, yeah, I would love to. You know, I guess I've dipped my toes in various things, I've looked at the pitfalls of liberal piety, I've done some work on Arab American literature, but I'm kind of oriented around Ethnic Studies and Indigenous Studies. Those are two designations that can take people in all kinds of interesting and useful directions. But lately I've been working on a comparative analysis of modes and strategies and discourses of decolonization in Palestine and North America. And looking at the ways in which Palestinians and Native Americans are in communication with one another, in some cases in communities with one another, and the ways in which their projects of decolonization inform one another in really meaningful ways.

KC: So, this is—as I kind of understand it, and I'm not an indigenous scholar myself—but this is an approach that we might call Comparative Indigenous Studies, is that fair to say?

SS: I think that's very fair, yes.

KC: And so, what's the place of something like Comparative Indigenous Studies as an important area of study in something like Native American or American Indian Studies?

SS: It's—you notice we don't use the direct nomenclature to describe it as comparative. Nearly all of the work in what we might call American Indian Studies or Indigenous Studies more broadly is fundamentally comparative. And it fits always a kind of transnational appeal, which doesn't necessarily mean transatlantic like my work is. We have hundreds—thousands, really—of distinct Native nations here on the North American continent, and the very act of putting them in conversation with one another in scholarship about indigenous communities in this country is part and parcel of a comparative framework. So, it's very difficult, actually, to do work within the field without looking at multiple national communities simultaneously. And so, a lot of people are developing really interesting methodologies for approaching multiple communities simultaneously.

KC: Well, and it also makes it very complicated, I think, just the number of different indigenous nations in the United States, let alone thinking globally. Will you tell us some of the initial kinds of things you're looking at, these relationships between indigenous communities in the United States and Palestine?

SS: Oh, happily. There's—it starts with some of the comparable, really, in some cases identical, discourses of colonization that we see in early America and then in Palestine at the onset of Zionism a few hundred years later. And there's a notion of chosenness, settler chosenness, a distinctive form of manifest destiny that is visible on both continents, a sense of—even in its secular incarnations—doing God's work or fulfilling some sort of godly or divine obligation. There's also, in North America, particularly among the Puritans, a desire to restore an unused or mismanaged land of milk and honey. So, a lot of the early settlers—English settlers conceptualize themselves as Israel in the wilderness and, in turn, conceptualized the Native encounters as, you know, the Holy Land tribes that God had slated for extermination in the Book of Joshua in the Old Testament, and so they became the Canaanites, essentially. And so, this kind of cosmology of the American settler as a reproduction of an ancient biblical myth and the reduction of the Native to a disposable Holy Land tribe very much influenced the tenor of the discourses of U.S. nationhood.

And so, if you move it back to Palestine, you see the same sort of reliance on divine obligation, the notion of an unused swampy land, an uninhabited land or a sparsely inhabited land. And these are features that are common to nearly every project of settler colonization in modernity, but they're particularly acute in North America and Palestine. And so, in turn, you know, there's a lot of solidarity organizing around Native and Palestinian communities, particularly Palestinian diasporic communities in North America. And we're looking at ways that both highlight and have the opportunity to undermine this very strong bond that exists between the U.S. and Israeli states, which we often hear both U.S. and Israeli politicians articulating as having a shared set of values, right? A shared set of Judeo-Christian values, a shared set of democratic values. And we're sort of looking at those shared values—which in fact exist, a set of shared colonial values, rather than democratic ones.

KC: Well, and this is a kind of interesting point, too. So, this concept of settler colonialism which can be used to describe both the U.S. and Israel-Palestine. And it is a concept—just listening to you now talk about the interrelationship between these two forms, they're more related, I guess, than I would have thought. Will you talk a bit about this idea of settler colonialism?

SS: Yeah, it might be more necessary in the context of Palestine because so much of the discourse about the so-called conflict that we hear in the United States and in Europe to a lesser degree, is that of inherent religious acrimony between Jews and Muslims. There's an idea that it's an ancient tribal rivalry between Jews and Arabs and all kinds of what I would consider mystical or mythical explanations. But, in fact, the Israel-Palestine conflict is pretty easily explained and it's straightforward. It's a matter of Jews colonizing the land of Palestine and in so doing implementing a disparate legal system in which rights and privileges are afforded according to the state's definition of a citizen's religion. So Jewish Israelis have more inherent rights inside Israel and certainly within the occupied territories than do Palestinian Arabs. And so, if we look at the situation in the context of settler colonization, in context of a colonial power acting to displace and dispossess an indigenous community, then it's much easier to make sense of what's happening, particularly the sort of violence that's described as mindless on the West Bank, which is anything but, which is actually very easily explainable. And the United States, I think most people are prepared to acknowledge to some degree that the origin of the nation-state exists in settler colonization, but I think far more—or, excuse me, far fewer people are willing to acknowledge that this project of settler colonization within the United States is in fact ongoing.

KC: It's interesting to kind of get a context for your work, and also this leads me to ask you, then, about the position that you applied for and earned at the University of Illinois. Will you talk a bit about how you decided to apply for a position there and what that position was?

SS: Yeah, it was an open—it was an open listing—or, sorry, a listing for an open position, and one of the desired features of the successful applicant was a focus on global or Comparative Indigenous Studies. So, they were looking for an assistant professor and an associate professor, and they ended up, I believe, from the search hiring one of each, me at the associate level, of course. And I put in an application based on my reading of the ad and its relationship to my particular skill set as somebody who is interested in thinking about American Indian Studies in a specific global framework, particularly in relation to Palestine. And I got a screening interview, I ended up with an on-campus interview, and the entire process, as do many academic job searches at the senior level, ended up taking around two years.

KC: And so, it wasn't—a lot of people don't understand how an academic job market works, which is not like you apply for a job, give someone two weeks notice, and head out. Often it does take this long. So, you first applied for this position when?

SS: I always get my dates confused [Both: *laughing*]. In early October or mid-October of 2012, and I interviewed on campus, you know the fabled campus visit where candidates suffer for around two days straight, in February of 2013. And I got offered the position in October, early October 2013, with a start date in January 2014, which I deferred until August of 2014 so I could complete the spring semester at Virginia Tech. I hope that timeline makes sense to listeners.

KC: Yeah, I think it's just important for people to hear the kinds of—the time frame, the deliberation, and, you know, these are not rash decisions that get made. And of course, just to—you weren't on this hiring committee, but you've been on hiring committees, I assume, and the process of vetting a candidate for a job, what does that typically entail?

SS: At the senior tenured level it entails tons of committee work. The search committee that was convened for the hiring process had to look at my stuff and vet my scholarship closely, vet my teaching record, they had to vet my service record, all of that stuff. And then it had to be approved by the dean of the college, and it had to be approved by the provost, and it had to be approved by the chancellor. And it also has to go through the normal tenure process at the University of Illinois, meaning all of the standard tenure committees that make those sorts of decisions internally had to look at my work and sign off on my tenure. It also involved external referees, at least three, maybe four, possibly five, I have no idea how many they used. They had to send out my dossier, a sample—a big sample of my scholarly work, my teaching record, et cetera—to external referees who judged the quality of the work and made a determination about whether or not I was worthy of receiving a tenured position at a prestigious research university. So, the application goes through an extraordinary number of eyeballs. Probably over a hundred people vetted my dossier, which is, again, normal for that sort of academic job-hiring process.

KC: Yeah, these are not, again, they're not rash decisions. Steven Salaita, a lot of people, when they talk about what happened to you, they use the word "unhire" to describe what happened. And in your book, you make a strong case for the fact that you were in fact fired. In addition to what we were just talking about, will you explain why "fired" is the appropriate word?

SS: Yeah, absolutely. Before I say that, I do want to encourage listeners to pledge. I don't know if you know this, I used to live in Madison for three years and was a very regular listener and lover of the station. So, it's a tremendous honor to be on your air actually. And it's a real gem of American broadcasting, which gets more and more corporatized. So, people, come on. But anyway, that's my pitch. Well, I think legally speaking it's a firing. A federal judge has affirmed that description in his ruling on the university's motion to dismiss the lawsuit,[8] which I think he rendered about three months ago,[9] I can't remember my dates exactly. He talks about all the ways that this specifically can be termed a firing. And just on a more personal or philosophical level, I prefer firing, as well. Unhiring just seems tame to me in ways that don't match the severity of the action. And at the same time there's a kind of dignity in being fired that doesn't exist in this tepid notion of being unhired that throughout history and throughout U.S. history, people who speak against centers of power don't get punished by being unhired, they get punished by being fired. And I'm very pleased to be able to situate myself into that particular history.

KC: And I'm wondering—I can't even imagine what must have been going through your head. You're sitting at home, it's early August, you're about to move across the country, and you get this email from then-Chancellor Phyllis Wise. First of all—I want to know what's going through your head, but did you even know that your name hadn't been sent to the board?

SS: No, I had no idea. I had no—I thought that every last hurdle had been crossed. It never came up in a single conversation I had with my department chair or with my colleagues.

KC: So, that part of it in itself is a surprise, but what was happening—what was your experience? And of course, getting an email in itself is a kind of strange way to get this kind of information.

SS: Yeah, I was really stunned. That's the best way that I can describe it. First of all, the letter is—and I—it's included in one of the appendices to the back of the book *Uncivil Rites*, so the documents are there for people to look at if they're interested in seeing them—but, it's worded in a really strange way. It doesn't say, "You're fired." And it doesn't go into any detail, it doesn't state any detail whatsoever, it doesn't even hint at a reason why this decision is being taken. It just sort of says, "Hey, the board's not going to approve, so don't even bother to show up, have a nice life." It was just a really, really weird bizarre moment. But I recognized, after I finished that email and understood what exactly that letter was telling me, that my academic career in the U.S. was suddenly in really serious jeopardy, and I knew it in that particular moment.

KC: Did you know, I mean did you have a sense of why this was happening at this point?

SS: Not really. I knew that there had been some—some of what I considered low-level grumbling about my Twitter feed—standard handful of right-wing websites had been trolling my Twitter feed about what a raging, murderous, homicidal anti-Semite I was, but come on. They're doing that stuff to professors all the time, there's an entire media industry devoted to that. One of your colleagues, Sara Goldrick-Rab, is quite familiar with that sort of nonsense. So, I figured there's a right-wing flare up and then it would go away. But I did put two and two together. I was like, "Well, it obviously has something to do with criticizing Israel, and those criticisms reached the wrong ears, and the people who heard them and weren't happy with them obviously acted on that unhappiness in some way."

KC: Well, and this is—having myself been a subject of this kind of targeting, it's like—it's really like your gut falls out, to think about those kind of moments. And so, eventually right, we realize there's this critique of your alleged incivility that's leveraged at you. And I wonder if you could talk about how that critique of your alleged behavior, because I think this point is debatable, and how you've had to negotiate this discourse of civility.

SS: It's been a long, intensive, but in lots of ways intellectually productive process for me, and I think a lot of other people who've been thinking about these issues and the way that our comments are framed by those who occupy centers of power or aspire to centers of power as opposed to those who challenge centers of power. So, we can look at it at a very basic legal level: there is no tradition in U.S. legal history at all, whatsoever, of a judge or court or anybody else with judicial authority deciding that civility, however it's defined, as a precondition for the exercise of free speech. And there is no tenet in the history of academic freedom in a U.S. context, in U.S. academe, that states that we must raise our arguments in extramural or scholarly environments using a certain tone and using a certain language. So, the first problem with the incivility argument is it contravenes every single tradition of free speech and academic freedom. But that's not where their problems end, that's probably where their problems begin. It's also profoundly racialized, the charge. It has a very long and violent history in discourses of U.S. colonization, so it's particularly rich that they decided to discuss concepts like civility and incivility in relation to an American Indian Studies program with seemingly no awareness of the violent history of that term vis-à-vis Native American communities. And it also normalizes a certain sort of emphasis on our demeanor or our etiquette, rather than on the content of our critique. And that's a huge problem because, as I point out in the book, some of the worst, most horrible violence in world history was planned or justified without a single inappropriate speech act having occurred.

KC: Well, and this is this irony, and I was thinking while reading your book about the concept of the kind of civilizing mission, the relationship between civility and civilizing, which is directly relevant to UIUC. So, another of the things you talk about in the book is the controversy over Illinois' mascot, and I wonder if you could talk a bit about that in relationship to what's happened to you.

SS: Yeah, it makes most sense. You know, the mascot Chief Illiniwek, who supposedly is retired—I mean, formally he's retired, it happened in 2007 at the behest, or really demand, of the NCAA.[10] But, Illiniwek thrives and survives in Champaign-Urbana, and his imagery is everywhere. And, you know, he's your standard issue, ridiculous looking Native mascot that people who have severe issues of majoritarian angst cling to as if it represents both their history and their future. And because of the presence of Illiniwek and the kind of racism that attends his very existence, the American Indian Studies program has long been in a sort of conflict with elements at the university and throughout the state of Illinois because folks associated with that program throughout the years, including its current faculty, have been adamantly opposed to the existence of the chief. And they've argued heartily for his abolition on grounds not only of racism but on grounds of the problematic campus climate that he creates for American Indian faculty, employees, and students. So, it's not just my Twitter feed that is relevant to this situation, nor is it simply academic freedom. I think it's important also to focus on the location of my firing, that it happened in an American Indian Studies program whose place on the campus and in the broader community was already tenuous based on a conflict of mores around racism and representation. And it's long been my opinion that it would have been a much more difficult decision to enforce—firing me, that is—had my hire been in another department.

KC: Yeah, I think this is a context that maybe is hard for people to understand that it *does* make a difference that it was an American Indian Studies program. And the question of sovereignty, which, you know, is constantly challenged for indigenous peoples globally but in the United States and how this functions, too, as a direct challenge to the kind of sovereignty of the academic department. I don't know if that's a frame you use to think about this.

SS: No, it's totally a frame that I use. I think you nail it. Because I think a lot of the subsequent response to the firing and the controversy that it created ends up reinforcing a broader paradigm of federal oversight of Indian affairs. I know that that probably doesn't make sense, so I'm going to try to explain briefly and I hope clearly. But a lot of UIUC's supporters are really motivated by a blind ideological commitment to Israel. And they won't just admit—and I wish they would—they won't just admit that "I hate the guy's politics so

I'm glad he got fired." They always have to create a rationale that makes their support of the university sound high-minded or ethical. And so, they go to the process and say that the hiring process was corrupt, the American Indian Studies program did it all wrong, they needed more responsible oversight, blah blah blah blah blah. Whereas if you think about how those narratives play in a broader context of U.S. history vis-à-vis Native peoples, it's actually a precise reproduction of the notion that Natives cannot govern their own affairs and therefore need to always exist under the aegis of a greater, more responsible authority, i.e., the U.S. federal government. So, it's almost like a metaphor for American Indian policy except it's not actually metaphorical. People are actually raising the argument that American Indian Studies, unlike any other department on campus, cannot conduct its own affairs and needs the special intervention of administrative bodies.

KC: Yeah, it's really interesting to hear you put it like that, and I hope people are listening closely to that. We only have about five minutes left here talking with Steven Salaita. I think we'd be remiss not to address in part something that you spend a bit of time addressing in your book, which is the question of anti-Semitism. So, the charge of incivility and also anti-Semitism. In your book you take a chance to respond to some of the tweets under question, the controversial tweets. And you write about your Twitter feed in general, quote: "Judge that feed as you wish. If you're being honest, however, you cannot judge it as violent or anti-Semitic (unless you define anti-Semitism as criticism of the Israeli state)."[11] Will you talk a bit about Twitter as a medium as you understand it and also what you meant by some of those controversial tweets?

SS: I would be happy to. I'll try to do it in less than five minutes. Twitter, as you can imagine, is a subject that I'm able to go on and on about. I'll invite people to read the book to—so they can follow along at their own pace without me boring them to death. But, Twitter relies in so many ways on shared sets of assumptions, intellectual assumptions or moral assumptions or geopolitical assumptions in some cases. And so, when I'm criticizing the ways in which anti-Semitism is used as a rhetorical device, then I have some expectation—in my mind a reasonable expectation—that people who are interested in my feed will have at least a basic understanding of that particular approach. It's very easy to decontextualize somebody's words on Twitter. It's very easy to woefully misread another person, and I would remind listeners—and I think this is an interesting point that often gets overlooked—that my Twitter feed has been monitored, closely monitored, as in every single tweet was being cached and stored, well before the incident in question.

And so, looking to interpret my tweets in the worst possible light in order to justify some sort of recrimination against me. But, it's very difficult in a context of 140 characters, or really in a context of a lot of social media, to raise a principled critique of state power, colonial violence, that doesn't offend or upset defenders of state or colonial violence. I don't know if I'm making any sense. So, it's almost inherent to the genre that people are going to get upset and argue. Because it's sort of designed in such a way that if you don't have the ability to articulate a long set of assumptions and present a long list of evidence to support your claims, that you very often end up unwittingly talking into an echo chamber.

KC: It's almost—it almost demands a kind of polemical engagement, I think is how I think of it.

SS: Of course, yeah. And I think a lot of users of Twitter, if they're being honest, would—those who are regulars on the platform would kind of roll their eyes about the charge of incivility and inappropriate language because Twitter is often just a cesspool of very harsh arguments [*laughing*]. I'm actually kind of on the nice end of Twitter when it comes down to it, and I think most people who use it regularly would recognize that the kinds of arguments that happen there tend to be very, very intense and unpleasant.

KC: Well, and that's helpful to respond to a question I was going to pose is, to play devil's advocate a bit, which is: if Twitter doesn't allow for a kind of contextualization, should you not use Twitter to engage in these complex issues? But I think you sort of answered that there, I don't know if you want to say a bit more?

SS: You know, yes and no. I think in the end, like anything else, it's a personal choice. I find value in the platform, I find enjoyment in the platform, but it's certainly not necessary, there are all kinds of other useful ways to get your message out. It's important also not to confuse Twitter with an act of scholarship because we're giving over a certain amount of inordinate power, once again, if only unwittingly, to administrators when we say "Oh, you know, tweets ought to count in terms of how we're evaluated as scholars." No, until administrators start counting our tweets as part of our dossiers for merit reasons and tenure et cetera, then it shouldn't count. We should see it as something extramural, something as distinct from the scholarly work that we do. And Twitter provides us an opportunity to raise arguments in a polemical way that we don't necessarily have the opportunity to do in a peer-reviewed article.

KC: Mhm, mhm. Absolutely. Well, and I hate to end this conversation here, I'd like to go on for another hour, but we're going to have to end it there. Steven Salaita, thank you so much for being here today.

SS: Oh, it's been my honor, thank you for having me.

KC: Again, our guest today has been Steven Salaita, author of the new book *Uncivil Rites: Palestine and the Limits of Academic Freedom*, which has just come out from Haymarket Books. Again, that's Steven Salaita, faculty member at the University of Illinois Urbana-Champaign, fired for controversial tweets with regard to Israel's attack on Gaza last summer.

NOTES

1. The final numbers were actually 2,251 Palestinian deaths, which included 1,462 civilians, and of those, 551 were children. "Key Figures on the 2014 Hostilities," United Nations Office for the Coordination of Humanitarian Affairs, June 23, 2015, https://www.ochaopt.org/content/key-figures-2014-hostilities.

2. Robert Mackey, "Professor's Angry Tweets on Gaza Cost him a Job," *New York Times*, September 12, 2014, https://www.nytimes.com/2014/09/13/world/middleeast/professors-angry-tweets-on-gaza-cost-him-a-job.html.

3. Jodi S. Cohen, "U of I Trustees Vote 8–1 to Reject Salaita," *Chicago Tribune*, September 11, 2014, http://www.chicagotribune.com/news/ct-salaitia-board-decision-20140911-story.html.

4. One month after this interview aired, in November 2015, the University of Illinois and Salaita reached a settlement. See Jodi S. Cohen, "University of Illinois OKs $875,000 Settlement to End Steven Salaita Dispute," *Chicago Tribune*, November 12, 2015, https://www.chicagotribune.com/news/local/breaking/ct-steven-salaita-settlement-met-20151112-story.html.

5. Ali Abunimah, "Salaita Firing Lands Univ. of Illinois on AAUP Censure List," *Electronic Intifada*, June 14, 2015, https://electronicintifada.net/blogs/ali-abunimah/salaita-firing-lands-univ-illinois-aaup-censure-list. The university was removed from the censure list in June of 2017. Peter Schmidt, "A Divided AAUP Lifts Censure on U. of Illinois," *Chronicle of Higher Education*, June 17, 2017, https://www.chronicle.com/article/A-Divided-AAUP-Lifts-Censure/240386.

6. Marc Parry, "Organizing to Defend a Professor's Freedom of Speech," *New York Times*, September 28, 2014, https://www.nytimes.com/2014/09/29/us/organizing-to-defend-a-professors-freedom-of-speech.html.

7. Marc Lamont Hill, review of *Uncivil Rites: Palestine and the Limits of Academic Freedom*, by Steven Salaita, in "Reviews," Haymarket Books, accessed June 27, 2018, https://www.haymarketbooks.org/books/792-uncivil-rites.

8. The judge does not explicitly say "this is a firing," but he makes a lot of points about why Salaita was engaged in a contract with the university and the university plausibly breached that employment contract. See *Salaita v. Kennedy et al.*, 15 C 924 (N.D. Ill. 2015), https://ccrjustice.org/sites/default/files/attach/2015/08/59_2015-08-06%20Order%20Granting%20in%20Part%20Denying%20in%20Part%20MTD.pdf.

9. This is correct.

10. Vincent M. Mallozzi, "Mascots in Court, Not on the Court," *New York Times*, March 4, 2007, https://www.nytimes.com/2007/03/04/sports/ncaabasketball/04cheer.html.

11. Steven Salaita, *Uncivil Rites: Palestine and the Limits of Academic Freedom* (Chicago: Haymarket Books, 2015), 9.

NORA BARROWS-FRIEDMAN
"In Our Power," February 25, 2015

https://www.wortfm.org/in-our-power/

KARMA CHÁVEZ: In late 2013, the American Studies Association, an academic organization of roughly five thousand academics, voted overwhelmingly in support of a resolution to endorse and "honor the call of Palestinian civil society for a boycott of Israeli academic institutions." The resolution also indicated that the "ASA supports the protected rights of students and scholars everywhere to engage in research and public speaking about Israel-Palestine and in support of the boycott, divestment, and sanctions (BDS) movement."[1] The ASA was the third academic organization to vote as such, with the Native American and Indigenous Studies Association and the Asian American Studies Association preceding it. A few others like the Critical Ethnic Studies Association have followed, and others have voted in contentious battles.

While academic organizations, led by professors, have only recently begun to move on such resolutions, student organizers, many who are Palestinian American, and many others who are Jewish American, have been organizing for more than a decade to pass divestment resolutions asking their universities to withdraw their investments from corporations that benefit from Israeli occupation and destruction of Palestinian homes. These students have built an incredible national movement, as local chapters of Students for Justice in Palestine have grown on university campuses nationwide. These students have engaged in bold actions, and many have suffered threats to their freedom of speech, have been charged with crimes such as disrupting public events, and have faced immense acts of intimidation by those who oppose them. Still they continue on. The story of such students is told in Nora Barrows-Friedman's new book, *In Our Power: U.S. Students Organize for Justice in Palestine*, from Just World Books, a small independent press.

"Nora Barrows-Friedman is a journalist, staff editor at *The Electronic Intifada*." "She has also contributed to Al-Jazeera English, Inter Press Service,

Truthout.org, *Left Turn* magazine, and various other international media outlets. From 2003–2010, she was the Senior Producer and co-host of *Flashpoints*, an award-winning investigative newsmagazine operating out of KPFA/ Pacifica Radio in Berkeley, California. Nora has been regularly reporting from Palestine since 2004."[2] Samantha Brotman of Jewish Voice for Peace said of *In Our Power* that it leaves "the reader both empowered and informed. Even seasoned activists would do well to read this book, as it is not only a source of inspiration, but it takes on the crucial task of placing the individual within a larger context. *In Our Power* should therefore be required reading for anyone in the world of Palestine activism."[3]

Nora Barrows-Friedman, welcome to *A Public Affair*.

NORA BARROWS-FRIEDMAN: Thank you so much, Karma.

KC: I'm excited to have you here. So, did I get anything wrong in that introduction, Nora?

NBF: That was like the sweetest, longest introduction ever. Thank you, it was great.

KC: I don't know if that's supposed to be a compliment, Nora, if it's the longest ever (*laughing*).

NBF: No, it was great, thank you.

KC: Well, I should say, we encountered each other last November at an event in Chicago and that was right when your book had come out. And so, I had ordered it from Rainbow Bookstore, another local enterprise you should support here in town, and it took a while for it to get in, so I just got it a couple weeks ago and called you immediately to get you on the show. So, I'm very excited to have you here.

NBF: Thank you, I'm excited to be here.

KC: Let's start with a basic question here for you. You've devoted a vast majority of your adult life to this, so why Palestine?

NBF: That's a really good question. Yeah, in 2003 I started interning at KPFA Pacifica radio station in the Bay Area. Actually, my first day of the internship was the day after Rachel Corrie was killed in Gaza trying to defend a Palestinian family's home. She was run over by an Israeli bulldozer, and it was also the day before the U.S. invaded Iraq. So, it was a really intense and heartbreaking week. I just—growing up in Berkeley with a very political background, with my family, it was just this point in time that I just felt we all had to do something. And so, I started working at the radio station, just helping out in whatever capacity I could, and that eventually led to me getting a position as a producer and eventually as a cohost. And especially in 2003, when it was the height of the Palestinian Intifada and also everything that was going on in Iraq and Afghanistan, my colleague Dennis, who's the host of *Flashpoints*, he literally handed me a stack of reports that he had printed out that morning when he got to the office and he said, "Here, you take Palestine, I've got to focus on Iraq." So, I was like, "Okay! Palestine, sure!" And within a few months, I had realized that—everyone has their own issue that they're really passionate about, and Palestine became my issue, and I started going there to report and to work with kids in a refugee camp, to set up a media station there. And then I just started writing for print as well as doing radio broadcasting, and here we are twelve years later. So yeah.

KC: Yeah, it's amazing to think about the sort of serendipitous start to focusing on Palestine. How many times have you travelled to the region?

NBF: Between—I've been there almost twenty times since 2004. I haven't been in a couple years, but that's because I've been focusing on the student solidarity movement in this country, which I think is so important to focus on and to report on. And really looking at the social movements of the past, whether it be the student-led antiapartheid South Africa movement or the student-led free speech movement, here we see another burgeoning and really strong and powerful movement for social justice and human rights that is really facing so many challenges. And yet these students with their immense amount of energy and determination and passion about this issue and about their role and responsibility as Americans, who, as taxpayers and as people who pay tuition to their universities that are invested in companies that do business with Israel, they really have taken on this role of trying to figure out how to be a wedge in that machine and how to make their voices heard. So that's what I've been focusing on the last few years.

KC: So how did you learn about the significance of the student movements?

NBF: Actually, it was always brewing in the background in the reporting that I did. Here in Berkeley, of course, we saw the growth especially of Students for Justice in Palestine at UC Berkeley. And, the activists, the journalists that I was hanging out with and forging these relationships with were getting more and more involved in student solidarity movements, and so whenever there was something happening in Palestine, there would always be a response on campus, really close to where I worked and lived. And so, especially in 2010 when UC Berkeley initiated its first real push for divestment, it really was a moving experience to be there with the students at these five-, ten-hour debates inside the student senate meeting rooms. And hearing just the unbridled passion that these students had—especially the Palestinian students, who were seeing what their tuition dollars were going to fund, to oppress, and to uproot and to ethnically cleanse their family ten thousand miles away. And so that really—I started covering the divestment movements around campus starting in about 2010, and it just kind of grew from there, and 2012 I was approached by Helena Cobban, who's the wonderful publisher of Just World Books, and she said, "You know you've been doing this great reporting, you should really just write a book." And I was like, "There is no way I'm going to write a book, that is way too much work. I've never even thought about writing a book before." And lo and behold two years later, a book was published. So, just because of—I was so moved by these students, I really, it was a pleasure for me to report on their activism no matter how big or small. For the *Electronic Intifada* in my daily work life and then being able to really go around the country, I went to eleven different states and spoke to nearly seventy students from more than thirty different universities. And just to hear their stories and their experiences and really try and investigate who these kids are, who these powerful movement builders are, and why their movement is so important. It was a lot of hard work and also a lot of fun to write.

KC: Well, and you can definitely tell the playfulness of a number of the students and their creativity. And I'm wondering if we could talk about—I was actually very surprised to know how early some of these groups, specifically Students for Justice in Palestine, got started. Will you tell us a little bit about the various groups that work under that name or other names?

NBF: Sure, yeah, so Students for Justice in Palestine, it began on UC Berkeley's campus right after the Second Intifada erupted and around the time when the U.S. was invading Afghanistan. And it was—at the time there were many, many groups on campus all kind of working independently but toward a similar goal of education and advocacy for Palestinian human rights, but there wasn't really like a centralized focus or any sort of organized campaign around the country. That kind of changed just in the past few years actually, when Students for Justice in Palestine chapters all over the country started popping up and students realized that there was a need for kind of a broader coalition. So, they formed National Students for Justice in Palestine, and right now I think there's over 150 different chapters on campuses around the country. There's still a chapter, of course, at UC Berkeley, there's chapters all up and down the West Coast and in the Midwest and on the East Coast. And also, coalitions within that broader umbrella of SJP National have popped up, so we have SJP West, which is, you know, West Coast SJP chapters, there's an SJP Midwest, there's SJP Chicago, even, which has a bunch of different chapters because Chicago has so many different universities. And so, students are really—it's become this really important way, not just to solidify the coalition, but also to provide each other with advice and working on strategic campaigns and letting each other know, "Well, this worked for us when we tried to do XYZ during Israeli Apartheid Week," or, "We ran into a lot of opposition when we tried this." Or even organizing for their annual conference, there's a lot of knowledge sharing and a lot of support, especially for the SJP chapters that are new or very scarcely resourced or who only have a few students, it's really been an incredible opportunity for students to support each other and help guide this movement to a bigger and broader space.

KC: That's really exciting to hear about that history and to think about both the local specificity but then how a kind of decentralized national organization was still a big part of this.

NBF: Yeah, absolutely. And this is on top of—I'm not exaggerating—a century of organizing here in this country for Palestinian human rights and for Palestinian solidarity. Primarily the work that was done at the beginning of the last century up until this point has been done by Palestinians, you know people who fled Zionist expansion in Palestine before the state of Israel was established, especially after the Nakba, after 1948, and then another wave of emigration happened after 1967, after military occupation. And so, Palestinians themselves have been very self-organized in this country, acting as kind of diaspora, community organizations and support for members of the community who are still struggling to get their rights of return and the basic human rights that are afforded to everyone else. So, this movement can't be disassociated from the incredible work that Palestinian Americans have done in the last century as well.

KC: Will you introduce us to a couple of the students who you spoke with, who they are, and why they're involved in this work?

NBF: Okay, let's see. So, one of the first students that I actually met on my whirlwind trip to collect as many stories as possible is this incredible woman named Rebecca Pierce. She just graduated from UC Santa Cruz here in the Bay Area, and she had been doing a lot of organizing to get—basically to get basic resources for Students for Justice in Palestine there and also to grow the organization and introduce divestment resolutions on campus. She's been one of the most exceptional voices of morality on this issue that I encountered, and she's incredible, she's a filmmaker, she's a social justice activist. She had to go really head to toe with—actually a woman who is on faculty at UC Santa Cruz who's also the head of this very vicious anti-Palestinian organization called AMCHA, which purports itself to speak for Jewish values, especially on campuses.[4] But actually, it's an organization that really seeks to crush student protest and to crush the Palestine solidarity movement on campuses and to really turn it into—she's trying to make it look like students who advocate for Palestinian human rights are anti-Semites, which is a very disturbing trend that's actually expanding across this country. When Israel advocacy organizations can't debate the facts about what Israel's policies do to Palestinians and the entire racist, ethnocentric, supremacist apartheid regime that it actually is, they resort to slander and demonization of the entire movement and trying to conflate criticism of Israeli policies with anti-Semitism, which is absurd and outrageous. And as you mentioned at the beginning, there's so many Jewish members of Students for Justice in Palestine and so many anti-Zionist Jewish advocates for Palestinian rights. You know, criticism of Israeli policy has nothing to do with hatred of Jews, it's patently absurd and false. And so, Rebecca has been a tireless advocate of speaking out as a Jewish woman, as a Black woman who is obviously taking on this absurd conflation by these outside political organization. She's one of the most determined, powerful, and passionate activists that I met.

There's also—gosh, there's so many activists I could talk about. I spoke with a graduate student at Portland State University, his name is Wael Elasady, and he's a Palestinian refugee, born in Syria and then moved to the U.S. He had never been to Palestine, his grandfather was born there, and he decided finally to go. He was really involved in antiwar organizing in the States but had never really been involved in Palestine organizing. But went to Palestine, actually visited the house his grandfather had been born in and was expelled from and is now being settled by an Israeli person there. And he went, and he visited that house, and his grandfather had drawn him a map of that village—he hadn't been there for sixty, seventy years, but his grandfather knew precisely the roads and the houses and the trees, and he was able to visit that, and after he came back he ended up starting a Palestine solidarity organization on campus called SUPER, Students United for Palestine Equal Rights, and although it's not called SJP, it's under the umbrella of the SJP national coalition, and he's been one of the most instrumental activists especially in the Pacific Northwest fighting for Palestine equal rights and the rights of students to organize on campus. So, I mean, there's almost seventy students, I could rattle off a lot about all of them, but that's just a tiny taste.

KC: Sure. And, I mean, the kind of interviews you did—one of the things I really appreciated about this book is that you have interviews interwoven with the chapters where you're explaining context about what has happened. And in *those* chapters, you get introduced to many more, I mean there's only a handful of the students you're actually able to profile in the interviews, but

I think you maybe hear from all seventy throughout the chapters, is that true?

NBF: Yeah, I did try to get everybody in who I interviewed, whether it's a full two-page Q & A or whether it's a two-sentence bit here and there. Yeah, I wanted—these students spent time out of their day of studying and organizing to speak with me, so I wanted to honor them as best that I could in the short book format that I had. So yeah, I tried to get everyone in.

KC: Which is no small feat with that number of interviews.

NBF: Right. It was a lot of late-night transcribing, I got really good at typing quickly.

KC: Yeah, I've been there, fully understand that. I wanted to talk a little bit about—so you already talked about this earlier, but I wanted you to expand on this. One of your chapters talks about the campus as a battleground, and I think you've kind of pointed to this, but I'm wondering if you could elaborate on why that metaphor of battleground seems to be appropriate.

NBF: Yeah, actually that was a word I believe was used by one of the main Israel advocacy organizations in talking about "the campus is a battleground for these ideological conflicts" or whatever, where they've identified this movement led by students as a very dangerous movement that could influence other communities on campus to sympathize with the Palestinian plight. And so there has been millions of dollars poured in by agencies affiliated with the Israeli government to try and crush student movements for Palestine solidarity on campuses across the country. So, these massive Israel lobby organizations like the Anti-Defamation League and AIPAC and the Zionist Organization of America, and then these kind of affiliated agencies like Stand With Us, which is an organization solely devoted to discrediting student activism on campus in Palestine issues, they actually take money from the Israel government.[5] So, we have these massive organizations with unlimited amounts of money against these student groups on campus that are incredibly underfunded. In fact, I was just speaking with a student today at a university on the East Coast who said that the administration has continuously attempted to block them from getting funds to hold events and for things like postering and flyering—things that student organizations usually have access to. It is an epidemic around the country that Palestine solidarity groups on campuses are being singled out for special treatment by the administrations which are under pressure by these outside political organizations to underfund or to put roadblocks in front of student organizing campaigns. And these organizations come to the administration saying that they're very concerned about Jewish students on campus, that they'll be discriminated against, that criticism of Israeli policy is equal to anti-Semitism. All of these fabrications that are meant to intimidate the administrations into really singling out these student organizations.

So, student organizations around the country literally have to hold bake sales and these very modest fundraisers just to get the resources that other student groups enjoy without any restrictions. And this is really, this points to the level of panic that these Israel lobby organizations, these massive agencies, are coming down to college campuses and trying to intimidate students and student government leaders and the administrations into crushing student protest precisely because they know that once students understand what's happening in Palestine, once these education campaigns keep going and these student groups ally with other communities on campus who are marginalized, who represent marginalized communities, that there is so much—there's a groundswell of support for Palestine solidarity and that frightens them. So, they're trying as desperately as they can to stop it in its tracks, even if that means censorship and violation of free speech and First Amendment rights for these student groups.

KC: Have some of the students who are involved in the Palestinian solidarity movement—have they talked directly with Jewish students who say that they feel threatened by some of the actions, or is there any conversation among those groups?

NBF: Yeah, it's different on every campus. Again, there are so many Jewish students involved with Students for Justice in Palestine chapters that the whole insinuation that Students for Justice in Palestine discriminates against Jewish students or seeks to harm Jewish students on campus is completely absurd and should be disregarded outright because it's false. There's nothing in Palestine solidarity student organizing that has anything to do with hatred of the Jewish people or anything. It's patently false, all these accusations. And there have been students who are groomed by these outside political organizations who are told that they will be harassed for being Jewish on campus if a divestment resolution passes in the student senate, who say that they will face threats and bigotry. Which is, again, it's absurd, but there's—these students, the Palestine solidarity students are very quick to portray this as what it is. It's a student movement for human rights, it has nothing to do with discrimination against any group, and the fact that Zionism is being conflated with Judaism is a real tragedy, and it's a problem. A political ideology based upon an idea that one group is supreme against another is what people are fighting. The students on campus are fighting for equal rights, are fighting for human rights, are fighting for the right to be recognized, and the right for self-determination, and that has nothing to do with anybody's religion. So, you know, it's different on every campus, but we do see this trend of these tropes repeating themselves over and over again trying to conflate criticism of Israeli policy with criticism of the Jewish people, and that's patently false.

KC: I guess in the last few minutes that we have here, I wanted to talk about questions of coalition and solidarity. Because it was really inspiring to see how students are building cross-movement coalitions. So, I was wondering if you could talk about who the students who are doing Palestinian solidarity work are building connections with and on what bases are they building those connections?

NBF: Yeah, well as I mentioned, these Israel-aligned organizations are increasingly panicked about the solidarity and building of bridges between different marginalized communities, including the Palestinian community on campuses. And just in the past few months, we saw Students for Justice in Palestine activists organizing alongside Black Lives Matter activists in Ferguson, Missouri, talking about the connections between state-sponsored violence on both communities. And also, the literal connections, I mean Ferguson police officers have gone to Israel to train with Israeli police.[6] And of course, we see weapon sharing, there are tear gas canisters that are made in the U.S. that are used on nonviolent protestors in the occupied West Bank. And so that's one connection that's being made currently, there's also—I talked to a bunch of students in the border states, in New Mexico and Arizona, who are organizing alongside student groups which work with undocumented persons along the border, with indigenous communities, with communities that are fighting against the militarization of the border and the enormous deportation policies that this administration has enacted. And so, we see Students for Justice in Palestine members locking themselves down to buses that deport—that transport persons who are going to be deported by the Obama administration. So that's a huge kind of cross-movement solidarity building that's happening.

We also see students from all different backgrounds—South Asian communities, East Asian communities, African communities, Jewish communities, LGBT communities on campus who are all noticing these similarities between the oppression of marginalized peoples from all over the world and from all different social, economic, gender backgrounds who are fighting also for equality and recognition and human rights. And so those—so when you see divestment resolutions being heard at the student senate level on campuses across the country, those resolutions are not just supported and brought forth by Palestine solidarity organizations, but they're supported by thirty, forty, fifty different allied student groups on campus who all support this notion of pulling tuition funds from companies that do business with an apartheid military occupation. And that's what's—another thing that's really beautiful about this movement is that students are making these connections themselves, they're understanding intrinsically that in order to fight for human rights for one group, you have to fight for human rights for every group. And it's a beautiful, very moving understanding of intersectionality, and these students are expressing that and embodying it and expressing it in their activism.

KC: And related to that, I thought one of the things that was really great about the way you ended the book was talking about the very nuanced ways that these students define solidarity as a practice. And so, you sort of touched on it there, but will you elaborate on that?

NBF: Yeah, it is very nuanced, it's very different for every student that I interviewed, but they said that solidarity isn't just words on paper, it's how you act in your everyday life and how you think about the world and how you ally yourself with different people and with different groups of people and different communities. Solidarity for some students I spoke with—especially those who are Palestinian American, solidarity is being an exile, is fighting for the rights of their family members ten thousand miles away. For some of the Jewish students, solidarity is listening to what Palestinians have to say, to recognize their history, to recognize their exile based on the fact that they're not Jews and what it means to be a person of privilege as a Jewish person, as a white person in this country when you're doing activism work and taking a back seat and listening to the voices that are leading, and not trying to lead, yourself. So, it's really—they are, they're really nuanced and very intimate and emotional these definitions. And I think that's a conversation that continues to happen in these student circles, there's a lot of discussion about privilege and about solidarity and about what it means to be a person in your own skin and in this country, which is heavily discriminatory and racialized and very, very privileging of one group over another. It's pretty incredible to see these discussions happening.

KC: And I have to say, as a scholar who teaches about social movement and about coalition and about activism, I thought it was really wonderful to read that, and it's something I can't wait to share with students in future classes. We only have about a minute left here, Nora, I'm wondering if you could say just a bit about—if people are listening today and they're inspired by the work that these students are doing, what are the ways you would recommend supporting these students?

NBF: That's a great question. Well, you can learn more at the National Students for Justice in Palestine, and I think it's sjpnational.org. If you're living in a city, there's a good chance that there's a university nearby, and there's also a good chance that there's a Palestine solidarity organization on that campus, so I'd encourage people to just get to know these students, to attend Israeli Apartheid Week, which is an annual week of events dedicated to educating campus communities about the situation in Palestine. And they need support from the community, as well. Their actions don't exist in a bubble as much as the opposition would like people to believe. This is a general human rights issue; this issue affects everybody as Americans, as taxpayers, and as people who support human rights.

KC: Well, we're going to have to end it there today. Nora Barrows-Friedman, thank you so much for being here today.

NBF: Thank you so much, Karma.

NOTES

1. American Studies Association, "Boycott of Israeli Academic Institutions" (resolution), December 4, 2013, https://www.theasa.net/about/advocacy/resolutions-actions/resolutions/boycott-israeli-academic-institutions.

2. "About," Nora Barrows Friedman, https://norabarrowsfriedman.com/about/.

3. Samantha Brotman, review of *In Our Power–U.S. Students Organize for Justice in Palestine*, by Nora Barrows Friedman, *Mondoweiss*, January 7, 2015, http://mondoweiss.net/2015/01/students-organize-palestine/.

4. See https://amchainitiative.org.

5. The organizations mentioned can be found at the following URLs: https://www.adl.org; https://www.aipac.org; https://zoa.org; and https://www.standwithus.com.

6. Rania Khalek, "Israel-Trained Police 'Occupy' Missouri After Killing of Black Youth," *Electronic Intifada*, August 15, 2014, https://electronicintifada.net/blogs/rania-khalek/israel-trained-police-occupy-missouri-after-killing-black-youth.

SARAH SCHULMAN
"Israel/Palestine and the Queer International," August 28, 2013

https://www.wortfm.org/israelpalestine-and-the-queer-international/

KARMA CHÁVEZ: The Israeli occupation of Palestine is one of the most important international crises of our times. A sensitive subject, to put it mildly. And one that has a complex history that most in the U.S., even the most educated, often misunderstand. A desire to take very seriously the devastation of the Nazi genocide, fears of anti-Semitism, Zionism, and Christian beliefs about end times, enduring racist perspectives about the Palestinian people, and a host of other intertwined factors feed into U.S. foreign policy toward Israel and Palestine, and many U.S. Americans' beliefs about the rightness of this occupation.

The occupation is a concern that crosscuts identity categories, but one of the most vocal groups against the occupation has been LGBT or queer activists. Over the past several years, Palestinian activists and their allies in places like Israel, the U.S., and Europe have called attention to what they describe as a unique way that the Israeli state promotes itself as tolerant, modern, and progressive even as it continues its brutal occupation and starvation policies and builds more settlements on Palestinian land. According to these activists, Israel has attempted to shine its image and justify its actions through positioning itself as safe and accepting of gays and lesbians, a practice deemed *pinkwashing.*[1] Israel is not alone, of course, but its use of gay rights as a public-relations strategy of sorts has far-reaching implications. The queer response, too, has significant implications for thinking about the content and contexts of politics.

Someone who has written extensively about the queer critique of Israel and Palestine is author and activist Sarah Schulman. Schulman is a Distinguished Professor of the Humanities at the City University of New York, College of Staten Island, and a Fellow at the New York Institute for the Humanities at New York University. She is one of the most well-known lesbian authors in the United States, who has written dozens of novels, plays, and works of nonfiction, including American Library Association Stonewall Book Award Winners *After Delores* (1988) and *Stage Struck: Theatre, AIDS, and the Marketing of Gay America* (1998), and other well-received works such as *Empathy* (1992), *Ties That Bind: Familial Homophobia and Its Consequences* (2009), and *The Mere Future* (2009). In 2012, Schulman published two works of nonfiction: a memoir, *The Gentrification of the Mind: Witness to a Lost Imagination*, and *Israel/Palestine and the Queer International*, which will be the subject of our conversation today. She has also been nominated for Lambda Literary Awards two dozen times, as well as been a recipient of a Guggenheim Fellowship and several New York Foundation for the Arts Fellowships.

Beyond her work as teacher and author, Schulman has been a fierce activist for lesbian writers and against the sexism and homophobia that permeate the literary world. Additionally, she was a member of ACT UP New York, and is currently working along with Jim Hubbard on the ACT UP Oral History Project to document the history of the important movement. She was also a founder of the Lesbian Avengers. Not sure how there are enough hours in the day for all of that. Welcome, Sarah, to *A Public Affair*.

SARAH SCHULMAN: Hi, thank you so much.

KC: It's great to have you here. And you've done a lot, did I get all of that right, or did I miss anything you want to make sure listeners know about you?

SS: That's okay, yeah that's fine.

KC: Good. Well, so I thought, before we get started on issues of Israel and Palestine, maybe we could talk a bit about your history in activism, as I think that informs the present day. So, you got involved with AIDS activism very early on, would you talk about that and your involvement early on?

SS: Well, I think it started way before that. You know, I come from a secular Jewish family in New York. I was raised by a refugee grandmother in the house, and her brothers and sisters had been exterminated in the Holocaust, so I grew up in a very politicized environment, and I was born in 1958, so my childhood was witnessing the '60s, and I think I've been involved politically ever since the beginning. So, primarily my work originally was on behalf of constituencies that I belonged to. I was involved in the reproductive rights movement, the women's movement, the lesbian movement, and AIDS activism. When I got, finally, involved in Israel-Palestine it was the first time I ever did solidarity work. And that was a very, very big shift. But I did start covering the AIDS crisis in the early 1980s because I was a reporter for a gay newspaper when AIDS began. So that gave me a sort of frontline seat. I covered issues like the closing of the bathhouses, the lack of testing of experimental drugs on women, pediatric AIDS, all of those really early social issues. And I just stayed in it ever since.

KC: And so, you're—I think it's interesting, you frame the AIDS activism not as solidarity work, because I think a lot of women in particular do frame it in terms of solidarity. Can you say a bit about that?

SS: Yeah, I didn't experience it that way. I mean, one thing is that prior to AIDS I had been involved in the abortion rights movement. And that was sort of the end of the traditional feminist movement. It was women's organizations of gay and straight women together, and I experienced the lesbian purge in the early '80s, and that was really at the end of that whole era. So, the next political commitment that I made was to ACT UP, and I came into it as a person who'd been in the gay community for a long time, still smarting from the homophobia of the straight women I had worked with and knowing that that would never be an issue. So, I came into it in a place of comfort.

KC: Yeah, that makes sense. And I guess that's really reflected in your book *Gentrification of the Mind*. Which, I have to say, I read it last December for the first time, and when I opened it up, I literally didn't put it down for the entire day.

SS: Oh, thank you.

KC: Cover to cover in one day, which, as my partner will tell you, is completely rare for me. But a very good read, and in that book, you talk about gentrification both literally, as in the coincidence—I guess coincidence is kind of the wrong word—but the coinciding of New York City's gentrification policies and promotion of real estate development at the exact same time as AIDS was ravaging communities. And people's apartments were open because they were dead, and the impact that has had on AIDS and AIDS activists. So, you talk about gentrification in the sort of literal sense, as you experienced. But you also talk about it more metaphorically, as in how it impacted the possibilities for queer cultural production, for example, but also how it's led to assimilationist politics. I'm wondering if you could talk about your project there and how that's led us to contemporary LGBT or queer politics.

SS: Well, it's a long story, but let me brief. I think it starts with World War II and the GI Bill. And the GI Bill was a way for the U.S. government to hand money to developers, to suburban developers, through the venue of veterans. So, they gave veterans very, very low interest loans so they could buy homes. But these newly developed suburbs were racist, so the only people who could move into them were whites or ethnic whites. So that's when you see this huge movement of urban whites out of the cities and into these newly developed suburbs, and this was called White Flight. And they were moving from urbanity, which is about the mix and difference of people into this new phenomenon which was American suburbs, which were highly stratified racially and had very conservative politics about sexuality and gender, and people were living in privatized houses, and there was car culture, and it was really the opposite of the city. So, then you have the open urban environment of White Flight in which rents are extremely low, people could get an apartment—they could get three months' rent for signing a lease, because there were empty apartments. And this is the period where you see great revolutionary movements coming out of cities. The Black Power movement, the women's movement, the gay liberation movement, these were not products of the suburbs. These were products of urbanity, of open space, and of people mixing and sharing radical ideas.

So then, in the '70s, you have this idea—and I'm talking about New York City—that it's gone broke. And the argument was made that it was because there were not enough rich people and there wasn't enough of the tax base to support the city. And this was the justification for gentrification, which was basically corporate welfare, it was tax money that was given to luxury developers to transform urban housing into high-end rentals and condos so as to attract the children of White Flight, the people who had grown up in this racial stratification, but had a sentimental attachment to the city because their parents had grown up there, or their grandparents lived there, or they would take the commuter train in and smoke pot, or, that kind of thing. And you see those people moving back. Now, this is the first time that you've ever had a massive influx of suburbanized culture—which had never existed before—into an urban environment. So, you're bringing in privatized white culture, which is what I call the "gated community mentality." It's a mentality of fear, it's a mentality that's willing to trade freedom for security, and it's a mentality that's been raised in homogeneity. And we have a significant policy to bring those people into the city and to replace the mix, the low-income people, the kinds of neighborhoods that were very dynamic and had produced these revolutionary political movements.

Now right in the middle of that is the AIDS crisis, starts in 1981. And if you look today at New York City, you can see that the most gentrified neighborhoods are the ones that had the highest rates of AIDS deaths. And the same is true nationally, the two most gentrified cities in America are New York and San Francisco. Because you had this very high number of deaths taking place in key neighborhoods in a very short period of time, and these apartments going to market rate. And you also have to remember that at that time there were no partner rights or anything like that. So, if a leaseholder died of AIDS, the other person living with them could not inherit the apartment. So, every time a leaseholder died of AIDS, the apartment went to market rate. And you start to see apartments that were $200 going to $1200, and this sort of turn over. Now, there's a cultural consequence to this. Because the kinds of people who can now move in and replace the dead are a very different kind of person. Because they have to be the kind of person who can survive in a high rental economy, who can get access to the money that's needed to get those very same apartments at six times the rate. So here you have people who are from wealthier backgrounds or have better relationships with institutions, are more likely to be able to earn well, or have family money behind them. They're not oppositional people, they're not refugees from sexual oppression who come to the city to be artists or to have sex or to escape religion. It's a totally different kind of person who thinks differently. And of course, they're racially homogenous. And then when you have this now for decades it undermines urbanity. Because cities produce new ideas because people who are different are living together in front of each other. So, the idea that people are different is an idea that can't be rejected. If you're living in a privatized house, you don't hear what's going on with your next-door neighbor. You spend your life in an apartment building, you go through cycles of people, and you understand that people have troubles and people have changes. There's a recognition of difference. Once you eliminate that, and people are coming in from a similar class and racial background, cities can no longer produce new ideas for the world like they were once able to. Because urbanity has been undermined.

KC: Well, and particularly with AIDS and the devastation of the queer community, the impact that you write about so starkly I think is the impact then on queer art and queer politics.

SS: Oh yeah, well those are both really fascinating subjects. Queer politics—I mean before AIDS we had the gay liberation movement, [and that term] was chosen because the movement conceptualized itself as being part of all the other liberation movements that were going on in the world in the 1960s, which were movements against imperialism and against colonialism. So, the goals of the gay liberation movement were to have the kind of social transformation where how people were sexually or in terms of gender, or how people bonded or made any kind of relationship, was available to all different kinds of people. It wasn't enforced by the state, and it wasn't promoted by the state. It was a much more open concept.

AIDS changed that because AIDS created enormous visibility for gay people. You couldn't hide that hundreds of thousands of people were dying.

Some of them were famous, some of them were walking down the street with Wasting Syndrome and KS [Kaposi's Sarcoma] and dementia. It couldn't be hidden. So, when the media had to acknowledge that gay people existed, what they looked and found were extremely radical movements, like ACT UP, for example, the AIDS Coalition to Unleash Power. They found movements of people who were willing to interrupt mass at St. Patrick's Cathedral with seven thousand people. And this was not the kind of thing that they could comfortably contain. So, you start to see the mass media creating its own kind of fake public homosexuality. They start to develop spokespeople who they're comfortable with who have no history in the grassroots community. And no credibility in the grassroots community. And you also start to see that advertising companies and marketing companies who had started niche marketing to people with AIDS to sell them medications now were developing ways to niche market to gay people. And they start to turn the gay community from a political movement into a group of consumers to be niche marketed to. In fact, one of the early marketing firms noted that gay people were the most brand loyal consumers in America. Because they had been abandoned by their families, they had been abandoned by the government, they had a mass death experience, but Absolut Vodka wanted them. So, this kind of emotional relationship as a consumer was developing. You start to see the advent of the transformation of gay liberation to gay rights being promoted by the kinds of people that were allowed in the media and by the cooptation of the Democratic party of certain sectors of the gay community. Now that's what's happening politically.

Artistically, you have across the board a professionalization of the arts taking place. So that—it used to be if you wanted to be a writer, you would move to New York, and you would write, and you would meet other writers, and you'd go hear writers, and you would read. And each artist would have an eclectic accumulation of influences and ideas in which they would produce individual voices. And there was nothing that was policing that. I mean there was the publishing industry of course, which was much more open at the time, but because of the economy, there was a lot more flexibility there. But with this gentrification and these containment processes, you start to see the professionalization of the arts, where this concept of the independent artist is removed and replaced by people who have to get MFA degrees. Which now, if you want to be able to earn a living as an artist and you want to teach, you have to have an MFA to be able to get a teaching job. And also, the MFAs are these—they're kind of like, I call them the Crips and the Bloods of the art world. The school that you go to becomes your brand. And the other people who share that brand, they identify with you and they promote you. So that you have this group identity. And of course, in order to get an MFA, number one you have to be admitted, but number two you have to be able to pay for it. They're extremely expensive. You have to be able to put the time into it, and you have to be able to finesse the homogenizing process of the program. So instead of being an artist out in the world who's reading eclectically, you're in a selected group of people who are similar to you and who are reading the same books together, who are listening to the same people together. And it produces what Chomsky calls "manufactured consent."[2] So, you now have this homogenized voice in the arts that's not only got access to all the goodies and the apparatuses of the arts but become the teachers and carry on the same value system. We have both of these things operating at the same time, and it's very hard for original work to be seen in that kind of environment.

KC: I wanted to pick up on this theme here, Sarah, of homogeneity and the notion of manufacturing consent. Because to me this is one of the big links between how someone like you goes from doing this work that you've done for your whole life into being an advocate around the issue of Israel and Palestine. So, I'm wondering if you could talk about the awakening you've had in relation to Israel-Palestine and then what led to the writing of your book *Israel/Palestine and the Queer International.*

SS: Okay, well let me just say really honestly that I came to this extremely late. I mean, I grew up in New York City, I come from a Holocaust family. I was not raised as a quote "Zionist" because our conception of Zionist was a person who actually moved to Israel. So that was the operative term that I was raised with. And I just never—I have a lot of relatives there—I just never did the moral and ethical work that was required to reexamine what I had been raised with as a child. I was raised with the idea that the land was empty, that everybody hates the Jews, that—the 1967 war, my father woke us up in the middle of the night, he was terrified, and he was like, "Kids, there's a war in Israel." And because I was born in 1958, which is thirteen years after the end of the Holocaust, which is not a very long time, those kinds of concepts are very terrifying to us. And we didn't—I didn't make the transition, because Jews had been the most oppressed people in the world. And then a few years later had a nation-state apparatus that allowed them to oppress other people. This happened within a matter of months. And it's very, very hard, emotionally, to make the transition, when you have either a group trauma identity or an individual trauma identity, to the fact that that's in the past. Of course, it does resonate with you, and you carry it all your life. But you also have to have responsible recognition of who you are in the present. And that was a process that I hadn't gone through, so I was one of these highly aware, highly active people who just had never done anything in relation to Israel and Palestine. And I am—I have to say honestly—I'm embarrassed and ashamed that that is true, but it is true.

Now in 2009 I published a book called *Ties that Bind: Familial Homophobia and Its Consequences*, which I believe is still the only major book analyzing homophobia in the family, which is sort of amazing since it's probably the most common experience of queer people around the world. But at any rate, as a consequence of that book, I was invited to give the keynote address at the Tel Aviv Lesbian and Gay Studies Conference. And I had been to Israel once because I wanted to see if I had any gay relatives. And I saw my relatives, and I didn't. And that was it, I didn't connect with it really in any way. This was years, years, years before. And I had no relationship to Israel, but I wanted to go because of homophobia in the Jewish family of course is very important to me and I wanted to have this conversation. And then a Jewish colleague of mine said, "You know, there's a boycott." I said, "What boycott?" She's like, "Well, at least find out about it." And I said, "Okay, I'll find out about it." So, I emailed people, including Judith Butler because I had heard her give a talk on Israel-Palestine a few years earlier that had made a big impact on me, it had been about the Palestinian right of return, and it was the first time I had ever heard that concept. So, I wrote to her, and she put me in touch with a bunch of queer Jewish academics. See, looking back on it now, I see that I only—I tried to solve the problem Jewishly, I only went to Jews. I didn't even know that I was doing that because that was my training.

But the ones—I chose the wrong ones because the ones I chose all led me to the understanding that there was a boycott that had been called in 2005 by Palestinians asking internationals, like myself, to not normalize the occupation by participating with Israeli state-funded institutions. And that includes universities, which are all government funded. And that included Tel Aviv University. So, through my conversations with a bunch of queer Jewish academics who were part of a movement called Boycott from Within, and with Butler, it became very clear to me that I could not accept the invitation. So, I declined publicly. Now at this point, through the help of some activists in Toronto, particularly Elle Flanders and John Grayson, who's currently in Cairo right now, I realized that sitting home wouldn't do anything and that I should go on what was called a solidarity visit. So, they helped me, and some Israeli leftists helped me set up a trip where I would speak in antioccupation venues in Israel. Because boycott doesn't mean don't go, and it doesn't mean don't communicate. It just means don't normalize state-funded institutions.

So, I went, and I spoke in a couple of antioccupation venues. Now, in the meantime I had made a public statement declining the invitation, and I received an email from Omar Barghouti from Ramallah in the West Bank, from an organization called PACBI, the Palestine Academic and Cultural Boycott of Israel. And it was like, "Dear Professor Schulman, thank you for your principled stance," and all of a sudden, I thought, "I wonder what he thinks about queers." Because of course in the U.S. left there's this history of supporting regimes like Cuba that were viciously oppressing gay people at the time. And, you know, I had never met a Palestinian queer, I had never seen sign of one, I didn't know that there were any organizations, but I knew somehow, they were there. And I didn't want to be involved with anything that would jeopardize them. So, through the people in Toronto, it was arranged that I would go to Ramallah and meet with Omar, and we would discuss queer politics.

So, I went to Israel, and I spoke at an anarchist vegan café, and I had about sixty people, including the organizers of the conference. So, I really did manage to communicate with people. And then I spoke at the Haifa Women's Center, which is a really cool space, and one of the groups that meets there is Aswat, which is Palestinian queer women. It's the Palestinian lesbian organization and queer women organization. And they had like forty people at my talk. So, this is my first exposure to the Palestinian queer movement. Now, through them and through Toronto, I made contact with a group called Al Qaws, which is the LGBT group that's in the West Bank as well as in Israel. So, what's interesting about Al Qaws is—first of all their leader, Haneen Maikey, is one of the most effective grassroots political leaders I've ever met in my life, and I've met many—it's the only Palestinian organization that exists on both sides of the wall. Because you know the wall affects the way people imagine. But because she's a great leader and because queer people think of themselves diasporically, and also because she comes from a village and doesn't come from one of the fixed ruling families of Palestine, she's been able to conceptualize this group in such a way that it transcends the wall.

So, I went to the West Bank, and the first stop was I went to Bi'ilin, which is the village that's in the movie *Five Broken Cameras*,[3] if you've seen that. And I went to a demonstration there. This is one of these villages where the Israeli wall of separation is between people's homes and their olive trees. And they have a demonstration every Friday. So, I went to this demonstration, and I have to say that 80 percent of the Israelis there were queer, interestingly. It's the people of the town, it's about 1,200 people, they march around, they sing, and they have Palestinian flags. And then the Israeli soldiers appear. And they just start shooting tear gas for absolutely no reason, nothing was happening. And the people from the town take these cut onions that they carry in their pockets and smell them to override the smell of the tear gas, which is a neurological tear gas that fools your brain into thinking that you're suffocating. And I'm sitting there, and I'm looking at these Israeli soldiers, and of course they look just like me, it's only my passport that kept me from being them, I have plenty of relatives who ended up in Israel from the Holocaust side of my family. And I just look at them and all of a sudden, I had this moment where I was thinking, "Who is we?" They were just not my "we."

And all my life, not Israelis but Jews, had been a group of people that I—I wouldn't say identified with, but I recognized myself as one of. And, you know, here suddenly—those were not my people, those soldiers. So, it was a really important moment for me. Because when you go there, you experience the occupation, you can't imagine what it's like. It was so much worse than I had imagined in so many ways. It's very important for people to go, there are a lot of delegations, and I really encourage people to go on delegations. Anyway, I got to Ramallah and I met with Al Qaws and I met with a bunch of other activists and they were great, and we had incredible conversations. And I knew that I was going to be meeting with Omar the next day. So, I went and met with him, and it really didn't—the first meeting didn't go well at all. In that, I was uptight, he was uptight, the whole thing was uncomfortable. And I couldn't tell if it was because I'm Jewish and therefore had too much power or because I'm a lesbian and didn't have enough power, I didn't know what the problem was. But at the end of the conversation, I just didn't want to leave on a bad note, so I said, "Omar, what can I do for you?" And he said, "You're creative, you'll think of something." Well, he was right.

So, then I went back to Al Qaws, and Haneen was there and some of the other great people there. And we decided that the important thing was that the queer community in the United States would become exposed to the queer movement in Palestine. And that they start to understand who these people are and what they're doing. So, we decided that I would organize a six-city tour for the leaders of these movements. And by that time there were now three organizations: Aswat, which is the queer women; Al Qaws, which is the LGBT group; and a third group called Palestinian Queers for Boycott, Divestment, and Sanctions, which is based in the West Bank. So, I came back, and I spent a year—I raised $40,000 and I organized a six-city tour, mostly by calling people on the phone who I've known or met along the line of my many, many years in the queer community. So, I organized the tour conceptually so that it would engage different pockets of the community. We started at Creating Change in Minneapolis, then they went to events situated in the Black gay community of Chicago, then they went to the Harvard Kennedy School, then they went to the opposite, the City University, the public university—by the time they got there, the momentum had built on Facebook so dramatically that the place was so packed that we had to turn away 220 people. Because these speakers were really, really effective. They were honest, interesting, complex, human, funny. You know, they just told the truth, and their truth was that they have an integrated politics where they need feminism, gay liberation, and an end to the occupation. And these things can't be separated. And they were very clear about that.

KC: I just want to jump in on that real quick because I wanted to—I think some people will find it interesting that these Palestinian organizations actually organize using the term "queer." And I wanted to read a quotation from Haneen, actually, about that term because I think it's really apropos. She says, "We use queer as a short cut to avoid the LGBT identity-based terms, and to refer and relate to different organizing approaches that focus on sexual and gender oppressions rather than on gay rights or homophobia," she said. "'Queer' was used by Al-Qaws to open to new definitions . . . we constantly work on shaping the term to suit our needs and struggle, and not to eclipse diversity of experience."[4]

SS: Right, exactly. And the discourse there has changed quite a bit since I was there. You know, there's been a lot more involvement of—I mean, let me just say this, by the time they came back from the tour they were contacted by Omar and he had heard really great things about what they had done. Apparently, they had the highest profile speaking tour of any Palestinian that we knew of in U.S. history. So, he started to work with them. And if you look at his website, you'll see that Palestinian Queers for Boycott, Divestment, and Sanctions is listed as a supporting organization, and it's also on the Arabic website, it's not just in English. And in fact, he came to New York, and he and I made a tape on Grit TV, which people can Google, it's Laura Flanders—G-R-I-T-T-V—in which he says that any future vision for Palestine has to include rights for LGBT people.[5] So, within this—Palestine is like any other place, it's a multidimensional society, it has all different kinds of people just like the United States. And there are sectors that have this kind of broad politic and those are the people that I personally am interested in supporting. It doesn't mean that I don't support other people—I think all Palestinians have the right to self-determination and all Palestinians have the right to autonomy just like every human being does. But when you look at which political factions you want to support, those are the people that I'm interested in. And the thing about the boycott for me—and now it's been a few years now that I've been involved in it—it just seems like the most essentially effective nonviolent strategy for change in the Middle East. I am completely open to hearing another strategy or another idea that could be as effective as the boycott, and so far, I haven't. So right now, that's where my affiliation is.

KC: Let's talk about the boycott for a moment though. And, full disclosure, I'm also an endorser of the academic and cultural boycott. But, there are a lot of people, even people on the left, some from various labor organizations, who have said, "The whole point of boycott—it will be ineffective, it won't actually affect the Israeli state, and it might actually hurt Palestinians who don't have access to resources et cetera, as a result of the boycott." Not the academic and cultural, necessarily, but the broader BDS movement. So, what do you say to someone who holds that position?

SS: Well, like I said, Palestine's a multidimensional society. And there's a lot of different factions like in any society, and people have different ideas for strategies. But this is a Palestinian-led strategy. So, if Palestinians are asking internationals to boycott Israeli state-sponsored institutions, it doesn't make sense to say, "No, we're not going to because it'll hurt you." That just doesn't seem viable to me. In terms of it being effective, well the Israeli government is extremely upset about it.[6] I mean they just put in $300 million into fighting the boycott.[7] They have a propaganda apparatus that's unbelievable. I know, because I've been a recipient of some of their stuff. You know, if you are an effective boycott supporter, they smear you and they—there was recently an article that was generated by them, it was called "Sarah Schulman Is A Paranoid Fraud." And it was on a lot of mainstream Jewish websites like *Tablet* and *Commentary* and this kind of thing.[8] The opening article, it claims that I'm a fraud because—exposé—I don't have a PhD.[9] I never said I have a PhD. Because I teach creative writing, so I'm qualified because of all of the books that I've published. But it's like they're looking for anything to smear you. It's highly organized, and also, there are laws inside Israel that make it illegal to support the boycott. So, they're clearly extremely upset about it, and they wouldn't be if it wasn't effective.

KC: So, I wanted to—because we're talking about the boycott and the state of Israel has responded pretty strongly to those who have actively and effectively supported the boycott, such as yourself. And I think one of the ways that that's happened, and this is what you wrote about in 2011 in the piece in the *New York Times* that received a lot of attention, one of the ways that they're aggressively countering this is through pro-gay politics. And I mentioned that a little bit in the front, but I'm wondering if you could expand on pinkwashing.

SS: Yeah, and, you know, around 2000—there's a global index of how popular countries are.[10] And Israel was somewhere between Sudan and Yemen[11] in terms of the estimation of the world. So, at that point they embarked on a remarketing campaign.[12] Saatchi and Saatchi, the prominent advertising firm did, I think, two or three years of pro-bono work.[13] That's millions of dollars of work, for Israel.[14] And they created something called "Brand Israel," that's what the advertisers call it. And it's a campaign to rebrand Israel in the mind of the world to be seen as progressive and culturally cutting edge.[15] So the first thing they did[16] was a photo spread in *Maxim Magazine* called "Girls of the IDF" or women of the Israeli Defense Forces.[17] And it was like sexy Israeli women soldiers in bikinis with guns on top of tanks.[18] And then they surveyed[19] the readers of *Maxim* the next issue and found that their image of Israel had improved.[20] They then started free trips to Israel for food and wine writers and architectural writers.[21] So these people got free trips, and they were wined and dined, and they saw all the beautiful art deco stuff in Tel Aviv, and they wrote these glowing reports.[22]

And what soon started was that in almost any profession you can get a free trip to Israel. I mean, the government is putting huge amounts of money into bringing influential professionals and giving them a very controlled view.[23] And of course there's also birthright, which gives Jews free trips to Israel as well.[24] But they were mostly focused on the demographic[25]—the world's most influential demographic is men ages sixteen to twenty-four. If men ages sixteen to twenty-four believe something, it is fact. So, they were gearing toward that demographic, because of course they have male power and they also have discretionary male income. And, of course, within that group, the ones who have the most discretionary income are gay men, also whom the Israelis see to be having more influence on cutting edge cultural development. So, you start to see low-cost air flights from London and Berlin to Tel Aviv.[26] Quite a bit of money going into gay tourism,[27] money going into Gay Pride in Tel Aviv,[28] and this kind of promotion of gay male culture. They're not pinkwashing to lesbians, it's mostly to men.[29]

Now, what's interesting about this is that there once was a time, very recently, where gay people were at the bottom of every society. And, you know, there's a lot of us who remember that. But that is no longer the case. And increasingly, through the phenomenon of Jasbir Puar's homonationalism,[30] you're seeing that societies with a lot of inequity are now granting gay rights to communities where people who have the dominant race or the dominant religion are now moving into and identifying with kinds of nationalist and supremacy ideologies. So, we're seeing in the Netherlands, for example, where gay people have the same rights as straight people, a lot more gay people moving into anti-immigrant, racist movements aimed primarily at Muslims.[31] You also see that in Britain. The English Defense League, which is a racist anti-immigrant group, has an LGBT column.[32] And so to say that you have Gay Pride, which once meant that you were a progressive society, doesn't mean that anymore. All it means is that you have Gay Pride.

So, this idea that Gay Pride is emblematic of modernity and means that a society is progressive is a sentimental idea from the past. Because the truth is, most secular right-wing movements in the world are no longer anti-gay. Most anti-gay stuff comes from religions. So, you can be quite conservative and quite racist and have gay rights, for people of your racial group. But Israel is making a false equation that Gay Pride means that they are progressive, therefore the occupation becomes irrelevant, or the occupation becomes whitewashed or, as we say, pinkwashed, by the fact that there's a gay enclave in Tel Aviv. But the truth is, there's absolutely no relationship between the fact that there's Gay Pride in Tel Aviv and the occupation. These two things are completely unrelated. They're exploiting not only the hard-won gains of the LGBT community in Israel but also the sentimental historic trauma of gay people who still experience themselves in a place that they may no longer be.

KC: Now, one of the things—I think you put that very clearly, and I think a lot of the people maybe who didn't understand how this operates probably do now or have a great resource in order to do that. But this kind of position—I mean, you know better than almost anyone, there are personal and professional costs. You mentioned earlier Judith Butler, the famous feminist and queer theorist who's also Jewish and who has spoken out extensively about Zionism, about the occupation, and has faced incredibly harsh criticism, as have institutions who have supported her. In fact, she was scheduled to keynote the Homonationalism and Pinkwashing conference that you held last April in New York and decided to step out, as I understand, after facing so many attacks for her work. And you write about a number of the obstacles put up in your way, including being prevented from reading your book *Israel/Palestine and the Queer International* at the LGBT—

SS: At the LGBT Center.

KC: Of all—I mean, queer is in the title, but you couldn't read at the LGBT Center in New York.

SS: Right. It was overturned, though, when 1,400 people signed a petition in forty hours, and I did read it there. But I just want to say that both Judith Butler and I are tenured professors, okay? Nothing can happen to us. The amount of risk, I think, is quite low to tell you the truth. And I'm sort of astounded, when you think of how many tenured professors there are in the United States. Tenured professors are the people with the most job security of anyone in the world, even more than kings and dictators. We're the only people with jobs for life. And the fact that so few are willing to come out forward on these very basic human rights issues is kind of pathetic. So, don't feel bad for us. And even for people—there are, of course, plenty of people in the U.S. who are punished in terms of their ability to earn a living by taking this position. But it's nothing compared to what Palestinians deal with every day. So, you know, getting nasty things written about you or threatening phone calls, or this kind of thing, is nothing compared to living under occupation. And I think we all are pretty clear about that.

KC: Well, and I think that's what's interesting about it, though, right? Is—so, the people who are in positions where—I mean, you have an audience, Judith Butler has an audience, for example. You have a status position, and you have a comfortable permanent job, as you said. And yet you've still had a lot of backlash. I wonder if you would talk a little bit about the chapter that you would've put into your book *Gentrification of the Mind* that was about Israel and Palestine, that you were essentially asked to remove otherwise not have the book published. Could you . . .?

SS: That's correct, I had to remove it. But it did become the new book. So that's, you know, that's how that happened. Oh, there's that—you know, listen, Americans do not understand what's going on with the occupation. They don't understand what it's really like. It's very hard to get good information. To me, I go to *Electronic Intifada* every day online, electronicintifada.com, and that's the best source for information on the occupation. There's the *Guardian* of London. But in terms of U.S. media, it's very hard to get good information. So, people are really under informed, it's a profoundly Islamophobic cultural moment, and Christian supremacist culture, and this cooptation of Jews into the rubric of Judeo-Christian, which is a concept I've never understood. So, there's a lot of obstacles to people understanding what's going on. And so, as a friend of mine says, there are Jews who believe that if the occupation ended tomorrow, they're going to the gas chambers. You know, there's a level of pathology. And this is so interesting because it has to do with the politics of fear—there is this idea, and I don't know if it's a post-Holocaust idea, I don't know where it's rooted—that if you say you're afraid, it doesn't matter what you do to another human being. But that is the ultimate justification for punishing, for using state apparatus, for shunning. Is to say that you're afraid and there's no method for addressing it. It's considered victimization to not fully obey the orders of a person who says they're afraid. This is a new phenomenon. But it's prevalent, and Israel uses it, and a lot of people use it. I think we're starting to see it, for example, with HIV criminalization. That's something that's happening in Canada and some of the United States, where the state is saying, "Hey, if you're negative and you have unprotected sex with someone who's positive and they didn't tell you, you can bring in the state, and you can punish them." You know, there's very much of a punitive move—and this is what happens when you get citizenship. Don't forget, all queer people used to live in illegality. And now some people have citizenship and have legally recognized families and are HIV negative, so they have the protection of the government and others don't. And they become the new queer, who's like the abject object on the outside of these protected systems. That's where we are right now.

KC: Well and I think—I think what you're saying right now, I think really, for people who've been listening to the whole show, they can sort of see how all of this ties together. You know, your queer politics, and how your queer politics have been informed particularly by, most recently, the Palestinian activists with whom you're in alliance. But how it kind of makes sense into this bigger picture of the relevance of queer politics toward issues that in some ways may seem disconnected from queer politics. And even how something like citizenship, which seems benign to a lot of people, is actually wrapped up in these discourses.

SS: Absolutely.

KC: I wonder if—it's been a sort of heavy conversation that we've been having today, I wonder if you might talk about, in the last few minutes we have, some of the positive reactions, both to your book as well as to the work you've done, including hosting that Homonationalism and Pinkwashing conference last April.

SS: Well, I have a very—my life is a life in which I get an enormous amount of positive reinforcement from people who don't have power. I write these books, and so many people interact with me about them and engage with me and care and argue with me, and it makes a difference to them. And it's a really alive and authentic relationship of depth, because it's about—my general subject is supremacy ideology and the issues of shunning and exclusion, and that's what I've been working on all of my life. So, people who are subjected to that really identify with it and care. And people who identify with those systems and need them are very, very hostile. And it's always going to be that way, but I'd rather be on this side of it than the other.

KC: Sure, sure. And as we move into this last couple minutes, what are some of the things that you're working on right now, and where do you see your work going in the next couple of years?

SS: Well, I have a new nov—well, first of all the twenty-fifth anniversary edition of *After Dolores* is coming out in September, that was my bestselling novel from a million years ago. I have a new novel called *The Cosmopolitans* that I've just finished. It takes place in New York in 1968, but I don't have a publisher yet. I'm working on a couple of movies, I'm writing a movie about the communist photographer Tina Modotti for the film director Lynn Hershman [Leeson]. And a couple of other projects with other filmmakers. And I'm about to go to Brazil and give a talk to five thousand people, which I've never done that before. Their topic was the challenge of feminism, and all I can ask myself is, "What is the challenge of feminism?" But anyway, that's what I'm writing today, as a matter of fact.

KC: And, I know the film you put out with Jim Hubbard, *United in Anger*.

SS: Oh yes, Jim and I coproduced a film that he directed, which is a history of ACT UP. We've shown it all over the world: we showed it in Beirut, Abu Dhabi, he took it to Bombay and Brazil, and we are about to take it someplace that I can't tell you yet. But once we do, we will announce it. We had the international premiere in Palestine, it's been a profoundly exciting experience. And I've also collaborated with Cheryl Dunye on two films, *The Owls* and a porn film, actually, called *Mommy is Coming*, which is rated triple X, which I wrote, and Cheryl directed, and which showed at the Berlin Film Festival. So, I'm into a lot of things, and I enjoy it. I love new ideas, I love trying things out, I love thinking for myself, and I love engaging with a community of people who do the same.

KC: Wow. Well we're going to leave it right there. Sarah, thanks a lot for being here today.

SS: Okay, thank you.

NOTES

1. Ghadir Shafie, "Pinkwashing: Israel's International Strategy and Internal Agenda," *Kohl: A Journal for Body and Gender Research* 1, no. 1 (2015): 82–86; Sarah Schulman, "Israel and 'Pinkwashing,'" op-ed, *New York Times*, November 22, 2011, https://www.nytimes.com/2011/11/23/opinion/pinkwashing-and-israels-use-of-gays-as-a-messaging-tool.html.

2. Edward S. Herman and Noam Chomsky, *Manufacturing Consent: The Political Economy of the Mass Media* (New York: Pantheon Books, 1988).

3. *5 Broken Cameras*, directed by Emad Burnat and Guy Davidi (New York: Kino Lorber, 2011).

4. Linah Alsaafin, "Though Small, Palestine's Queer Movement Has Big Vision," *Electronic Intifada*, July 12, 2013, https://electronicintifada.net/content/though-small-palestines-queer-movement-has-big-vision/12607.

5. Laura Flanders, "GRITtv: Omar Barghouti: Equality Now, Not after Liberation," April 11, 2011, Internet Archive, https://archive.org/details/GRITtv_-_Omar_Barghouti_-_Equality_Now_Not_After_Liberation.

6. See, e.g., Ben White, "Behind Brand Israel: Israel's Recent Propaganda Efforts," *Electronic Intifada*, February 23, 2010, https://electronicintifada.net/content/behind-brand-israel-israels-recent-propaganda-efforts/8694.

7. There is no record of the Israeli government "just" committing $300 million to the fight against BDS. Over the past couple of years, the Israeli government has spent tens of millions on it. But

there was no indication of this spending by the government in or before 2013. For an example of recent news about the Israeli government's spending, see Carlos Ballesteros, "Israel to Spend $72 Million against BDS Movement," *Newsweek*, December 31, 2017, http://www.newsweek.com/israel-bds-campaign-lobby-online-public-speakers-766996.

8. The "they" in this sentence is not meant to imply that the Israeli government directly smeared Schulman. As Schulman noted about the sentence, the "they" refers to the many aspects of the propaganda apparatus that defends the Israeli state against criticism. The article Schulman refers to is titled "Sarah Schulman of 'Pinkwashing' Fame is a Paranoid Fraud.'" This was originally published on a right-wing blog called *Elder of Ziyon*. See "Sarah Schulman of 'Pinkwashing' Fame is a Paranoid Fraud," *Elder of Ziyon*, June 16, 2013, http://elderofziyon.blogspot.com/2013/06/sarah-schulman-of-pinkwashing-fame-is.html. Although that article was not published on *Tablet* or *Commentary*, negative pieces on Schulman were published in both venues. See James Kirchick, "'Pinkwashing' Conference Head Claims Dissenters are 'Israeli Operatives,'" *Tablet*, June 14, 2013, http://www.tabletmag.com/jewish-news-and-politics/134712/pinkwashing-sarah-schulman?all=1; Seth Mandel, "The Real 'Pinkwashing' Scandal," *Commentary*, June 17, 2013, https://www.commentarymagazine.com/culture-civilization/the-real-pinkwashing-scandal/.

9. The *Tablet* article attacked Schulman for not having a higher degree than a Bachelor's. See Kirchick, "'Pinkwashing' Conference Head."

10. This is accurate, and she is likely referring to the BBC's annual poll of countries' popularity. However, fact checking did not find a record of the poll for 2000.

11. The BBC polls that fact checking discovered did not poll people on Sudan or Yemen—they did poll people on North Korea and Iran, and Israel was consistently ranked only slightly ahead of those countries. See "BBC Poll: Germany Most Popular Country in the World," *BBC*, May 23, 2013; "Poll: Israel Viewed Negatively around the World," *Jerusalem Post*, May 17, 2012, https://www.jpost.com/National-News/Poll-Israel-viewed-negatively-around-the-world.

12. The *Forward* reports a pro-Israel advertising group did start looking into Israel's "brand" in around 2002, though the "Brand Israel" campaign was not adopted by the Israeli government until 2005. See Nathaniel Popper, "Israel Aims to Improve Its Public Image," *Forward*, October 14, 2005, https://forward.com/news/2070/israel-aims-to-improve-its-public-image/. For a slightly different history, see Pinkwatcher, "A Documentary Guide to 'Brand Israel' and the Art of Pinkwashing," *Pinkwatching Israel*, June 13, 2012, http://www.pinkwatchingisrael.com/2012/06/13/a-documentary-guide-to-brand-israel-and-the-art-of-pinkwashing/.

13. The *Electronic Intifada* has reported this, so it seems that Saatchi did do this work, but it is unclear how many years they did this work. See Rima Merriman, "Israel's Image Problem," *Electronic Intifada*, December 6, 2006, https://electronicintifada.net/content/israels-image-problem/6579; "Saatchi & Saatchi," Powerbase Public Interest Investigations, accessed June 18, 2018, http://powerbase.info/index.php/Saatchi_%26_Saatchi.

14. This claim is not verifiable.

15. Elinor Garely, "Brand Israel: Not by PR Alone," *eTurboNews*, June 3, 2014, https://www.eturbonews.com/91352/brand-israel-not-pr-alone; Popper, "Israel Aims to Improve."

16. The "Brand Israel" campaign actually did many things before the *Maxim* photo shoot. See, e.g., Hannah Griffin, "Public Diplomacy, Nation Branding and the State of Brand Israel" (master's thesis, 2013), http://cic.biu.ac.il/cic.biu.ac.il/originals/1447085863Public%20Diplomacy,%20Nation%20Branding,%20And%20The%20State%20Of%20Brand%20Israel%20-%20Hannah%20Griffin,%202013.pdf; Nathaniel Popper, "Israel Aims to Improve its Public Image," *Forward*, October 14, 2005, https://forward.com/news/2070/israel-aims-to-improve-its-public-image/.

17. Ben Harris, "Toronto Film Fest Calls Israeli PR Strategy into Question," *Jewish Telegraphic Agency*, September 16, 2009, https://www.jta.org/2009/09/16/arts-entertainment/toronto-film-fest-calls-israeli-pr-strategy-into-question.

18. The link to the original photo spread is dead at *Maxim*. None of the photos in this CNN segment show tanks or guns in the *Maxim* spread, but it is unclear if the original full set of photos did. See "Israel Pimps Soldier Girls in Maxim as Tourist Attraction," YouTube video, 2:31, posted by "grandtheftcountry," June 21, 2007, https://www.youtube.com/watch?v=HtfPoGWS8jY.

19. *Maxim* did not conduct the survey, another company did. See David Kaufman, "Best Face Forward," *Adweek*, March 17, 2008, https://www.adweek.com/brand-marketing/best-face-forward-95248/.

20. Kaufman, "Best Face Forward."

21. Gary Rosenblatt, "Marketing a New Image," *New York Jewish Week*, January 21, 2005, http://jewishweek.timesofisrael.com/marketing-a-new-image/.

22. Publication of such reports could not be verified.

23. "A Free Trip to Israel–Custom-Made for You!" *Jewish Journal*, February 23, 2007, http://jewishjournal.com/culture/lifestyle/education/14451/.

24. "Welcome to Birthright Israel," Taglit Birthright Israel, accessed June 18, 2018, https://www.birthrightisrael.com/countries.

25. The demographic is 18–34, not the 16–24 that Brand Israel focuses on. See Rosenblatt, "Marketing a New Image." See also Schulman's detailed history here: Sarah Schulman, "A Documentary Guide to 'Brand Israel' and the Art of Pinkwashing," *Mondoweiss*, November 30, 2011, http://mondoweiss.net/2011/11/a-documentary-guide-to-brand-israel-and-the-art-of-pinkwashing/.

26. As of June 2018, Kayak advertised flight prices from Tel Aviv to Berlin averaging $317 and as low as $136. See "Find Cheap Flights from Tel Aviv Ben Gurion Intl to Berlin (TLV-BER)," Kayak, accessed June 18, 2018, https://www.kayak.com/flight-routes/Tel-Aviv-Ben-Gurion-Intl-TLV/Berlin-BER.

27. "Israeli Government Allocates $5 million to Address Needs of LGBT Community," *i24 News*, October 8, 2016, https://www.i24news.tv/en/news/israel/society/127316-161008-israeli-government-allocates-5-million-to-address-needs-of-lgbt-community.

28. "Tel Aviv to Hold World's First Bisexuality Themed Pride Parade," Israel Ministry of Foreign Affairs, May 10, 2017, http://mfa.gov.il/MFA/IsraelExperience/Lifestyle/Pages/Tel-Aviv-to-hold-first-world's-first-bisexuality-themed-LGBT-pride-parade.aspx.

29. Although this claim is not verifiable, a quick search of Tel Aviv and gay and lesbian tourism overwhelmingly brings up images of men and sites geared toward gay men.

30. Jasbir Puar, *Terrorist Assemblages: Homonationalism in Queer Times* (Durham, NC: Duke University Press, 2007).

31. Rebecca Staudenmaier, "Gay in the AfD: Talking with LGBT Supporters of Germany's Populist Party," *Deutsche Welle*, March 17, 2017, http://www.dw.com/en/gay-in-the-afd-talking-with-lgbt-supporters-of-germanys-populist-party/a-38002368.

32. Matt Broomfield, "The English Defence League LGBT Division: The Dark Side of the Rainbow," *Left Foot Forward*, July 19, 2013, https://leftfootforward.org/2013/07/english-defence-league-lgbt-division/.

JEFF HALPER

"*War against the People,*" May 4, 2016

https://www.wortfm.org/jeff-halper/

KARMA CHÁVEZ: For those on the left who do Palestinian solidarity work and challenge the policies of the Israeli state against Palestine, many often ask how does Israel get away with it? Condemned multiple times by the United Nations for its gross human rights violations; often compared with the apartheid state of South Africa for its ongoing occupation of the Palestinian territory, the brutal treatment of those in Gaza and the West Bank, and the second class status it offers to Palestinian citizens of Israel; and the subject of an international boycott, divestment, and sanctions movement that has gained steam in the last decade, Israel remains a strong ally of nearly all major western countries and many non-Western ones. To condemn Israel in this political climate in the U.S. is to commit the equivalent of political suicide.

How does Israel get away with it? This is the question posed in a new book by a leading figure in the Israeli peace movement, Jeff Halper, in *War against the People: Israel, Palestinians and Global Pacification*, published by Pluto Press in 2015.

> Long-awaited, *War against the People* is a powerful indictment of the Israeli state's "securocratic" war in the Palestinian Occupied Territories. Anthropologist and activist Jeff Halper draws on firsthand research to show the pernicious effects of the subliminal form of unending warfare conducted by Israel, an approach that relies on sustaining fear among the populace, fear that is stoked by suggestions that the enemy is inside the city limits, leaving no place truly safe and justifying the intensification of military action and militarization in everyday life. Eventually, Halper shows, the integration of militarized systems—including databases tracking civilian activity, automated targeting systems, unmanned drones, and more—becomes seamless with everyday life. And the Occupied Territories, Halper argues, is a veritable laboratory for that approach.
>
> Halper goes on to show how this method of war is rapidly globalizing, as the major capitalist powers and corporations transform militaries, security agencies,

> and police forces into an effective instrument of global pacification. Simultaneously a deeply researched exposé and a clarion call, *War against the People* is a bold attempt to shine the light on the daily injustices visited on a civilian population —and thus hasten their end.[1]

As Andrew Feinstein put it, "This is an important book for anyone who cares about peace, the plight of the Palestinian people, and the role of Israel in the world of war. Halper's fascinating book places the Israeli occupation of the Palestinian territories at the heart of its role in the transnational military-industrial complex and what he calls the pacification industry. A brave, analytical, and innovative book from an admirable activist and thinker."[2]

Jeff Halper is the cofounder of the Israeli Committee Against House Demolitions, an anthropologist and former professor at the University of Haifa and Bun Gurion University. He's the author of several articles and books, including *An Israeli in Palestine: Resisting Dispossession, Redeeming Israel* and *Obstacles to Peace: A Reframing of the Israeli-Palestinian Conflict.*

Jeff Halper, welcome to *A Public Affair.*

JEFF HALPER: Thanks for having me.

KC: For sure. So, Jeff, there is a lot to cover from your very, just, information-rich book, which I learned immensely from, so I really want to thank you for it. But I guess I wonder if we could just start getting to know you and how you got involved with the Israeli peace movement.

JH: Well, I'm kind of a native son. I grew up in northern Minnesota—Hibbing. And I was very active in the '60s, in the anti-Vietnam war movement, in the civil rights movement, and other things. And part of the '60s that we sometimes forget about is kind of the emergence of identity politics, beginning with Alex Haley's *Roots* in the African American community and then of course Cesar Chávez and La Raza and then the Native American movement, and I got caught up in that. My Jewish identity became very important to me—I would say in some ways more than my American identity. There was an alienation, also, from American life under—when the '60s collapsed, certainly, and we get Nixon, I really didn't find anything transcendent in American life, and it wasn't important enough, to me, to fight for. I was looking for another field of battle. And my Jewish identity became important to me in the sense that an ethnic identity becomes important to different groups in this country. But I'm not religious in any way. So, there was no real place for me as a—in a sense it was an identity shift from being an American Jew to an Israeli before I went to Israel, even. So, when I went to Israel, it spoke to me. I mean, I liked the idea of a Hebrew language, of—not nationalism, exactly, but a place where you could develop a national culture. I liked the whole idea, but I was always aware of course that there's an occupation, displacement of the Palestinians. I never went as a Zionist. I tell young people today, everything global. We didn't really have that word in the '60s. Uh, you had a globe [*laughing*].

KC: [*laughing*] Right.

JH: But the world was a big place. You flew—say, if you flew from Minneapolis to Madison, you wore a suit to the airport. It was—the world was a big place. So, our word, I think, in the '60s was the revolution. And the revolution could be anything you wanted it to be—it could be political, it could be love, it could be crystals, it could be music, it could be drugs. There were all kinds of expressions of whatever your revolution was, but that was, in a way, our attempt to try to grasp a wider system. And so, going to Israel I felt that I was going—on the one hand I was meeting some of my own needs as a, as a Jew that was looking for roots, let's say, that I didn't have in northern Minnesota—but at the same time going to another front in the revolution. So, the first—as soon as I got to Israel, I got involved with the Israeli peace movement, and I've been active for forty some years now in Israel, the last twenty years as the head of the Israeli Committee Against House Demolitions.

KC: Well, and so—and I do want to talk about the committee, but I wanted to talk about—so you mentioned Zionism, you don't identify as a Zionist. I wonder how as a non-Zionist Jew, living in Israel, how you relate to the sort of construct—and Zionism, of course, is very complex, with many definitions—but how it is that you relate to the concept of Zionism that seems to be most accepted by the Israeli state.

JH: Well, Zionism, certainly from the Palestinian perspective, is settler colonialism. It was people from Russia and Poland coming into Palestine, someone else's country, and saying, "This is our country, you get out." So, I completely understand and accept the Palestinian narrative. On the other hand, there's also—I don't know if I want to call it a Zionist narrative. I mean, Zionism has become this loaded term.

KC: Sure.

JH: Basically, the Jews were a kind of a group that kept a national identity. In other words, they lived a thousand years in Russia and were never considered Russians. They didn't see themselves as Russians, and they had their own language, which is Yiddish. And they weren't considered by the Russians to be Russians. Or the Germans, or Poles, or whatever. And I think at the time in the nineteenth century, late nineteenth century when nationalism was developing all over the world, certainly in Europe, I think the Jews got caught up in that. And some Jews said, "Well, we're a national group with rights of self-determination like every other group." And, of course, then their territorial reference was Palestine, or what they would call the land of Israel. It was a movement—I think it had a logic to it, and like I said, it spoke to me, in a sense. In an identity sense—the fatal flaw, until today, of Zionism was that it was exclusive. And that comes out of Eastern Europe, Eastern European nationalism is very different from the West. You don't have a concept, until today, in Russia, or Poland, or Hungary of a citizen, democracy, and so on. You have—these are very turfy, kind of tribal sorts of nationalisms. You see it with the refugees coming into Europe, the xenophobic—you know, Hungary and Serbia and all these countries just closing their borders, and they can't tolerate anybody from outside of their own particular national group. So, in a sense, Jews were a victim of that on the one hand, but they also adopted that form of nationalism.

So, Zionism is really an Eastern European tribal nationalism. That just like Russia is exclusively for Russians, the idea that Palestine or the land of Israel was exclusively for Jews. And they never recognized the existence of a Palestinian people or their national rights until today. So, I think for me the challenge is—and this is why I call myself anti-Zionist actually, because I don't think Israel can be or should be a Jewish state. I am, in a sense, a cultural Zionist in the sense that I'd like to see a Hebrew Israeli culture emerging, the language and the literature and so on, that's what brought me there in that country. But *not* to be exclusive to Palestinian nationalism, in a sense to live together, to enrich and enable each other's nationalisms in a sense in a binational country. So, it could actually—done right, it could actually be a good case study of how you take a culturally plural area and find a political arrangement in which different groups have their own cultures, their own self-determination, their political rights, but nevertheless find a way to share the country.

KC: Well, in your—one of your early books, *An Israeli in Palestine*, you sort of talk about this in a lot more depth.

JH: That's right.

KC: And so, exactly the part that you just said, being really against the ethnocracy that is Israel now and advocating really a deep democracy. Of course, you also admit the pipe-dream status, if you will, of that kind of vision. And I'm wondering after doing the research for this book, *War against the People*, that you just put out—do you feel more or less hopeful for the possibility of the kind of democratic state you describe?

JH: Well, yeah, I don't think it's a pipe dream. I think we have to—if you're going to be political, you have to constantly find ways to resolve the conflict in a just way. You can't be fatalistic, certainly. And if something sounds like a pipe dream or sounds fantastic or has no support, you've got to find a way to say, "Well, wait a minute, maybe there's a fundamental flaw in how I'm conceiving of it. How can I build this in a way that makes more sense?" And then have a strategy of how do we get people on board. And I think that's what you can do with the idea of a democratic binational state that sounds fantastic to me—fantastic in the fantasy sense. In that, Israel wouldn't be a Jewish state, Israel would be transformed into a state of all its citizens and the entire country, live with Palestinians, I mean, that really sounds pipe dreamy. But I think in the real world, the two-state solution that's always been presented as the realistic one is gone. Israel eliminated, completely, the two-state solution by building settlements, by annexing East Jerusalem, by—really today there already is one country, so we're halfway there. Now, the country we have between the Mediterranean and the Jordan River, Israel and the occupied territory, which is really one country, is an apartheid state. There's one population, the Israeli Jewish population, that has all the rights and all the power and all the land. And the Palestinians are a people without rights, without land, that have all been—they're half the population of the country, the Palestinians, but have all been confined to 10 percent of the land. And then half the Palestinians are refugees. So that's intolerable.

But the fact is that already the two-state solution is gone. And one state exists. So now our task is to take that one apartheid state that Israel created and say, "We can have one state. The Palestinians have always dreamed of one state. That's fine, but it can't be apartheid." It has to be a democratic state of equal rights for all its citizens, which shouldn't be such a revolutionary idea for Americans. You're fighting wars all over the world to bring freedom and democracy. Here the Palestinian people are saying to you, "Please, a little freedom and democracy would be very nice thank you." And somehow that's too radical, the idea that that country could be democratic. But it has to be. Now, just one—there's no way to get there today. That's why it seems to be like a pipe dream. It's a nice idea, but how would you ever get there. And there really is no mechanism.

The PLO [Palestinian Liberation Organization], which would've been the mechanism for the Palestinians developing a strategy and negotiating with Israel, is gone. And so, there's no mechanism for that. But everything depends on the Palestinian Authority. And I think the Palestinian Authority—which is very oppressive to its own people, it's a collaborationist regime, it's Israel's policeman—is going to collapse. And I think it's going to collapse sooner rather than later. It's lost all its credibility among its own people. When that happens, that's the game changer. In other words, there's nothing we can do except in a sense wait until that happens. But once that happens, in all the chaos that emerges, that's when you get the possibility of new solutions, new approaches that don't exist today. So, when that happens and the whole thing starts to collapse—the occupation, I think Israel will start losing control, you would have to start in a military way reoccupy Gaza. So, in that whole—in the general context of the meltdown in the Middle East, I think the two-state solution is gone, you can't go back to that, and so the only realistic, in that context, option is one democratic state. So, I think it makes a lot of sense if you factor in the collapse of the present political reality and you begin to see a new reality emerging in which you need a solution and new things are possible.

KC: So, Jeff I'm interested in—and I think that the analysis you offer has a lot of prudence and you've been watching it for—since the beginning and I'm wondering—the work that you've done in founding the Israeli Committee Against House Demolitions, how do you see projects like that as any way leading to this kind of vision that you imagine?

JH: In terms of Israel-Palestine?

KC: Yeah, absolutely.

JH: Well, it's—I don't know. Next question [*laughing*]. Because, I'll tell you why—we're Israelis. Critical Israelis, I would say anti-Zionist Israelis, which is not a big camp in Israel. But we're really dependent on our Palestinian partners. Because the Pale—I can't get up and say what the solution is. I can't speak for the Palestinians. And they're in a very difficult situation. First of all, they're living under the Palestinian Authority, which is an Israeli-created authority. So, they're living under the dead hand, and it's very brutal, actually, toward their own people, the PA. So that prevents a lot of new voices from emerging. They're very fragmented. Israel, and the U.S. especially, there's five different Palestinian peoples, from the camps to the diaspora to Israel to the West Bank to Jerusalem to Gaza. And again, without a PLO, they have no mechanism for really getting together and strategizing. So, in a sense, the only thing we can do as the Israeli Committee Against House Demolitions is to continue to resist the demolitions—the occupation. We focus on the issue of house demolitions. Because that's a good—that really brings out—it exposes the way the occupation works, Israel's intentions, and the human cost. Israel's demolished almost fifty thousand Palestinian homes in the occupied territories since 1967. And it has nothing, this policy, to do with security. It's not terrorism—it's simply a proactive displacing of the Palestinians from their lands.

So, we resist the occupation. We—I'm on a speaking tour right now of about a month, Madison is one stop, so we're raising these issues. Among the—to try to mobilize at least the people around it. We have the BDS campaigns—boycott, divestment, sanctions—that we work with a lot. And we have our Palestinian partners. The problem is that they're in a very difficult position in terms of getting together, like I said, and trying to formulate, for themselves, solutions. So, we're in a very difficult and important political conflict but without an end game today. I can't sit in front of you and say, "This is where we should be going, this is a solution." And that's what makes us weak, in a sense, and unable to really move forward. Because until the Palestinians formulate where they're going, everybody has to wait on that.

KC: Mhm. We actually have a caller who wants to respond to some of your comments. So, let's get—Yanev, you're on the air, welcome to *A Public Affair*.

YANEV: Hi, thank you. So, I took issue with a few of the comments that you've made about Zionism. I think Zionism itself is a national ideology, that's true, and I agree with what you said about the Eastern European origins being somewhat intolerant of other ethnicities to this day, but I think that in and of itself is a very idealistic movement that maybe—I don't think it denies the existence of Palestinians, I think it just ignores them in the way that many nineteenth-century Europeans did with indigenous populations. But, to a larger extent—to a larger point, I think Zionism doesn't have any of that, I think, baked into it. I think it was a very—and is still, to this day, a very idealistic movement that just wants to have—to establish a home for the Jewish people which have not had a home for 2,000 years. So, to that extent I don't think that the effect on the Palestinians was intentional, but I think that—to another point that you made, there are Palestinians living in the state of Israel. Israel *is* a democracy. Twenty percent of the—of the residents of Israel are Palestinian Muslims. And they do have full voting rights, and they do have representation in the Knesset, in the Parliament. And, to what you're saying about a binational state, those representatives of the Palestinians in the Knesset regularly make statements that claim they want to destroy Israel, that deny the Holocaust, et cetera, that are more in line with the most racist sentiments expressed against the state of Israel around the world. So, in that sense you can also see the successes of binationalism and multiculturalism around the Middle East, such as Syria, such as Iraq, where you have multiple ethnicities that were forced together by Europeans—by secret European arrangements that redrew the map of the Middle East after World War I, creating these artificially created constructs that force the Kurds, and the Shiites, and the Sunnis, and the Alawites, and other ethnicities to live in artificially created space. And now they're at each other's throats. So, I don't think there's a good precedent for any kind of multiculturalism or binationalism in the Middle East, which is extremely tribal to this day. And forcing that on Israel and the Palestinians would be cultural suicide, I mean, you have to remember that the conflict itself came about for many, many reasons, but a huge contribution—a huge contributor to it was not that the Jews came and decided to kick everyone out and were anti-Muslim. The problem is that the Middle East back then, as it is today, was an extremely intolerant place, and the decision of the Middle Eastern powers was that there was not going to be a Jewish state, and there was conflict because of xenophobia.

KC: Well, you've got a lot of points in there, Yanev. I'm going to have to turn it over to Jeff to respond to you, but I really, really appreciate the call.

YANEV: But I think—my point—my point is that it's very simplistic to say that this is an apartheid state, that the conflict originated with Zionism, and that is just not true.

KC: Thanks for the call, Yanev. Would you like to respond, Jeff?

JH: Well, there's so many slogans there, it's like a list of talking points that—you hear this all the time, there's nothing new. It's too complex actually to get into. But, first of all, the idea that the Middle East is not multicultural is absolutely ridiculous. I mean, Jews lived in the Middle East for four thousand years, they lived very well with the Arab populations, including the Muslim populations. It's true, the conflicts today, including a lot of the conflicts that the Jews are involved with, have to do with neocolonialism. You know, in a sense, this fellow is right in that he's blaming these conflicts on the fact that the Europeans messed up the Middle East and created artificial borders and set one people against the other. But to say that that is the way people lived in the Middle East is ridiculous! People lived very well, the Christians, and Muslims, and Jews all lived very well in the Middle East. It wasn't Europe, where you had anti-Semitism, where you had Holocaust, where you had ghettoization. It was—I'm not saying it was all perfect and ideal, but under Islam it was much much more tolerant and multicultural than it is. And the whole idea that Israel is somehow a model, that every little group creates an exclusive state and gets the other people out and gets the Kurdish state and the Jewish state and a Druze state and an Alawite state—I mean, that's crazy. We've got to figure out how to live together in the mosaic that is the Middle East.

Now Zionism was—just in a word, it's true, Zionism wasn't against Arabs. The Arabs were irrelevant. And that is—that was one of the problems, of course. You were coming into the Middle East, into a country that—it's very nice to say that Jews should have their own country, but it wasn't an empty place. There was a people there. So, you have to accept the fact and take responsibility for the fact that you displaced an entire people. And it's going on until today. This isn't something that happened, "Too bad, it was a historical thing, now we should just forgive and forget." It's ongoing. And the denial of Palestinian existence, let alone national rights, goes on today. Israel today absolutely denies—it's not just ignoring—it denies the national rights of Palestinians, and it even denies their very existence. We don't talk about Palestinians in Israel, we talk about Arabs. So that Israel, unfortunately, became—there was a sort of idealism, but it was a myopic idealism of us. It was like, narcissistic. Us, going into this land with no people and setting up a wonderful democracy and completely ignoring what we've done to the other people, violating the rights of the other people, and the terrible crimes that were committed in the name of this idealistic movement. And we have to decolonize Zionism if Israel wants to remain. Israel cannot remain as a Jewish state, that simply—it can't happen. And to cast the Palestinian citizens of Israel, who are 20 percent of the population, as enemies, first of all, is terrible.

But in addition to that, just one more thing I'll say is that there is—it is not a democracy. It's true, Palestinian citizens have the right to vote, but they're confined to certain parties. And, 94 percent of the land of Israel—of the state of Israel—is reserved only for Jews.[3] So if you're a citizen of Israel and you're not Jewish, you are excluded from living on 94 percent of the land.[4] So it's true, the Palestinian citizens of Israel are 20 percent of the Israeli population,[5] but by law and zoning they're confined to 3.5 percent of the land.[6] So don't think the situation of Palestinians inside Israel is any better, really, than that of Palestinians in the occupied territory. And there's all kinds of laws now that are threatening their civil rights and their citizenship.[7] And you know there's a law in Israel, it's been a law for years now, that if you're an Israeli citizen and you marry someone from the occupied territory or from an Arab country, you cannot bring your spouse to live with you in Israel,[8] which is a fundamental violation of the human right to have a family. And of course, it's presented like that—framed like that, but in fact it means—who marries, in Arab countries? It's Palestinians. And you often have cousins marrying—you often have Palestinians inside Israel marrying Palestinians in the occupied territory, so it really means that Palestinians are not allowed to live with their families. Even if they're citizens of Israel, you can't marry who you want to marry and bring them back. So, in so many fundamental ways, Israel is simply not a democracy. There's the formal mechanisms of voting, but that's about it. That's where it pretty much ends.

KC: Well, Jeff, I want to get into your book because we only have about twenty-twenty five minutes left in the show, and we could do three hours—five, six, hundred hours on this show—and I would love to because I think that all of these issues are so important. But I do want to ask you, moving into your book *War against the People*, what is it that led you to your investigation of questions around security and militarization in order to answer the question, "How does Israel get away with it?"

JH: Well, that was the question nagging me in the back of my mind all these years that I've been an activist on the ground. We're in—we're fifty years after the end of colonialism—fifty or sixty years. We're in a world where concepts of human rights and international law has some mileage, people are aware of it. And here there's an occupation—in the Holy Land, no less, so if you're religious that's kind of ironic—on the southern border of Europe. There's never been a conflict as documented and as visible, transparent as this one with a European power oppressing a colonized people, massive violations of human rights and international law, brutal. And yet, Israel is America's closest ally in the Middle East. You hear all these things, it's the only democracy in the Middle East. Israel's international status improves all the time. How do you explain that? How can you explain a country that really is—has a brutal occupation for fifty years. And yet this—it's almost like a Teflon kind of a country, that none of the criticism sticks to it. Well, the usual explanations just didn't work for me.

AIPAC, which is the Israeli lobby in Washington, which is powerful, but the United States isn't run by—no matter what people say—by the American Jewish community. Christian fundamentalists are important, I mean look at Ted Cruz and so on. But, they have a certain constituency, but they don't run the country. Guilt about the Holocaust might work in Germany, but it can't explain policies in other parts of the world in support of Israel. So, when I started to look at the occupation, I started to look up at Israel's role in the world in general. And it turns out that Israel is the world's fourth,[9] fifth,[10] sixth[11] largest arms exporter. Israel is the fourth largest nuclear power in the world.[12] And Israel has fought over the last century what generals call a "war amongst the people." I call it war *against* the people, that's the title of my book, against the Palestinian people. So today in the world, the wars that are being fought are what are called asymmetrical wars, counterinsurgencies. They're wars against people, they're not against armies. You don't have any more battlefields and tank battles, armies meeting each other. You've got wars against people, non-state actors in particular.

So, the United States—and I put this also within the capitalist system, as capitalism goes into crisis and there's tremendous income disparities, more and more people are being excluded from the capitalist system. I think two thirds of humanity is defined by corporations as surplus, that are simply to be written off. The resource base is shrinking, but you need the resources that are usually under the feet of the world's poorest people. So, you have to sort of extract those resources while excluding them. People are being impoverished, including in this country. You have the Occupy movement and so on. So, in this kind of a crisis, capitalism is—the ruling classes are more and more at odds with and actually securitizing themselves against the people. Whether it's their own people in this country or peoples abroad. And those are the kinds of wars that are being fought.

And Israel, because of its expertise in fighting the Palestinians—and in fact you can look at the occupied territory as a laboratory, where you've got millions of people, four and a half million people, that you can experiment on. You've got six hundred checkpoints, so of course Israel's the world's leader in surveillance systems and in airport security. You've got—you can't explain the invasion of Gaza in 2014 with the Hamas—these little Hamas rockets. The military response of Israel was so disproportionate, it can't be explained in military terms. This has to be a testing of weapons. And in fact, in my book, I list all the new weapons that Israel tested—not only Israeli weapons but American and European weapons—on Palestinians, they're the guinea pigs.

So, what I'm saying, in short, is that Israel gets away with it because of the *quid pro quo*. Israel provides, on the basis of its suppression of the Palestinians, weapons, tactics, technologies, surveillance systems, that it sends out to the elites all over the world in order to control their own restless people that are being excluded and oppressed. And, in return, the international community is closing its eyes and allowing Israel to maintain the occupation. That's the big *quid pro quo* that's going on, so you have to look—in a way, Israel over Palestine is a microcosm of the Global North over the Global South. So, I talk here about global Palestine, in a sense that—you know, we have a saying in the Israeli peace movement that we're all Palestinians. We mean it, of course, in the sense of solidarity. But you could say literally you—we—are all Palestinians in the sense that tactics perfected on the Palestinians in Gaza are used in this country, in Ferguson by your militarized police forces, by your security agencies, and so on. And so literally you're being Palestinianized as your police forces and security forces are being Israel-ized. So that what's happening to the Palestinians is very relevant in terms of your own civil liberties here. But if you put it within the wider capitalist framework, it gives you a window to understand how—how the ruling classes are enforcing their hegemony through these wars against the people.

KC: We do have a caller here that I'm going to bring on—Mike, welcome to *A Public Affair*.

MIKE: Yeah, thanks, Karma. This is sort of my question or comment—it kind of comes in two parts. I think another reason why the support for Israel is so strong is because the Zionist myth has been inculcated so much among Americans—Jews and other Americans. And it comes—you know there's the one statement, "It's a land without people that needs to go to a people without land," that's quite well known, but there's also a corollary to that, which has also been strongly sold and believed and that's that the holy land, it was this land flowing with milk and honey but then all of a sudden along came these "lazy" Arabs who turned the whole country into desert and therefore they don't deserve this country because they ruined it. Which is obviously not true, but it's a myth that has been extensively sold to people. And then the second part of my question is this: why were other areas, which were available, not considered for a Jewish state? I know there were areas in Africa that were proposed for that purpose, there were also areas of land that became available in Europe as a result of the border changes in the aftermath of the second World War, so I guess that would be the second part of my question, why weren't other areas considered for a Jewish state besides where Israel is today? I will take my answers off the air, and I look forward to hearing you tonight, take care.

JH: Okay, thank you much.

KC: Thanks, Mike. So, what about these two points here?

JH: Well, first of all, it's true that Israel has become Americanized. Israel is as American as apple pie. And it's interesting, if you look at the presidential discussions—one candidate is falling over the other one in both parties on who is more pro-Israel. So, one of the greatest PR pieces of material in history was the book *Exodus*. Maybe a little less in this generation, but certainly in my generation, in the '60s—'50s-'60s— this was translated into every language, it was read by everybody. And it was a very emotional story of Zionism and the Jews, and the Arabs are the bad guys, they don't even have names, they're gangs and so on. But that book, with all its influence, was made into a movie starring Paul Newman, music by Harry Mancini, sung by Andy Williams. The words to the song "Exodus," which was a number-one hit in those days, were written by Pat Boone. [*singing*] "This land is mine/God gave this land to me/da da da da." So, Israel became American. I mean, Israel's Pat Boone and Paul Newman. So, I think that that's—I think it's true that that's what happened, is that Israel has become part of the domestic—it's not a *foreign* policy issue. But again, I think that's part of it, but I think there's also interests here that explain better why the United States is in support of Israel, but that's certainly a part of it.

And the second part of the question, of course, is that, I think for the Zionists, obviously the land of Israel was their focus. There were other countries suggested, the British tried to get Uganda. Luckily, that didn't work. The Rothschild family tried to get the Jews in northern Argentina. There was even a suggestion of some island off of Niagara Falls. Maybe Salt Lake City, since, you know, the Mormons are very Zionistic-y. But all of those things fell through, and I think for the Zionist movement, the only meaningful place was the land of Israel.

KC: Mhm. Which makes—makes a lot of sense for very historic reasons. So, we don't have a lot of time left here, Jeff, but a couple things I wanted to have you elaborate on in relation to your book. Some of the really—and the book is so concept rich and there's so many things that are really relevant. Building on what you're saying about the kind of globalization of Palestinians, we're all Palestinians, and one of the things you talk about in your book is this concept of the matrix of control.

JH: That's right.

KC: And you write in your book, "The occupied Palestinian territory has been transformed into probably the most monitored, controlled, and militarized place on earth. It epitomizes the dream of every general, security expert and police officer to be able to exercise total biopolitical control."[13] And I wonder if you'll—so in addition to the kind of direct military stuff you're talking about with Gaza, particularly in 2014—I wonder if you'll elaborate on this idea of the matrix of control and the concept you use of warehousing.

JH: Well, you know, the concept—the big concept I have in the book is pacification. And again, the capitalist system—and we don't talk about the capitalist system very much, Naomi Klein is one of the few that does in a popular way—but this is a system that we're living in, and there are ruling classes, and there are corporations, and it's a real thing, it's not a conspiracy. There isn't some capitalistic club—there are clubs as well—there are certain logics and strategies, but I'm not trying to do this in a conspiratorial way, but there is this kind of a system that's under—that's both under crisis and that's being resisted by people that have been excluded. And it's very active in enforcing its hegemony. The thing is, there's not one particular enemy. It's not like ISIS is here or there's communists over there or there's liberation movements somewhere else. Two thirds of humanity has been excluded from the system, the whole Global South. Including the Global South in this country—talk about peoples of color, you're talking about immigrants, poor people, refugees—maybe less here and more in Europe, but—so that—and of course, with the Occupy movement, young people that feel excluded from the system and alienated and so on. And the enemies of capitalism are all over the place, they permeate everywhere, you see.

And the language of security and terrorism is the language which is applied, partly to delegitimize, of course, any form of resistance. So that the thrust of what the powers that be are doing is to pacify us. And that's a global project, to pacify people abroad in what's called counterinsurgency operations and people at home in securitization. So, the United States is being transformed, I think, from a democracy into a security state. People forget this in a way, but you're living in a state of emergency here. The Patriot Act is fifteen years old. And you've had *very* serious restrictions on your civil liberties. You don't see it and feel it as long as you're sort of living your very narrow life and staying within the perimeters. But the minute you step out and become a little bit critical, or you want to be critical, and you go to the library to read some critical works, you're going to find out that they're on top of you, the security services. So, this is, I think, the idea of pacification. It's war against the people, it's war against us. And what I'm trying to do in the book is to show how it's done.

There are technologies today—we know [George Orwell's novel] *1984*. But there are actually technologies today in which you can completely saturate Madison with—not only with cameras, of course you have drones. You have all kinds of technologies, digital technologies, that build databases on every single individual. And you have technological systems today that plot your patterns and who you're with that eliminate—and this is what security companies and security agencies dream of—to eliminate all spaces of anonymity. That there is *nowhere* that you can go that the state and the authorities don't know where you are and who you're talking to and what you're talking about. It's the dream of technological complete control. And we're getting close to that. The spaces of resistance and the spaces of freedom are getting less and less and less. And that's really what my book is about. So, Israel is doing this on the Palestinians—and again, it's exporting the occupation abroad.

So that, what's interesting for example, is that you had the bombing in Brussels last month—with all the criticism of Israel and the occupation, Israel's saying, "You shouldn't be criticizing us, you should be imitating us. Because what we have—a system in which we have a democracy, we're the only democracy in the Middle East, and the bad guys, the Palestinians who are the terrorists, of course, are under control. That's the kind of system you need in the United States and in Europe." And in fact, one government minister said, "Now maybe the Belgians will stop eating chocolate and join the real world."[14] So the real danger of Israel and the occupation is that it might succeed in convincing the powers that be—Congress and the administration in the Pentagon and others—that in fact this kind of complete securitization is the only way—not only can we secure ourselves, America, but in a larger sense it's the only way you're going to secure the capitalist system for the elites, the 1 percent of the capitalist system, that have to fortress themselves against the rest of the world. So, this, I think, and this is not an area that the left knows much about, and that's the reason why I wrote it. Let me say one quick thing.

KC: Sure.

JH: If you take the military and security agencies, Homeland Security and police together as one package—because they're not separate anymore, you've got militarized police and you've got police-ified military and it's all one thing—those areas together, that's a $2.5 trillion-a-year industry. So, there's *tremendous* interest, tremendous money to be made, tremendous interest in using it. And it has to have a tremendous impact on societies, economies, conflicts, and so on. And it's an area that we in the left don't know much about. I mean, what do I know about the military? [Both: *laughing*] I wrote a book about something I know nothing about. But I said to myself, "You know what? The fact that I know nothing about these—securitization and these systems and these technologies, and the fact that I don't know very much about a $2.5 trillion-a-year industry is a pretty big blindspot in my political understanding of things." And so, I'm trying to urge us to be more aware of how capitalism is actually enforcing its hegemony than we are.

KC: Well, and I have to say, that's one of the things I appreciate most about the book, an admittedly at points dense reading because you are, you're giving us a lexicon that we have no access to. And so, I think on the left, we have a kind of blanket critique of militarization of the police and these kinds of things, but we don't actually understand how these systems work.

JH: Right.

KC: And I guess, we have just about two minutes left in the show, is—for those who are listening and want to do something, is that kind of your big takeaway? Or what's the big thing you'd want people to take away?

JH: Well, I think to be aware. But there's a real problem here is that the left is not organized—we'll never organize the left, that's impossible [KC: *laughing*]. But we have no infrastructure, we have no way of communicating with each other, strategizing with each other. And especially connecting the dots! So, people in women's issues are here, third-world debt is here, Israel-Palestine is here, climate change is here, queer issues are there. And everybody's self-contained. You can't do everything, but there's no cross-cutting things. And no global, everything is local. I think this whole idea of "think global, act local" is not a good idea. We have to act global as well. So, I'm putting together—I'm working with some other activists to put together an organization that we call The People Yes! Network. "The People, Yes" was a poem by Carl Sandberg, written in the '30s about how working people have built the world, not Napoleon and the big figures of history.[15] And The People Yes! Network wants—we want to try to provide an infrastructure—because you're never going to organize our left, I know our left. But provide an infrastructure of common strategizing, analysis, developing campaigns, especially the global perspective, that would unite groups all over the world. I mean a genuinely global infrastructure. Because I think unless we organize better and articulate better, really as a movement, we're not going to get very far. And we're not a—the left today worldwide is not an effective political agent. And I think that's what we have to address. So, in a way, I have this analysis, but I have nothing to plug it into, you see? Even if you're dealing with Israel-Palestine, there's a lot of groups around, there's Students for Justice in Palestine, there's local groups in Madison, there's Jewish Voice for Peace. If you're getting into this military, security, policing stuff and this huge industry in capitalism, there aren't groups around that this is their agenda. And yet this is the metaissue from which all our other issues are coming from. So, I'm trying to address that with The People Yes! Network, and we have a website if people are interested.

KC: Yeah, what is the website?

JH: Just look up tpyn.org[16]

KC: Great, tpyn.org.

JH: It's just starting out, but that's where I'm sort of going with this.

KC: Well that—we're going to have to wrap it up there, Jeff Halper, but thanks so much for being here today.

JH: Thanks for having me.

KC: Again, our guest today was Jeff Halper, who is the author of a new book called *The War against the People: Israel, Palestinians, and Global Pacification.*

NOTES

1. Book description of *War against the People: Israel, the Palestinians and Global Pacification*, by Jeff Halper (2015), University of Chicago Press, http://press.uchicago.edu/ucp/books/book/distributed/W/bo22356644.html.

2. Andrew Feinstein, endorsement of *War against the People: Israel, the Palestinians and Global Pacification*, by Jeff Halper (2015), Pluto Books, https://www.plutobooks.com/9781849649735/war-against-the-people/.

3. The situation is more complicated than Halper puts it here. The Israeli state controls 93 percent of the land. The Jewish National Fund, which does exclusively sell land to Jews, owns 13 percent of that state land, but controls about half of the governing authority that decides how to lease lands. So, most of the state land is not explicitly reserved only for Jews—that is, there is no regulation or law saying that. However, in practice, Adalah says 80 percent of the land is denied to Arab citizens. See Human Rights Watch, "Discrimination in Land Allocation and Access" in *Off the Map: Land and Housing Rights Violations in Israel's Unrecognized Bedouin Villages*, March 30, 2008, https://www.hrw.org/reports/2008/iopt0308/4.htm.

4. Human Rights Watch, "Discrimination in Land Allocation."

5. Dov Waxman, "Israel's Palestinian Minority in the Two-State Solution: The Missing Dimension," *Middle East Policy Council* 18, no. 4 (2011): 68–82.

6. Palestinians own 3.5 percent of the land, but nobody is asserting that they are confined only to that land. See Ilan Peleg and Dov Waxman, *Israel's Palestinians: The Conflict Within* (Cambridge: Cambridge University Press, 2011): 41.

7. "Israel: New Laws Marginalize Palestinian Arab Citizens," Human Rights Watch, March 30, 2011, https://www.hrw.org/news/2011/03/30/israel-new-laws-marginalize-palestinian-arab-citizens.

8. "'Ban on Family Unification'—Citizenship and Entry into Israel Law (Temporary Order)," Adalah, 2003, https://www.adalah.org/en/law/view/511.

9. It depends on the year as to where Israel ranks in terms of arms exports. See Laurie Copans, "Israel is 4th Largest Arms Exporter," *Washington Post*, December 11, 2007, http://www.washingtonpost.com/wp-dyn/content/article/2007/12/11/AR2007121101535.html?noredirect=on.

10. "Israel Claims Fifth Place among Arms Exporters," *Flight Daily News*, February 23, 2000, https://www.flightglobal.com/news/articles/israel-claims-fifth-place-among-arms-exporters-62369/.

11. Gili Cohen, "Overtaking China and Italy: Israel Ranks as the World's Sixth Largest Arms Exporter in 2012," *Haaretz*, June 25, 2013, https://www.haaretz.com/.premium-israel-ranks-world-s-no-6-arms-exporter-1.5286178.

12. It is difficult to fact check information that is not publicly available, but there seems to be a consensus that Israel has around eighty nuclear weapons, which does not place it as the fourth largest. See "Nuclear Weapons: Who Has What at a Glance," Arms Control Association, last modified March 2018, accessed June 11, 2018, https://www.armscontrol.org/factsheets/Nuclearweaponswhohaswhat. Others have put the total around two hundred, but those numbers are not confirmed. If Israel has two hundred nuclear weapons, that would place it at fifth. President Carter estimated it at three hundred—the highest number given. See Noam Sheizaf, "Former President Carter: Israel has 300 Nuclear Bombs," *+972*, January 31, 2012, https://972mag.com/former-president-carter-israel-has-300-nuclear-bombs/34285/.

13. Jeff Halper, *War against the People: Israel, the Palestinians and Global Pacification* (London: Pluto Books, 2015), 143.

14. This is not a direct quotation, but Israeli Minister for Intelligence and Transportation, Yisrael Katz, did make such a comment. "Israeli Minister Lambasts Belgium for 'Eating Chocolate' and Not Fighting Terror," *RT*, March 23, 2016, https://www.rt.com/news/336955-brussels-israel-minister-chocolate/.

15. Carl Sandburg, *The People, Yes* (New York: Harcourt, Brace, 1936).

16. This website is incorrect. The network can actually be found at https://medium.com/the-peoples-yes-network.

APPENDICES

Appendix A: Referenced Palestinian and Palestine Solidarity Organizations

Al Qaws: For Sexual and Gender Diversity in Palestinian Society
http://alqaws.org/siteEn

Al Midan Theater
https://www.facebook.com/almidan-theater

Arab American Institute
https://www.aaiusa.org

Aswat—Palestinian Gay Women
https://www.aswatgroup.org

Boycott, Divestment, Sanctions (BDS) Movement
https://bdsmovement.net

BOYCOTT! Supporting the Palestinian BDS Call from Within
https://boycottisrael.info

Coalición de Derechos Humanos
https://derechoshumanosaz.net

Hirakuna
https://www.facebook.com/Hirakuna

Institute for Middle East Understanding
https://imeu.org

Isha L'Isha–Haifa Feminist Center
isha2isha.com/english

Israeli Committee Against House Demolitions
https://icahd.org

Jewish Voice for Peace
https://jewishvoiceforpeace.org

Kohl: A Journal for Body and Gender Research
https://kohljournal.press

Madison-Rafah Sister Project
madisonrafah.org

No to Pinkwashing
www.nopinkwashing.org.uk

Palestinian American Research Center
parc-us-pal.org

Palestinian BDS National Committee
https://bdsmovement.net/bnc

Palestinian Campaign for the Academic and Cultural Boycott of Israel
https://bdsmovement.net/pacbi

Palestinian Queers for BDS
https://www.facebook.com/PQBDS

The People Yes! Network
https://www.facebook.com/thepeopleyesnetwork

Pinkwatchers
www.pinkwatchingisrael.com

Students for Justice in Palestine
https://www.nationalsjp.org

U.S. Campaign for the Academic and Cultural Boycott of Israel
https://usacbi.org

U.S. Palestinian Community Network
https://uspcn.org

WORT-FM
https://www.wortfm.org

Appendix B: PACBI Call and Guidelines and Referenced Academic Boycott Resolutions

Call for an Academic and Cultural Boycott of Israel

Palestinian Campaign for the Academic and Cultural Boycott of Israel

Issued July 6, 2004

Whereas Israel's colonial oppression of the Palestinian people, which is based on Zionist ideology, comprises the following:

- Denial of its responsibility for the Nakba—in particular the waves of ethnic cleansing and dispossession that created the Palestinian refugee problem—and therefore refusal to accept the inalienable rights of the refugees and displaced stipulated in and protected by international law;
- Military occupation and colonization of the West Bank (including East Jerusalem) and Gaza since 1967, in violation of international law and UN resolutions;
- The entrenched system of racial discrimination and segregation against the Palestinian citizens of Israel, which resembles the defunct apartheid system in South Africa;

Since Israeli academic institutions (mostly state controlled) and the vast majority of Israeli intellectuals and academics have either contributed directly to maintaining, defending or otherwise justifying the above forms of oppression, or have been complicit in them through their silence,

Given that all forms of international intervention have until now failed to force Israel to comply with international law or to end its repression of the Palestinians, which has manifested itself in many forms, including siege, indiscriminate killing, wanton destruction and the racist colonial wall,

In view of the fact that people of conscience in the international community of scholars and intellectuals have historically shouldered the moral responsibility to fight injustice, as exemplified in their struggle to abolish apartheid in South Africa through diverse forms of boycott,

Recognizing that the growing international boycott movement against Israel has expressed the need for a Palestinian frame of reference outlining guiding principles,

In the spirit of international solidarity, moral consistency and resistance to injustice and oppression,

We, Palestinian academics and intellectuals, call upon our colleagues in the international community to *comprehensively and consistently boycott all Israeli academic and cultural institutions* as a contribution to the struggle to end Israel's occupation, colonization and system of apartheid, by applying the following:

1. Refrain from participation in any form of academic and cultural cooperation, collaboration or joint projects with Israeli institutions;
2. Advocate a comprehensive boycott of Israeli institutions at the national and international levels, including suspension of all forms of funding and subsidies to these institutions;
3. Promote divestment and disinvestment from Israel by international academic institutions;
4. Work toward the condemnation of Israeli policies by pressing for resolutions to be adopted by academic, professional and cultural associations and organizations;
5. Support Palestinian academic and cultural institutions directly without requiring them to partner with Israeli counterparts as an explicit or implicit condition for such support.

Endorsed by:
Palestinian Federation of Unions of University Professors and Employees; Palestinian General Federation of Trade Unions; Palestinian NGO Network, West Bank; Teachers' Federation; Palestinian Writers' Federation; Palestinian League of Artists; Palestinian Journalists' Federation; General Union of Palestinian Women; Palestinian Lawyers' Association; and tens of other Palestinian federations, associations, and civil society organizations.

PACBI Guidelines for the International Cultural Boycott of Israel

Palestinian Campaign for the Academic and Cultural Boycott of Israel

Published July 16, 2014

Being that part of the Palestinian BDS National Committee (BNC) tasked with overseeing the academic and cultural boycott aspects of BDS, the Palestinian Campaign for the Academic and Cultural Boycott of Israel (PACBI) has advocated, since 2004, for a boycott of Israeli academic and cultural institutions. This is based on the fact that these institutions are complicit in the Israeli system of oppression that has denied Palestinians their basic rights guaranteed by international law, or has hampered their exercise of these rights, including freedom of movement and freedom of expression.

Cultural institutions are part and parcel of the ideological and institutional scaffolding of Israel's regime of occupation, settler-colonialism and apartheid against the Palestinian people. Israeli cultural institutions (including performing art companies, music groups, film organizations, writers' unions and festivals) have cast their lot with the hegemonic Zionist establishment in Israel, and notwithstanding the efforts of a handful of principled individual artists, writers and filmmakers, these institutions are clearly implicated in supporting, justifying and whitewashing Israel's occupation and systematic denial of Palestinian rights.

The cultural boycott campaign against apartheid South Africa has been a major source of inspiration in formulating the Palestinian boycott calls and their criteria, despite some crucial differences. In particular, the Palestinian boycott, unlike the South African cultural boycott, is institutional and does not target individuals as such.

Freedom of Expression

Given that the BNC, through the PACBI guidelines presented below, rejects censorship and upholds the universal right to freedom of expression, the institutional boycott called for by Palestinian civil society does not conflict with such freedom. PACBI subscribes to the internationally-accepted definition of freedom of expression as stipulated in the United Nations' International Covenant on Civil and Political Rights (ICCPR).

Anchored in precepts of international law and universal human rights, the BDS movement, including PACBI, rejects on principle boycotts of individuals based on their identity (such as citizenship, race, gender, or religion) or opinion. Mere affiliation of Israeli cultural workers to an Israeli cultural institution is therefore not grounds for applying the boycott. If, however, an individual is representing the state of Israel or a complicit Israeli institution, or is commissioned/recruited to participate in Israel's efforts to "rebrand" itself, then her/his activities are subject to the institutional boycott the BDS movement is calling for.

While an individual's freedom of expression should be fully and consistently respected in the context of cultural boycotts, an individual artist/writer, Israeli or otherwise, cannot be exempt from being subject to "common sense" boycotts (beyond the scope of the PACBI institutional boycott criteria) that conscientious citizens around the world may call for in response to what they widely perceive as egregious individual complicity in, responsibility for, or advocacy of violations of international law (such as war crimes or other grave human rights violations), racial violence, or racial slurs. At this level,

Israeli cultural workers should not be exempted from due criticism or any lawful form of protest, including boycott; they should be treated like all other offenders in the same category, not better or worse. This is in accordance with the Universal Declaration of Human Rights, on which the BDS movement's principles are based, and which states:

> In the exercise of his rights and freedoms, everyone shall be subject only to such limitations as are determined by law solely for the purpose of securing due recognition and respect for the rights and freedoms of others and of meeting the just requirements of morality, public order, and the general welfare in a democratic society.

International Cultural Boycott Guidelines

During years of intensive work with partners in several countries to promote the cultural boycott of Israel, which is supported by an overwhelming majority of Palestinian artists, writers, filmmakers and cultural institutions, PACBI has thoroughly scrutinized many cultural projects and events, assessing the applicability of the boycott criteria to them and, accordingly, has issued open letters, statements or advisory opinions on them. The three most important conclusions reached in this respect were: (a) many of these events and projects fall into an uncertain, grey area that is challenging to appraise, (b) it is important to emphasize that the boycott must target not only the complicit institutions but also the inherent and organic links between them which reproduce the machinery of colonial subjugation and apartheid, and (c) strategically, not every boycottable project must be met with an active boycott campaign, as activists need to invest their energies in the highest priority campaigns in any given time.

Based on this experience and in response to the burgeoning demand for specific BDS guidelines for applying the international cultural boycott of Israel to diverse projects, from film and literary festivals to art exhibits to musical and dance performances to conferences, PACBI lays out below unambiguous, consistent and coherent criteria and guidelines that specifically address the nuances and particularities in the field of culture. These guidelines are mainly intended to assist international conscientious artists, writers and cultural workers, as well as cultural organizations and associations to be in harmony with the Palestinian call for boycott, as a contribution towards upholding international law and furthering the struggle for freedom, justice and equality. Similar guidelines for the academic boycott have been issued by PACBI.

International cultural workers who fail to heed the call for boycott, crossing the BDS "picket line," and then attempting to visit Palestinian institutions or groups in a "balancing" gesture, contribute to the false perception of symmetry between the colonial oppressor and the colonized. Although visits to the occupied Palestinian territory by international supporters and advocates of Palestinian rights have always been welcomed as a source of encouragement and support, Palestinians believe that solidarity entails respecting the boycott call, which is an authoritative call of the oppressed, and not combining a visit to Palestinian institutions or groups with activities with boycottable Israeli institutions. International visitors who insist on including Israeli cultural institutions in their itinerary, as a form of "fig-leafing," should not expect to be welcomed by Palestinian cultural institutions.

In general, PACBI urges international cultural workers (e.g. artists, writers, filmmakers) and cultural organizations, including unions and associations, where possible and as relevant, to boycott and/or work towards the cancellation of events, activities, agreements, or projects involving Israel, its lobby groups or its cultural institutions, or that otherwise promote the normalization of Israel in the global cultural sphere, whitewash Israel's violations of international law and Palestinian rights, or violate the BDS guidelines.

In all the following, "product" refers to cultural products such as films, artworks, plays, among other art forms; "event" refers to film festivals, conferences, art exhibits, art performances (including music and dance), tours by artists and writers, among other activities.

Specifically, these are the BDS guidelines for assessing whether events or products are in violation of the Palestinian cultural boycott of Israel:

(1) As a general overriding rule, Israeli cultural institutions, unless proven otherwise, are complicit in maintaining the Israeli occupation and denial of basic Palestinian rights, whether through their silence or actual involvement in justifying, whitewashing or otherwise deliberately diverting attention from Israel's violations of international law and human rights.

Accordingly, these institutions, all their products, and all the activities they sponsor or support must be boycotted by cultural organizations and cultural workers worldwide. As in the cultural boycott of South African apartheid, international artists and cultural workers are urged not to extend recognition in any way to Israeli cultural organizations by exhibiting, presenting, and showcasing their work (e.g. films, installations, literary works); lecturing or performing at or in cooperation with complicit Israeli cultural institutions or events, and granting permission for the publication, exhibition or screening of such work by such institutions. Likewise, activities and projects involving individuals explicitly representing these complicit institutions should be boycotted. It must be emphasized that a cultural product's content or artistic merit is not relevant in determining whether or not it is boycottable.

(2) A cultural PRODUCT is boycottable if it is commissioned by an official Israeli body or non-Israeli institution that serves Brand Israel or similar propaganda purposes[1]

Israeli cultural products (as opposed to public events) that are funded by official Israeli bodies but not commissioned or otherwise attached to any political strings are not per se subject to boycott. "Political strings" here specifically refer to conditions that obligate a fund recipient to directly or indirectly serve the Israeli government's or a complicit institution's rebranding or propaganda efforts. Israeli cultural products that receive state funding as part of the individual cultural worker's entitlement as a tax-paying citizen, without her/him being bound to serve the state's political and propaganda interests, are not boycottable. Accepting such political strings, on the other hand, would clearly turn the cultural product into a form of complicity, by contributing to Israel's efforts to whitewash or obscure its colonial and apartheid reality, and would render it boycottable as a result. *Using this logic, we consider all non-Israeli (e.g., international, Palestinian) cultural products that are funded by official Israeli bodies or international "brand Israel" organizations to be commissioned and to be politically motivated, therefore being subject to boycott.*

The clearest example is the well-documented fact that many Israeli artists, writers and other cultural workers applying for state funding to cover the cost of their—or their cultural products'—participation in international events are obligated to contribute to Israel's official propaganda efforts. To that end, the cultural worker must sign a contract with the Israeli Foreign Ministry binding her/him to "undertake to act faithfully, responsibly and tirelessly to provide the Ministry with the highest professional services." The contract also states that, "The service provider is aware that the purpose of ordering services from him is to promote the policy interests of the State of Israel via culture and art, including contributing to creating a positive image for Israel." All cultural products, whether Israeli or international, that are commissioned by an official Israeli body (e.g., government ministry, municipality, embassy, consulate, state or other public film fund), or by an Israeli rebranding project or organization, deserve to be boycotted on institutional grounds. Such products are commissioned by the Israeli state or by colluding institutions specifically to help the state's propaganda or "rebranding" efforts.

(3) A cultural EVENT/ACTIVITY is boycottable if it is partially or fully sponsored by an official Israeli body or a complicit institution.

As in the previous guideline, the general principle is that a public event/activity carried out under the sponsorship/aegis of or in affiliation with an official Israeli body or a complicit institution constitutes complicity and therefore is deserving of boycott. The same may apply to support or sponsorship from non-Israeli institutions that serve Israel's branding/propaganda purposes.

(4) Normalization Projects are boycottable.

Cultural activities, projects, events and products involving Palestinians and/or other Arabs on one side and Israelis on the other (whether bi- or multi- lateral) that are based on the false premise of symmetry/parity between the oppressors and the oppressed or that assume that both colonizers and colonized are equally responsible for the "conflict" are intellectually dishonest and morally reprehensible forms of normalization that ought to be boycotted. Far from challenging the unjust status quo, such projects contribute to its endurance. Examples include events, projects, publications, films, or exhibitions that are designed to bring together Palestinians/Arabs and Israelis so they can present their respective narratives or perspectives, or to work toward reconciliation, "overcoming barriers," etc., without addressing the root causes of injustice and the requirements of justice. Other factors that PACBI takes into consideration in evaluating such products and events are the sources of funding, the design of the product or event, the objectives of the sponsoring organization(s), the participants, and similar relevant factors.

Given that the only normal—and indeed welcome—relationship between those from the oppressor community and those from the oppressed community is one that recognizes the basic rights of the oppressed under international law and involves a common struggle against oppression, joint projects that meet the following two conditions are not considered forms of normalization and are therefore exempt from boycott:

(a) the Israeli party in the project recognizes the comprehensive Palestinian rights under international law (corresponding to the 3 rights in the BDS call); and
(b) the product or event is one of "co-resistance" rather than co-existence.

Public debates between Palestinians/Arabs and Israelis are also excluded from the boycott if organized without any cooperation with Israel, its lobby groups, or its complicit institutions.

(5) Fact-finding missions and study tours that receive funding from Israel, its complicit institutions, or its international lobby groups are subject to the boycott.

On the other hand, balanced, independent fact-finding missions or study groups, even those that include meetings with complicit Israeli academic institutions, are not boycottable, provided that no institutional link (e.g., seminars, workshops, exhibits, etc.) of any sort is established with complicit Israeli institutions.

The cultural boycott of Israel should continue until Israel is in compliance with the three basic demands outlined in the 2005 BDS Call.

To end their collusion in Israel's regime of occupation, settler-colonialism and apartheid and become non-boycottable, Israeli cultural institutions must fulfill two basic conditions:

(a) Publicly recognize the inalienable rights of the Palestinian people as enshrined in international law (including the three basic rights in the 2005 BDS Call) and

(b) End all forms of complicity in violating Palestinian rights as stipulated in international law, including discriminatory policies and practices as well as diverse roles in whitewashing or justifying Israel's violations of international law and Palestinian human rights.

Resolution to Support the Boycott of Israeli Academic Institutions
Association for Asian American Studies
Passed by Membership April 2013

Whereas the Association for Asian American Studies is an organization dedicated to the preservation and support of academic freedom and of the right to education for students and scholars in the U.S. and globally; and

Whereas Arab (West Asian) and Muslim American communities, students, and scholars have been subjected to profiling, surveillance, and civil rights violations that have circumscribed their freedom of political expression, particularly in relation to the issue of human rights in Palestine-Israel; and

Whereas the Association for Asian American Studies seeks to foster scholarship that engages conditions of migration, displacement, colonialism, and racism, and the lives of people in zones of war and occupation; and

Whereas the Association for Asian American Studies seeks to advance a critique of U.S. empire, opposing U.S. military occupation in the Arab world and U.S. support for occupation and racist practices by the Israeli state; and

Whereas the United Nations has reported that the current Israeli occupation of Palestine has impacted students "whose development is deformed by pervasive deprivations affecting health, education and overall security"; and

Whereas Palestinian universities and schools have been periodically forced to close as a result of actions related to the Israeli occupation, or have been destroyed by Israeli military strikes, and Palestinian students and scholars face restrictions on movement and travel that limit their ability to attend and work at universities, travel to conferences and to study abroad, and thereby obstruct their right to education; and

Whereas the Israeli state and Israeli universities directly and indirectly impose restrictions on education, scholarships, and participation in campus activities on Palestinian students in Israel; and

Whereas Israel imposes severe restrictions on foreign academics and students seeking to attend conferences and do research in Palestine as well as on scholars and students of Arab/Palestinian origin who wish to travel to Israel-Palestine; and

Whereas Israeli institutions of higher education have not condemned or taken measures to oppose the occupation and racial discrimination against Palestinians in Israel, but have, rather, been directly and indirectly complicit in the systematic maintenance of the occupation and of policies and practices that discriminate against Palestinian students and scholars throughout Palestine and in Israel; and

Whereas Israeli academic institutions are deeply complicit in Israel's violations of international law and human rights and in its denial of the right to education and academic freedom to Palestinians, in addition to their basic rights as guaranteed by international law; and

Whereas the Association for Asian American Studies supports research and open discussion about these issues without censorship, intimidation, or harassment, and seeks to promote academic exchange, collaboration and opportunities for students and scholars everywhere;

Be it resolved that the Association for Asian American Studies endorses and will honor the call of Palestinian civil society for a boycott of Israeli academic institutions.

Be it also resolved that the Association for Asian American Studies supports the protected rights of students and scholars everywhere to engage in research and public speaking about Israel-Palestine and in support of the boycott, divestment and sanctions (BDS) movement.

PASSED. No OBJECTIONS. No ABSTENTIONS.

April 20th, 2013 by the General Membership of the Association for Asian American Studies.

Declaration of Support for the Boycott of Israeli Academic Institutions

Native American and Indigenous Studies Association

Approved by NAISA Council December 2013

The council of the Native American and Indigenous Studies Association (NAISA) declares its support for the boycott of Israeli academic institutions.

A broad coalition of Palestinian non-governmental organizations, acting in concert to represent the Palestinian people, formed the Palestinian Campaign for the Academic and Cultural Boycott of Israel. Their call was taken up in the United States by the U.S. Campaign for the Academic and Cultural Boycott of Israel. A NAISA member-initiated petition brought this issue to NAISA Council. After extensive deliberation on the merits of the petition, the NAISA Council decided by unanimous vote to encourage members of NAISA and all who support its mission to honor the boycott.

NAISA is dedicated to free academic inquiry about, with, and by Indigenous communities. The NAISA Council protests the infringement of the academic freedom of Indigenous Palestinian academics and intellectuals in the Occupied Territories and Israel who are denied fundamental freedoms of movement, expression, and assembly, which we uphold.

As the elected council of an international community of Indigenous and allied non-Indigenous scholars, students, and public intellectuals who have studied and resisted the colonization and domination of Indigenous lands via settler state structures throughout the world, we strongly protest the illegal occupation of Palestinian lands and the legal structures of the Israeli state that systematically discriminate against Palestinians and other Indigenous peoples.

NAISA is committed to the robust intellectual and ethical engagement of difficult and often highly charged issues of land, identity, and belonging. Our members will have varying opinions on the issue of the boycott, and we encourage generous dialogue that affirms respectful disagreement as a vital scholarly principle. We reject shaming or personal attacks as counter to humane understanding and the greater goals of justice, peace, and decolonization.

As scholars dedicated to the rights of Indigenous peoples, we affirm that our efforts are directed specifically at the Israeli state, not at Israeli individuals. The NAISA Council encourages NAISA members to boycott Israeli academic institutions because they are imbricated with the Israeli state and we wish to place pressure on that state to change its policies. We champion and defend intellectual and academic freedom, and we recognize that conversation and collaboration with individuals and organizations in Israel/Palestine can make an important contribution to the cause of justice. In recognition of the profound social and political obstacles facing Palestinians in such dialogues, however, we urge our members and supporters to engage in such actions outside the aegis of Israeli educational institutions, honoring this boycott until such time as the rights of the Palestinian people are respected and discriminatory policies are ended.

Resolution on the Boycott of Israeli Academic Institutions

American Studies Association
Passed by Membership December 2013

December 4, 2013

Whereas the American Studies Association is committed to the pursuit of social justice, to the struggle against all forms of racism, including anti-semitism, discrimination, and xenophobia, and to solidarity with aggrieved peoples in the United States and in the world;

Whereas the United States plays a significant role in enabling the Israeli occupation of Palestine and the expansion of illegal settlements and the Wall in violation of international law, as well as in supporting the systematic discrimination against Palestinians, which has had documented devastating impact on the overall well-being, the exercise of political and human rights, the freedom of movement, and the educational opportunities of Palestinians;

Whereas there is no effective or substantive academic freedom for Palestinian students and scholars under conditions of Israeli occupation, and Israeli institutions of higher learning are a party to Israeli state policies that violate human rights and negatively impact the working conditions of Palestinian scholars and students;

Whereas the American Studies Association is cognizant of Israeli scholars and students who are critical of Israeli state policies and who support the international boycott, divestment, and sanctions (BDS) movement under conditions of isolation and threat of sanction;

Whereas the American Studies Association is dedicated to the right of students and scholars to pursue education and research without undue state interference, repression, and military violence, and in keeping with the spirit of its previous statements supports the right of students and scholars to intellectual freedom and to political dissent as citizens and scholars;

It is resolved that the American Studies Association (ASA) endorses and will honor the call of Palestinian civil society for a boycott of Israeli academic institutions. It is also resolved that the ASA supports the protected rights of students and scholars everywhere to engage in research and public speaking about Israel-Palestine and in support of the boycott, divestment, and sanctions (BDS) movement.

December 16, 2013
The members of the American Studies Association have endorsed the Association's participation in a boycott of Israeli academic institutions. In an election that attracted 1252 voters, the largest number of participants in the organization's history, 66.05% of voters endorsed the resolution, while 30.5% of voters voted no and 3.43% abstained. The election was a response to the ASA National Council's announcement on December 4 that it supported the academic boycott and, in an unprecedented action to ensure a democratic process, asked its membership for their approval.

NOTE

1. One such organization is the America-Israel Cultural Foundation, whose mission includes depicting the State of Israel "as a thriving cultural environment that stimulates creativity and artistic life." See http://www.aicf.org/about/mission. The organization takes credit for having supported and promoted all major cultural institutions in Israel, such as the Israel Philharmonic Orchestra and the Israel Museum. See http://www.aicf.org/about/impact/institutions.